Midcentury
Tales
from Rural Ohio

D1430630

Midcentury *Tales*

from Rural Ohio

BIRTH, GROWTH, AND NEAR DEATH

R. C. Steinle Williams

ORANGE *frazer* PRESS

Wilmington, Ohio

Published for the copyright holder by:
Orange Frazer Press
37½ West Main St.
P.O. Box 214
Wilmington, OH 45177

For price and shipping information, call: 937.382.3196
Or visit: www.orangefrazer.com

Book and cover design:
Orange Frazer Press with Catie South

Library of Congress Control Number: 2023906180

First Printing

In Memory of my Parents

Elsie Loretta Philomena Steinle
Harold Jean Williams

With Thanks and Love

Table of Contents

Preface

The inspiration for this book—not to sound too grand—was John Colville's memoir *Footprints in Time*, which he wrote toward the end of his life. I have had an interest in the military and political history of the first half of the 20th Century, particularly British and how they affected American foreign policy and action. I learned about Colville because he was Winston Churchill's private secretary through World War II and during Churchill's later years in office. He and I were both educated at Cambridge University. There the similarity ends. Colville was an upper-class Brit, educated at Harrow, a posh public (private) school, and at age twelve was appointed Page of Honor to King George V. He later led the effort to establish Churchill College Cambridge to honor the former prime minister. I am a lower middle-class, blue collar, mongrel from the corn fields of Ohio and do not make any pretense to his felicity with language or his importance to British history and letters. It was the self-deprecating tone of his memoir and the warmth with which he described his family, education, travels, political insights, and career that I found impressive, and the fact that he waited until his later years, as have I, to put personal memories to paper.

Here you will find a world that no longer exists, rural Ohio mid-20th Century. No cellphones, no personal computers, no internet, no ghastly "social media," no 300 TV channels—no color TV for a good part of it—no whole genome DNA sequencing, no gravity waves, no space telescopes, and no men on the moon, though NASA was trying, despite their rockets exploding at regular intervals. What we did have were the shadows of World War II, Korea, and the Cold War, the beginning of Rock and Roll, Jim Crow segregation, Communist hunting, the rise of the far right, the beginning of the Vietnam War, and restless undergraduates at our best colleges who were to lead a social revolution in just a few years, protesting the war, burning bras, and destroying earlier sexual mores. In October 1962 we almost blew up the world with nuclear weapons.

Amid all of this, in 1947, I was born and matured in a community, Delphos, Ohio, that was only found by chance because a stranger or trucker was travelling east or west on Route 30, became extremely annoyed by all the red lights on Fifth Street, and said "what is this damn place anyway?" I now stand, after more than seventy years, in the same position as my paternal grandmother and great aunts with whom I grew up and who were born at the end of the 19th Century, a time without automobiles, airplanes, radio, Mendelian Genetics, antibiotics, or television. We were contemporaries, they and I; together we represent the overlapping of generations, knowledge, stories, and culture totaling 140 years. This book is a meditation on time, the continuity of families, and the role of randomness in our lives. Here I explore this in the four or five occasions that, with high probability, would have seen me dead, not the least of which was enlisting in The United States Marine Corps in the middle of a war. I wish I had the faith of friends who believe in a halo of invisible, unknowable beings especially looking after them. But I do not, and do not expect them in this book. I do have a long-term, loving wife and a career that has given me over fifty years of creativity, education, joy, and satisfaction. In the roll of the dice of life, I have cleaned the table with nearly every throw.

I want to especially thank my editor, Lauren Simek Ph.D., for putting her education in English literature to work on my drafts. My very good friend Clint Joe Miller, now deceased, read an early version of the book and engaged me in spirited conversations with corrections as to time, person, and dates. I miss him every day. My gratitude as well to the publishers at Orange Frazer Press who read the manuscript and offered much help as to language and tone. For selected actors in this book who are still living, I have changed their names. They know who they are, as do our living classmates and friends. These are my stories and how I remember them. Any mistakes are solely mine.

Midcentury Tales

from Rural Ohio

CHAPTER 1

In the Beginning

Delphos

I grew up in the farm fields of Ohio. My crib may as well have been between two rows of corn plants. The town was an idyllic village called Delphos. It was small because of its size and, yes, because of its attitudes and prejudices that were common in the 1940s and 1950s in such a place. When one approached Delphos from the east, west, north, or south, the most prominent feature above the many hardwood trees was the steeple of St. John's Roman Catholic Church. It rose from the town's geographical center, with its four clocks facing each direction and its bells chiming the hours and the evening prayers, calling the devout to say the Angelus and celebrate that invisible Virgin in the sky who protected them. The town was founded by a German Catholic priest, who had a large celebratory monument over his grave. However, the town was also home to Lutherans, Presbyterians, and Methodists, as well as Holy Rollers and Evangelical Christians of various flavors, who rejected paid indulgences, the cults of the Saints and Mary, and the tyranny of the Pope. One could hardly travel a couple of blocks without seeing a house of worship. Nonetheless, the clear divide was between the "one true Roman Catholic religion of nearly two thousand years" tradition and everyone else. There was the Catholic school and the public, non-Catholic schools, the Catholic funeral home and the non-Catholic one, the Catholic cemetery and the non-Catholic ones, and the Catholic families and the non-Catholic homes. My family was highly mixed. Mother practiced a pious, conservative Roman Catholicism that was derived from her mother's family, the Fortners. Her Steinle side was a mixed bag of religion, some Catholic, some Protestants, some care-less. Father was an agnostic, as was his father, as far as I know, while his aunts and various relations were protestants who seldom went to church. My immigrant paternal grandmother's father was a Jewish tailor, Albert Kaskel, whose family was from northern Germany. I take after my father and the religion-care-less relatives, with a strong interest about my German Jewish ancestors and their fates during World War II.

The town was little more than a mile square with parks on the north and south ends and small factories dotted throughout. While Delphos was, well, small, it stood like the hub of a wheel with spokes leading out to even smaller farming communities that relied on the resources of the larger town. Manufacturing and agriculture thrived in the post-WWII years, creating wealth that supported a vibrant downtown. Small businesses were many and varied: meat markets (2), groceries (2), a jewelry shop, drugstores (2), banks (3), a large dry cleaner, a newspaper, the post office, doctors' offices (4), furniture stores (3), a poultry store, car dealerships (4), an appliance store, and a newsagent who kept the *Playboy* magazines under the counter. There was also a cigar store (where we could also buy ammunition for our .22-caliber rifles), a surplus store for WWII goods, a movie theater (a favorite of us children), W. T. Grant's, Woolworth's, Western Auto (also a favorite at Christmas with a huge toy selection on the second floor), cafes and restaurants, and at least six bars that served booze and good food. All of this and more was dedicated to the care and feeding of about ten thousand persons in town and the many surrounding farm families.

Delphos sits on the southeast corner of what once was the Great Black Swamp, a wet, malarias marsh that projected like a large southwest-pointing finger from the western extent of Lake Erie. Once drained and inhabited, the glacial soils proved extremely fertile. In the mid-1800s farmers reclaimed the land and flourished. They still do. An echo of the Great Swamp is found throughout the village and rural landscapes. Fields must have drainage tiles installed to drain the land to prepare it for plowing, tilling, and planting. These direct their water to the ditches, the creeks, and finally the rivers. A couple of miles east of Delphos, the Auglaize River runs north to the Maumee, while on the rural west side the Little Auglaize River drains the fields and meets its larger sister farther north.

One of the benefits of living on the edge of a drained swamp is the summer green. The landscape is a mixture of farm fields and woods. As a child I became fascinated by my 360-degree view from our car as we traveled through the countryside. On the horizon I saw nothing but a wall of forest. This was an optical illusion, because much of the land had been cleared for agriculture, and what I was observing were the numerous patches of hardwood forests that, in their random distribution across the land, appeared to present an unbroken aspect. These woods and waterways were my joy and the playgrounds of my youth. Woods lined the rivers, acted as breaks for the prevailing northwestern winds, and served as homes for the many small mammals, birds, and reptiles that populated the area. Primarily deciduous hardwoods, the trees would reveal in April the tint of a light green followed by the deep emerald color of June, July, and August. Amplifying the color was the four-to-five-month farming season that year after year produced green, luscious fields of corn, soya beans, wheat, oats, and hay. It was easy to be green.

Odd Couple

My parents were born and grew up in Delphos; but that was where the similarity ended. They were an odd couple. She was from a Catholic family and very conservative. He was non-affiliated and a bit of a bounder. Mother said that only at the age of sixteen did she begin to have a regular period, and even then she was still not sure of the mechanics of procreation. Her witnessing her older sister giving birth was a bit of a shock. My father loved the bottle his whole life, and as a young man had a normal fascination with the opposite sex. One of his stories had him in the back of a strange car recovering from an alcoholic sleep on the way to Cincinnati to be married to a woman who was virtually a stranger. Another had him pulling a drunken friend out of a brothel, where the friend was loud and abusive, to save him from further embarrassment—a friend who was a pillar of the Catholic Church and a prominent Delphos businessman. Father returned the man to his new wife; she in turn accused him of leading her husband to perdition.

My parents attended separate schools, she the Catholic ones, he the public. Yet they knew of each other, as children do in a small town, especially in the 1930s, when there were dance clubs where young people socialized. The pious side of my family did not appreciate Father's attention to Mother when they began to date. My maternal grandmother, Philomena, had died in the Spanish Flu epidemic of 1918, leaving behind four very young children who were then raised in the home of their maternal grandparents with a somewhat distant father in the house next door. Their mother's sister, Aunt Laura, who set the standard for Catholicity in the family by sending both of her sons to the seminary, led the charge against my father. She had sent her obnoxious—by testimony of Mother, who liked nearly everyone—younger son Bertie out of the eighth grade on the pretext of a vocation from God. (More likely it was from

God to Aunt Laura.) Before he had the chance to experience a good level of sexual excitement at puberty, Laura had guaranteed that he was on the road to celibacy and, therefore, holiness. Bertie was also a pedantic ass with delusions of great education and learning. In later years, when family visited whatever unfortunate parish he directed, part of the ceremony was hearing Bertie's monologues on, for example, how the Germans were not so bad in WWII and how that thing about the Jews was greatly exaggerated. Being of German ancestry, he still had a fondness for the old country. Laura directed Bertie onto Mother, where he tried every trick of emotional and spiritual blackmail, sprinkled with large doses of Catholic guilt, to dissuade her from marrying my heathen father. Luckily she, in her own quiet, dignified way, told him to go to hell—where today, if there is such a place, he likely must be, sitting next to the devil himself, continuing on as an apologist for the Fatherland.

When my parents were married in September 1940, one year into the European war, the ceremony had to be performed in the rectory of the parish. "Mixed marriages" could not be performed in the church building. Father Joseph, Aunt Laura's older son who was indeed a scholar and good person, was the celebrant. After a reception with a small number of close family and friends, the newly married couple honeymooned briefly in Florida. When they returned, they took up residence in the house next to my paternal grandparents. My grandfather had purchased the home and had rented it to a couple who now moved across the street. Father was an only child, in fact the only child to be born in his generation among his father and his father's siblings, Nell and Zola. His parents and aunts therefore prized and showered him with every rural middleclass advantage, even during the depression. As a young adult he was given a house and a job. My grandfather, Evan, was the superintendent of The New Delphos Manufacturing Company where he employed his son.

World War II played a very large role in the birth and growth of my generation because many of our fathers had been in uniform. Mine had not. He went to Columbus for his draft physical in 1942 and was diagnosed with high blood pressure, which meant a medical exemption. To celebrate, he went on a bender, and Nell and Zola, who lived in the capital, had to pull him out of a bar and send him home to his new wife and son, my brother Jake, who had been born just before the Battles of the Coral Sea and Midway. Mother later related to me her terrible distress during this time. She did not know where her husband was, whether he would be leaving her and Jake to risk his life in the war. And where had he disappeared after the induction physical? Upon his return, she was very angry but relieved. No gold star would grace our front porch window. Yet in future years, it was not unknown for veterans in the factory to comment somewhat caustically about their boss's lack of service during the war. I felt these comments deeply when I overheard them.

A second son, Luke, was born in the interregnum of VE and VJ day in 1945. Having had success with two healthy sons, my parents decided to try for a girl. Mother loved children, especially little girls. She very much wanted a daughter whom she could dress in pretty clothes and treat as a young lady and who would add a little estrogen to the testosterone in the growing family. But such was not her luck. I was the third male, born in the fallow season in the Midwest—when the sky was nearly always gray, the ground brown, and the trees just contrasting black sticks—some sixteen months after the end of the war, in early winter 1947. After my birth, Mother had no idea what she had borne because at that time mothers were often anesthetized and slept through the procedure. When waking from the drugs, she saw Father come through the door of the hospital room, his eyes meeting hers. He just sadly shook his head "no." It was another boy. Worse, he was deformed. His left leg was congenitally bent off center.

The Cripple

Family scuttlebutt had it that my somewhat severe paternal grandmother, Emma, thought that two boys in my parents' nuclear family were enough. A third child was not necessary or desirable. After all, she had had only one. Mother's sister Helen later told me that Emma referred to me as "the cripple" when I was born, which tells the reader everything they need to know about my relationship with Grandmother. Two weeks later, the pious side of my family baptized me into "the one true Catholic faith." It was quick because babies who died before the holy waters had washed away original sin would languish for eternity in limbo. It seems that this God of love that priests constantly extolled could not tolerate an innocent child in his presence without the intervention of His earthly ministers. Hence, I began my journey with the two themes that were thrust upon me and were to dominate my early years, malformation and religion—what later in life I just called "my disabilities."

The medical diagnosis was a severe clubfoot that required medical intervention. There was no cure. The goal was to bend the poorly formed and distorted lower limb back into a normal orientation with the body. This would result in the patient having a relatively normal gate. The leg and tendons, particularly the Achilles tendon, would retain their congenital nature. The affected lower leg and foot were smaller, with foreshortened tendons that were prone to severe tendonitis when stressed by hiking or running. The first therapy soon after my birth was a series of plaster casts that slowly bent my leg back in line. At home I shared a room with my oldest brother Jake, who later recalled how I ran my cast day and night along the rungs of my crib, making a rattling sound that delighted me but proved the first of many annoyances for him. Therefore, I would spend hours during the day and night entertaining myself. When the last cast came off, braces were put on that delayed my walking for months.

After the braces, I wore special shoes to keep the affected limb from bending inward. My parents took me back and forth during this time to an orthopedist in Lima some thirteen miles to the east, where the specialists and hospitals were. A small city of about fifty thousand souls, that Father called "Little Chicago", because it shared its industrial, crime-ridden, and tough natures with its larger namesake to the northwest. There the doctor examined me and gave my parents instructions for the coming months. After about two years I toddled around like other young children and was on my way to a semi-normal growth and development of my lower limbs.

Memories of this time revolve around the doctor's office and my shoes. His office was dark but roomy with a long narrow space. He had me walk and then run so he could observe my progress. I have no idea how often I was there. Father told me later that the doctor would never take a payment from him. Dad always liked to pay in cash and became irritated with unpaid bills. At the end of the appointment the doctor would merely say, "We'll talk about payment next time. Don't worry about it." Finally, near the end of my visits, Father insisted on the doctor giving him a bill. He was concerned that it was going to be too large to pay in cash and he would need to make arrangement for a loan. Father hated loans. The doctor said, "Mr. Williams, that will be fifty dollars." My dad was incredulous: after those months of specialty care he would charge him so little? Fifty dollars in 1950 translate approximately to five hundred dollars in today's currency. But still, try to get a clubfoot repaired for that amount of money today. The orthopedist realized that my father, a factory worker, had three young sons and not much money and gave him essentially *pro bono* medicine. My foot and I are eternally grateful.

When it came to my shoes, the only adequate words were heavy and clunky. To support the ankle on my left foot, I wore high-top shoes, almost small boots, for a good bit of my childhood; I was in combat boots from an early age. To the sound of clump, clump, clump, I made my heavy way across the floor. The first streamlined shoe that I remember wearing was a low-cut set of football spikes in the last two years of high school.

All of this was done for me without much comment. There was no "oh poor son" talk in the family. Their expectations were no different than for my brothers. Quiet, subtle events would occur without my knowledge, however. I spent a large part of my life as a child in Delphos on a bicycle. The town was flat and small and easily traversed. In a couple of minutes, we could be on the country roads and among the fields. When Father purchased my green, full-sized Schwinn cruiser, he took the rear wheel and hub to the bicycle shop and installed a gear that would make me pedal harder when I took off from a standing stop. I always wondered why my bike was so difficult to get going, especially when I tried my brothers' bikes. He did it, of course, to build up the strength in my left leg. But it was not something that we discussed.

As I began elementary school my foot was to the point that the casual observer could not notice. I did have a little hitch to my gate, a bit of a bounce coming off the good leg. But I managed to play with my friends and participate in intramural sports in the normal way. I was even moderately fast when running. Psychologically, it was a different story. An early history of disability imprints a person. Hardly a day went by as a child, young adult, or adult that I did not think about my leg at least once. After all, I used it all the time to move. In the Boy Scouts, about the age of eleven, I noticed that my bad leg would get quite sore on the six-mile hikes to the Auglaize River and back. On the way out I would be able to walk in comfort. But by the time we were heading west back to town on the verge of 30N highway, I would begin to feel a sharp pain in my left Achilles tendon with every step. I loved to hike; it pained me physically and mentally to do so, however, because the pleasure of being outside and physically active was ground raw by the pain in my foot. It was only much later as an adult, after my hiking boots in the Grand Canyon gave me a similar sore foot, that I learned of the foreshortened tendon and the simple fix of a small prosthetic lift in my left boot.

Unfortunately, there was no easy fix for my brain. The residue of disability was like a weak acid that permanently etched my mind and conditioned many of my future choices. Downhill skiing, jumping out of perfectly good airplanes with a parachute, and riding a motorcycle with exposed legs were out of the question. I loved the idea of such a two-wheeled chariot—a Triumph or Harley—me sitting on the seat, hands on the throttle and brake, racing down the road at eighty miles an hour. I ached for a bike. But then as a teenager, when I was in the hospital for a minor operation, my roommate was a man who had been hit broadside by a car on his motorbike and had just had his third operation. Lines of stitches snaked up and down his leg and he still could not walk. Looking at him and his condition evoked in me a deep primal horror of permanent immobility. I became very cautious about my legs and any activities that might affect them. Nevertheless, this etched brain possessed a second side, the competitive masculine pride that was unable to accept the congenital defect. All through Boy Scouts, high school football, and The United States Marine Corps Platoon Leader Corps, boot-camp, infantry training regiment, and quarterly physical fitness exams, I imperfectly persevered. Protect the legs and ignore the disability.

School

As a member of the baby-boom generation I was in a large class, large for the small town where I was born. Mother enrolled me in the Catholic school that she had attended as a child, which was part of the church's campus. First grade found me in the building that had the name of my great-grandfather, who had helped build it, on the cornerstone. My class was divided into three sections of about forty-five each who traveled from year-to-year together as a unit, each assigned a teacher. My memories are dim for the first two grades other than to see shadows of two black-clothed women, heads covered in a black bonnet with white fringe, with large rosary beads tied around their waist to hold in the yards of black cloth that nearly brushed the floor and polished the tops of their ugly black shoes. They would sit at the front of class at a very large wooden desk when not teaching at the blackboard. We would sit at our hinged-top desks in neat vertical columns, boys on one side and girls on the other. Order was by alphabet or by class standing, depending upon the teacher. We did not talk unless spoken to or move away from our desks unless given permission.

For the third grade, I had my great-aunt Laura as a teacher. She had known me and my brothers and cousins since we were born; we had visited her home often, helping with errands and allowing her to spoil us. During that school year Mother felt that I had taken advantage of that familiarity in the classroom and had behaved badly. Maybe it was the stolen kiss from Kathleen in the cloakroom, or the many notes that I passed to another student before I walked her home after school, or my pleading the need to poop in order to get out of mass and sit by myself in the boys' restroom, or my fighting on the playground during recess, or my verbal familiarity with Aunt Laura in class that verged on disrespect. She was slated to teach the same section again for the fourth grade. But Mother had had enough. She talked to the pastor of the church, who was also the head of the schools, and had me transferred at the beginning of the fourth grade to a different section of students taught by the infamous nun who was known for a severity of temperament even greater than her severity of dress. Here I would have to toe the behavior line; and here

I met students whom I had not known before, including the beautiful Julia, whom I would date in high school.

Fifth grade's teacher was a wonderful, older, civilian non-nun, who was married to a wealthy businessman in town who made trailers for hauling grain and was a professional acquaintance of Father's. She was someone who would become a close, life-long friend. In later years I would see her in Florida where she and her husband were retired and lived just down the street from my snowbird parents. She was a staunch Republican and fulminated over the candidacy of JFK in 1959 and 1960. She deprecated Kennedy's treatment of his wife during the campaign—prescient, in the light of history. How could she have foreseen the sad story of Tricky Dick's presidency when she voted for Nixon in his close loss to Kennedy?

Sixth grade brought a young, attractive, blond, single woman teacher who subsequently married the football coach and moved away. Miss Anne was particularly critical of my fighting and pugnacious attitude and told me that someday my clock would be cleaned. (How right she turned out to be.) She was, however, a welcome relief from the black-robed sisters. I could see that she had breasts underneath her blouses, and her skirts often settled just above her knees, pleasant sights for a pubescent boy. My older brother had also had her in the sixth grade. Her family's farm was just west of Delphos and was where her brother, for reasons that we did not understand, went to the barn and shot himself in the head. Luke and I walked to the funeral home to pay our respects during the awful ritual of body-viewing and commiseration. The parlor was very hot and had the heavy, oppressive scent of flowers. To our horror, when we approached the casket to see her brother, the wax that the funeral directors had used to fill the hole in the middle of his forehead was beginning to melt; it formed an ovoid depression where the bullet had entered the skull. This was our first experience with mental illness, violent death, and suicide. It left us deeply disturbed and reinforced our empathy for our teacher.

For the seventh and eighth grades, I was condemned to the attention of nuns again. The seventh-grade teacher, a real harridan with the unpronounceable name of a saint, rapped my knuckles with a ruler when I was rebellious and rude (which was often) and made us bring in old Christmas and birthday cards that we recycled for test paper. The eighth-grade nun caused a conflict in my newly testosterone-fueled body because she was young, had a very pretty face, and was "hot" under those folds; I was sexually attracted to her. It did not help that she singled me out of the class for special treatment and engaged me in adult conversations after school when I was cleaning the erasers and imagining what her body looked like with the folds removed. When a fourteen-year-old boy gets a large erection—and at that age all boners are enormous—he is not supposed to be fantasizing about a nun. I suppose I should have taken that little sin to confession. But I did not. How could I tell a priest that I was lusting after a nun?

Those eight early years of school were dominated by the severe black dress and personalities of the religious celibates who taught us, the strict rules and regimentation that controlled our young lives, the North-Korean-like indoctrination through the rote memorization of the dictates of the catechism, and the stifling mold that tried to press us all into little religion-besotted automatons who learned their reading, writing, arithmetic, and Jesus. My anger emerged through poor behavior in the classroom and fights in the hallways and playgrounds.

The Factory

As I thus attempted to break the mold and to fashion for myself a different set of beliefs and behaviors, thank goodness I had my father. He professed no religion and quietly and subtly encouraged my rebelliousness. He was also physically close to me when I was at school. The New Delphos Manufacturing Company was just across the playground. As the superintendent, he had his own stall in a covered garage that faced the school and that was reserved for the executives. We rode with him early in the morning and walked across the railroad spur and street to find our classrooms and begin the day. When the morning session ended at 11:20 A.M., we joined him again at his garage door. The factory whistle blew at 11:30, and we made the five-minute car ride home to Sixth Street, where Mother had our main meal on the table.

After eating, I often cycled back to school, which started again at 12:40. I parked my cycle in the galvanizing department of the factory, whose gates opened across from the school and which served as my second home. Children who are raised in service families are called military brats. I was a factory brat. I had free range of the many buildings and was allowed to stand or sit in a corner and watch dangerous jobs, even when many tons of metal were being moved or parts were being formed in huge hydraulic presses and the probability of an accident was not zero. I was the son of the superintendent and had privileges that other children did not. The men quickly learned who I was, and I became a common sight, particularly in the galvanizing department.

Father's first promotion had been as foreman of the galvanizing process. As very small children, we occasionally accompanied him in the evening or on the weekend when the factory was running the line. Here a large sheet of black metal was put between two revolving rollers that first directed it into a tank of hot, dilute acid to clean and etch the surface and then through more sets of rollers that put the sheet through a vat of molten metal, a combination of tin and zinc, that gave it a "galvanized" coating to better protect it from rust. After a couple of cooling steps, the sheet was manhandled by two employees onto the top of a growing pile at the end of the line. These sheets then were transferred to the cutting room to be fashioned into the correct form for stamping in the press room and from there to the various departments for assembling and finishing of the metal products.

When the galvanizing line was running, it was a feast of sights, sounds, and scents for a young boy. At the center of the action the line supervisor sat in a tall leather chair, maybe eight to ten feet in the air, and watched the process that was flooded with bright light. With the sound of the forced air coolers and the gas burners that heated the acid and metal, it was like standing next to a jet plane warming its engines while great clouds of noxious vapor rose from the acid tanks and metal pots. Many bad things could happen, like a sheet getting twisted in the rollers. The supervisor needed to act quickly to shut down the rollers and free the obstruction; if he did not, permanent damage could be done to the equipment. And accidents did happen. The large rectangular sheets of metal had an unpredictable mass and were dangerous to handle. If one end was dropped while being lifted, the resulting torque of the mass suddenly whipped the sharp sides of the sheet in an unpredictable curve.

By the mid-fifties the factory decided that it was uneconomical to galvanize its own metal and began to buy it from the steel companies that fabricated it. Then the line and its equipment were replaced with slabs of concrete and by two items that fascinated me as a child, trucks and a large mechanical overhead crane. Trucks with metal-laden flatbed trailers from the steel company pulled into the gates of the galvanizing department and then into the tall, wooden building below an I-beam, attached to which was the crane. Cables descended from the crane and were attached to two iron pieces with projecting prongs that fit on either side of the metal pile with the prongs firmly slid underneath. It then slowly and gently lifted from the bed while the crane moved along the I-beam to place it in its appropriate place on the floor. This was repeated until the truck was empty.

The piles of galvanized sheets that arrived on the truck bed were held together by black metal straps and covered by dark canvas tarps. When it was raining, I relished the delicious scents of truck, oil, tires, gasoline, and wet tarp, especially when combined with the sounds of the diesel engine and the air brakes as well as the sights of the tractor and trailer's multicolored signal lights.

I had my own small-scale trucks with which I played as a young child. When I was a bit older, I begged my father to do a ride-along in the semi-rig that the factory used to distribute its products. John, their semi-trailer driver, was a tall, thin, friendly man who smoked pungent cigars and was kind enough to tolerate me in the cab of the tractor. Depending on the size and shape of the load, two trailers could be hooked to the tractor, one a flat bed with removable sides and the other an enclosed trailer like one sees by the hundreds on the road. Each had double axles and could carry a heavy load. The company driver picked me up at home early in the morning, usually between 3 and 4 A.M., and transported me to the loaded semi sitting inside the factory building. We then drove to our destination, usually another business or warehouse some hours away and delivered the load. This meant waiting while the men at our destination removed the boxes or items on the flatbed and checked them against the manifest. Then we headed back to Delphos. I participated in off-loading the boxes, or, when we were using the flatbed, I was responsible for the canvas tarps that covered the load and that needed to be folded and chained to the bed before our return. I was in heaven in and around trucks and very much enjoyed participating in the adult world of work.

At the end of the school day, I often ran down the stairs and pushed open the metal door to see Father, fedora on his head, leaning against the gates of the galvanizing department waiting for me. We wandered togeth-er through the factory to a local office or across the street to his office on the corner. After a few minutes of casual conversation, the buzzer would sound for him to call the main office. Another fire needed to be put out, another problem fixed. Off I would go, fetching my bicycle, and complet-ing the circle of my early years: from home, to school, to factory, to home. Healed cripple, rowdy student, factory brat, I made my way through the first years of my life in the middle of the cornfields. Little did I know at the time what an idyllic and insulated life it was, one surrounded by a loving, protective family but also one that allowed me to develop an in-dependent spirit and explore new experiences and opportunities. It was a Midwestern bubble in the forties, fifties, and early sixties. Only later was I to learn the harsh emotional and physical landscape that lay outside it. For the time being, it was enough that I was young, loved, and happy.

CHAPTER 2

Extended Clan

One of the Clan

I grew up in the middle of the warm, noisy, embrace of an extended family of seventeen children on my mother's side. In addition to our nuclear family, she had two sisters with children—Aunt Elizabeth with a girl and five boys, and Aunt Helen with a girl and a boy—and a single brother, Charles. My late maternal grandmother, Philomena, who died of the Spanish Flu, had a brother whose wife also perished in the epidemic of 1918. She left a young girl similar in age to Mother who spent a great deal of time with her and her siblings at their grandparents', where they lived as children. "Aunt Jane," however, had attended the public school with my father and had converted to Catholicism only when she married. Although a first cousin of my mother, we always treated her as her sister, and her two girls and four boys were incorporated into our extended family with equal status.

Given the many cousins it was inevitable that some of us would make the journey through school together. Four pairs of first cousins were in the same classes in our respective years. Many pictures exist in the family albums with a pair of kids in the snow-white suits or dresses that marked a first communion. These allow us to date the photos because this holy event always occurred in the spring of the second grade. In a picture from the day of my own first communion, Helen's daughter Barb and I are standing in her backyard with the sun glaring off our outfits and her bright red curly hair and freckles. It was one of the few times that we did not have scrapes, dirt, and torn clothes.

What prominence we had as a family in Delphos must be credited to Mother's father, Charles Steinle. He was a nineteenth-century man who had joined his father, Felix, in the family business, which had existed since the 1870s on East 2nd Street just north of the Catholic cemetery and east of St. John's Schools. They owned and ran the Steinle Brewing & Ice Company, brewed Steinle's Famous Delphos Beer, and distributed it throughout the area. Between the years 1918 and 1920, Charles Steinle suffered a double tragedy. First his young wife, Philomena, died and left him with four children under the age of ten. Unable to care for his children himself, he moved them next door where their mother's parents raised them. Then, on January 1, 1920, the Volstead Act delivered a second blow, implementing the eighteenth constitutional amendment that banned the sale and consumption of alcoholic beverages. Charles's brewing skills were suddenly superfluous, the resultant product illegal. He kept the establishment alive on near-beer, soft drinks, and ice.

He was a distant father who lived close by. At dinner, he would walk next door and eat with the family, a time when the children were especially careful to be quiet and good. He did not marry again and concentrated his attention and energies on his business.

Grandfather's position as a German Master Brewer, who created a product enjoyed by the largely German community, made him a prominent man in Delphos. Success and money brought prestige in the Midwest, where you were what you did, and the measure of your worth was in dollars and cents. Small-businessmen, country doctors, and lawyers formed the nobility in this meritocracy. In the early-twentieth-century rural areas and small towns there was little inherited wealth among the immigrants who drained the fields, grew the crops, built the homes, businesses, and churches, and created wealth. Small manufacturing firms flourished. A network of railroads that included the Nickel Plate and Pennsylvania lines crisscrossed our town and gave these growing companies communication with suppliers and clients. Around all this new money rose the service industries, including clothing stores, drugstores, plumbers, carpenters, roofers, undertakers, schools, and teachers. After work, recreation frequently took the form of consuming Grandfather's beer. He was thus at the center of the town's community life—and its large thirst for alcohol.

He and other successful business owners started the private Delphos Club, where the prominent men in town dined and drank once a week and played a couple of rounds of cards. It was located on the second floor of a late-19th Century building on the corner of Main and Second streets and was reached by a steep set of creaky wooden stairs polished to a bright dark finish. The club was also where business was done, and status created. Little of importance occurred in Delphos without the knowledge of one of the members. Trust was established here; loans negotiated; contracts created with a smile and handshake; opportunities offered to friends and relatives of members; gossip exchanged that could brand either good or bad; children vetted for appropriate dating stock. It was strictly a male society. Wives of the members used the facilities only to play bridge and pinochle in the afternoons and plan the occasional evening dinners and dances for couples.

In 1933, during the Roosevelt administration, when Prohibition was repealed by another amendment, Grandfather again began brewing beer and distributing it throughout the region. With spirits again legal, the large brewing establishments moved to buy up the smaller ones to limit competition and create companies with interstate reach and power. At some time after the end of Prohibition, I do not know what year, Grandfather Charles had to make the choice of becoming larger or selling out. Expanding the business meant finding local investors. My father told me that the money had been there. It seems that his friends and relatives with resources, however, thought his management skills did not match the high quality of his beer. If they provided the capital for expansion, they wanted control of the finances and distribution. He would be the Master Brewer only and share all profits. He refused and eventually sold out to a firm in Dayton in return for which he became the local sales representative. In January 1947, when Mother was in the hospital at the time of my birth, her father was also there being treated for heart disease. He would come down the hall and visit with her and see the new baby. Six months later he died.

Warm and Goofy

Mother and her sisters and brother were very close. They related to us, in later years, stories that would suggest a happy childhood brought up by loving grandparents with the assistance of nannies, with a prominent father and an extended maternal clan nearby. As adults, they all lived in town, and Mother's siblings' homes were just a couple of streets away, so we often saw them. The oldest, Aunt Elizabeth, married first. She and her husband Don lived in the large house that they purchased from her father's estate— at a song, or so said Father. It was the family home where Mother and her siblings were born and raised until their mother's death. It had two floors, a full basement with cistern, an open porch, and a large attic.

Aunt Elizabeth can best be described as the goofy sister. Often Mother and I entered the home to hear "and who are these people coming in my front door" accompanied by various physical gestures of befuddlement. Her housekeeping skills were minimal and compounded by the activities of four to six young children that kept it in a perpetual state of disorder and chaos. Uncle Don engaged in many home improvement projects but was extremely slow in their execution. So, in addition to general disarray, there were often construction materials, wall boards, or paint cans about. We children were fascinated by the facility with which Aunt Elizabeth could produce dinner when we visited. She would be wandering around the house, making random gestures and seemingly unrelated comments about this and that until just shortly before our young stomachs required food. Then suddenly she would disappear into her cluttered kitchen with dirty dishes and pans everywhere and in a very short time produce a meal not only for her large family but also for the various cousins who were hanging about. It was a warm home full of activity and laughter, the friendliest and most comfortable home to visit among the relatives.

A great advantage of the old family home was that it was close to the Overhead. In the early twentieth century, an interurban trolley line originated in the east at Lima, ran down Second Street, and headed west out of Delphos into the country, and on to farms and towns fifty miles further on. Where the line crossed the railroad via an overpass were ramped wooded areas that rose to concrete berms on each side of the double train track of the Pennsylvania Railroad. The iron rails had long ago been removed along with the bridge. The remaining concrete supports, what we called the Overhead, had been abandoned by adults long ago, but were accessible if one took Second Street to where it dead-ended at the woods, picking up the grown-over trolley bed there and following it for a hundred yards. Only two minutes from Aunt Elizabeth's home, we could play in the narrow woods until we heard the distant horn of a train coming and then rush along the path to the Overhead to watch the train's light become larger and larger until right below us was the sound, fury, dust, and smell of the long procession of articulated cars. They moved by quickly at fifty or sixty miles per hour, the engineer blowing the horn before the town's intersections. Quickly the sound moved away, even before the last of the cars had passed. Occasionally we were rewarded with the wave of the crewman on the porch of the caboose where he would be enjoying a smoke or a chew under the red light. Passenger trains going from Chicago to New York often sped by, as did freight trains going anywhere and everywhere. Each train produced a burst of excitement that punctuated our woodland games and roughhousing.

Big Red

Mother's second sister, Aunt Helen, always intimidated me a little as a child because she was tall, about five-feet-nine-inches, with bright red hair usually piled high on her head, which made her appear even larger and more imposing and starkly contrasted with her white nurse's garb. But it was her blunt, no-nonsense personality that impressed us kids, so different from her two sisters and brother. She did not suffer fools gladly, nor had she ever met a male who was her equal or from whom she would take abuse or—as we were to learn later in life—long emotional entanglement. She was also a free spirit and had few inhibitions about what she said. When my young brother developed the habit of putting himself to sleep by hitting his head on the pillow to the tune of "Irene, Goodnight," she told my conservative, orthodox Catholic mother that it was a form of masturbation, which left my mom speechless and aghast and us children in hysterics.

Aunt Helen was also fond of life's physical pleasures. When we were adults, she described her trip to New York City in December of 1941 right after the attack on Pearl Harbor. Her first husband had drowned in

Lake St. Mary's, leaving her a single mother with a two-year-old boy. Her friend Arthur—whom she had dated before her marriage and who was the brother of Aunt Elizabeth's husband Don—was in the Navy on a floating dry dock, was about to ship out to war, and the likelihood of the two of them soon seeing each other again was small. There was also, of course, the chance that Arthur might die in the war. Aunt Helen's trip brought condemnation from the pious half of my family; a single woman traveling six hundred miles to see a single man was not an appropriate activity. They all knew the purpose of the trip was not only emotional comfort, but physical as well. Arthur survived the war, and they married, he only to die of cancer soon after in 1948, leaving a one-year-old daughter, Cousin Barb. From this time, Helen raised two children on her own.

Fortunately, unlike her siblings, Helen had sought higher education after high school, attending the nursing school at St. Rita's Hospital in Lima. When I was very young, she was a staff nurse for the general physician and surgeon in Delphos. Then she took a job at St. Rita's where she reigned supreme over all staff and patients as head nurse on the fifth floor. This was the floor where only male patients were allowed. Many stories existed in our family about young nurses and visitors who had rubbed Big Red the wrong way on floor five, nurses who had made a bad medical decision, been late for work, lazy, or insubordinate, or visitors who overstayed their welcome or who tried to challenge the absolute authority of the head nurse. These folks were quickly dispatched with sharp words and a cursory manner. Big Red was a professional perfectionist and would let nothing compromise medical standards on her floor. And the male patients had better behave as well. Word had it that, when a patient got aroused during Big Red's ministrations, she would take her thumb and middle finger, give his member a painful flick, and tell him to behave himself. A shrinking violet my aunt was not!

I was the beneficiary of her authority on the fifth floor when, in my early teens, I went to the hospital and had my appendix removed. For four days after the surgery, I was very sore, with limited mobility. At that time an appendectomy was major abdominal surgery. I received the most solicitous attention from young, pretty nurses who did everything they could to ingratiate themselves with Big Red's nephew. Well, almost everything. When they woke me in the middle of the night to take my rectal temperature, I was not amused. It was an indignity to have to roll over and reveal that orifice to the nurse and then feel a cold glass rod covered in jelly being pushed up my ass at 2 A.M. Also, it was painful, to say the least, because the incision burned like hellfire when I moved. However, the nursing staff redeemed themselves in the evenings. One of them would come into the room with a bottle of lotion in her hand and say, "Mr. Williams, it is time for your backrub." I suppose this was to help prevent bed sores; or it was an attempt to improve my grouchy attitude. What it did was excite my young male body, making me thankful I was lying on my sore stomach. Those wonderful, soft, young, female hands massaging my skin and muscles and filling the room with soothing words and gentle laughter sent me into heights of rapturous pleasure. It was the first time that a woman had spent that much time trying to make me feel good.

Helen's house always resembled the size and style of a hat box. With two bedrooms, a TV room, living room, tiny kitchen, full basement with poured concrete walls, and a garage, it was made up of every sort of rectangle that one could imagine putting into a house sited on a lot that was three times longer than it was wide. Father told me that she had purchased the house in cash with the military life insurance policy she had received after Arthur's death. He and Uncle Don had counseled her to invest the money for the future and float a mortgage for the building of the home. But Helen was never one to save. Spending was her style. And it left her short of cash and in debt for most of her life.

The home was located at the opposite end of town from ours, in one of the new developments that sprung up in Delphos after WWII to house the returning service members and their families. It was a mixed neighborhood. Across the street was the much grander, multilevel house of one of the local doctors. Next to the doctor lived an electrician and his large family with children whose names all began with the letter "V." (The father of the Vs used to call me "Elephant," something that really pissed me off and made me want to punch his smiling face.) The street was a dead end. The residents decided that they did not want traffic to run through their private enclave and built a concrete barrier to block exit to the east; "to protect the playing children" was the rationalization. But I always felt that there was a touch of snobbism and exclusivity in the choice.

Barb and I, born two weeks apart, she without a father, grew up pretty much as brother and sister. My mom and dad helped Big Red with finances and child rearing, the former with a lot of grouching from my father about irresponsibility, the latter with an openness and love that always impressed me. Father treated Barb with a tenderness that was foreign to me. We spent a lot of time at each other's homes. Our respective basements were our playgrounds during the cold and wet winters. Aunt Helen was a meticulous housekeeper and loved flowers and shrubs. Grass, trees, and bushes tastefully surrounded the home and filled the long backyard where many family parties took place. After Christmas Eve midnight mass, she hosted a breakfast for the church-going adults and children. Burning candles, the scent of food (wonderful to children who had been fasting for communion all day), a glowing tree surrounded by wrapped packages that took up much of the cramped living room, and all of us screaming and happy children on the one night of the year we could be up and active through the early morning produced a cozy atmosphere in that small space.

Aunt Jane's Bottom

Aunt Jane married a prominent Miller whose family owned and ran grain mills where corn, oats, wheat, soybeans, and other products were bought, sold, and stored. Jane and my father had also known each other for years because they had been classmates. She and Uncle Bob lived in the country about three miles east of town, next to the Auglaize River, where they raised sheep and had a chicken coop.

My lasting impression of Aunt Jane was her speech: it was loud, sometimes shrill, opinionated, and often very earthy and funny, with a sprinkling of profanity. Once, when asked by her granddaughter why Jane's son, the girl's father, was always getting strange women pregnant, she responded, "Because he thinks with his dick!" She was very interested in politics and current affairs and affected the posture of a small-town intellectual, which she probably was. Her job as proofreader for the local daily newspaper kept her well informed. Speaking of posture, she was quite unconcerned about the finer points of manners and etiquette; she usually sat on her couch with one leg's ankle on the other knee, beer in hand and a cigarette in her mouth, in a position that was hardly "ladylike." Her acute sense of injustice and Democratic inclinations precipitated fulminations of spiteful words when tweaked. Three of her children had had trouble with the police, incidents that received the attention of the paper and town gossips. When she learned of prominent people working the system to protect their children from the newspaper and vicious mouths, she would rail against them like an inflamed preacher invoking hell fire and damnation.

Mom and Dad would often take us kids to the river to see Jane and Bob. Each visit had a familiar ritual, the adults sitting in the wood-paneled living room drinking beer, conversing, and laughing, while we children headed for the river. My strong impression of their house was the odor. In parts of the outlying country the well water contained large amounts of sulfur that stained sinks and toilets and left the house with the slight fragrance of rotting eggs. It was compounded by Uncle Bob, who cleaned his chickens' eggs in the basement before putting them in cartons for sale to the local egg wholesaler. Freshly laid eggs often have organic matter that needs removing; in the process of cleaning them a small number cracked and leaked, and a few fell and broke on the cement floor. When I visited, I could not drink from the tap; the combination of the atmosphere and the taste of the water made me gag.

I preferred to spend my time outside when we visited. Their house was on a small hill and next to the road that ran parallel to the river. The gentle slope to the water ended about thirty yards from the river's edge and was known in the family as "Aunt Jane's Bottom." It was here that my wealthy Aunt Frances, also a cousin of my mother, hosted a family party every Fourth of July. Our parents would put large tables and many chairs next to the river. Food was prepared by all the families and shared. Father's yearly complaint was that Mother's fried chicken was so good it was eaten first, and he had to choose a leg and a thigh from one of the other relative's trays that was inferior in taste and texture. Aunt Frances's son filled the back of a pick-up truck with ice-cold sodas and bottled beer. We also had a five-gallon keg of draft beer that was iced and fitted with my father's tap, a device with a long tube and air pump that was inserted into the top of the keg that pushed the beer through a set of iced coils when the faucet was turned on. Many pictures in our old family albums show a large gathering of adults and small children grouped next to the Auglaize River gazing into the lens. At any one time, there would be at least a dozen kids from the four families. We were mostly boys. As high energy, easily bored children we were always looking for excitement and mischief. There are family stories about the older cousins whose girlfriends arrived in pretty, white summer outfits that soon became wet and the color of the muddy river water, thanks to childhood pranks that tipped the rowboat or pushed them down the bank. Occasionally more sedate, urban children who were distant cousins would attend the party. Clean clothes on shy, prissy-looking young males and females were like waving a red cape in front of us little country toughs. We would incorporate them into our hikes, games, and swims, but I cannot remember any of them returning a second time.

Dynamic Cousin

An important member of our extended clan was the Auglaize River itself, which played as significant a role in our young lives as any other person. In every season we would be found around it, in it, or on it. In the summer a well-trodden path went from Aunt Jane's Bottom to the small, broken dam that was about a mile from her house. In a rowboat, a canoe, or on foot we made our way to this concrete wall that served as our playground. A familiar path took us through the backyard of the neighboring farm, up and over wooden fences with barbed-wire tops, and along a farmer's field until we emerged at the edge of the river that led to the dam. The water flowed over the top and went cascading about fifteen feet to the rocks below. Why it had been built, I could never understand. It was small and did back the water up to the south but not to a large depth, never more than five or six feet. The east side had been battered by flooding and debris that broke the concrete. Also, on the east side of the shore by the dam was a small dirt bluff about twenty feet high that flooding had eroded into a concave shape. Above the dam we swam; across it we walked with the water running over our ankles and legs, a test of skill that was an initiation for the younger children; on the lower side of the dam, we stood under the waterfall and hid from the outside world. Laughing, jostling one another, tripping relatives who were snaking their way over the top; it was a wet children's party.

How none of us ever became sick and died is a mystery. In the fifties and sixties, before Congress passed the Clean Water Act, farmers and cities used rivers as refuse dumps and cesspools. Uncle Bob raised sheep. When one died, it was not uncommon for us to find the remains along the bank where he had deposited it. When the water rose, they were carried downstream along with all the chemicals and bacteria from the putrefaction. We also made our way to the dam by wading in the middle of the river and swimming the parts that were too deep. It was not unusual to feel the end of a pipe that came out from the shore and then a squishy patch of mud-like material into which we sank up to our ankles, the end of a farmer's plumbing for his house. While we had some consciousness of this as children, it passed as an everyday rural occurrence and held no sense of danger. The spectrum of antibodies and immunological memory cells in my body must be large from those years. Doctors now warn parents of the dangers of keeping their houses too sterile with the antibiotic chemicals in off-the-shelf cleaners. Children need to have their young immune systems exposed to viruses and bacteria to develop good immune health. As children, we had no such problems.

The river was indeed a living, breathing part of our family, an ecology with fish, turtles, snakes, and crawdads in the water and an abundant tree, plant, and animal life lining its shores. We fished for catfish and crappies and hooked freshwater turtles on long lines baited with raw meat. Mother had been raised in a hunting and fishing family and could make delicious meals from old recipes that she had learned from her grandmother. The one thing that she refused to do was clean game or fish. They had to come to her fresh and ready to cook. Therefore, we children soon learned how to gut, skin, and scale. The river was full of food.

It also had the most dynamic personality of any family member. For four seasons it changed in a familiar cycle, year after year. In the summer the water was low and brown, with insects buzzing at its surface and the trees and shrubs at its edges deeply green with foliage. Fall was my favorite, with multicolored hues on the shore, cool, clear water in its bed, and no insects to harass us. Winter presented bare branches, snow, and thick ice, opportunities for skating and hiking. Spring rains along with the thawing of the ice created huge floods that cleansed the river and deposited large piles of organic debris along the paths that followed the river's course. This varied, mercurial member of the family nourished us, played with us, and surrounded us with beauty and peace in all seasons, a valued member of our extended clan.

Embattled Uncle

Bogie

Staying with Aunt Helen and acting as a sort-of surrogate father to
Barb, was Mother's brother, Charles Steinle Jr. Everyone in the
family, however, called him Bogie. Every family probably has one like
him. Single his entire life, a "dedicated bachelor," hating the structure
and discipline that work imposed on his habits, he must have had five
or six jobs when I was growing up, all interspersed with long periods of
unemployment. He was a clerk for the local company that made insulation
from old newspaper; he was a bank teller in Lima; he was an accountant
and clerk for the tombstone sellers in town; he worked for Uncle Don
at the stone quarry; and my father found him a job in the office of his
factory. Nothing lasted very long. He always had a story, an excuse: this
person was mean to him; another was a duplicitous shit with whom he
could not get along; the bank in Lima was looking at him suspiciously,
suspecting him of fraud or worse. Bogie was a paranoid. He was often
without money and lived where he could: above the old building that
had one of the hardware stores in town, in a couple of rooms in a house
across the street from the library, or on Helen's couch when he had no
other place to go. Mother would slip him money and invite him to the

house to eat. Father would give him his old clothes to wear and fix him highballs with the expensive Old Grandad whiskey he favored. Uncle Don would slip him a few bucks and provide him with cigars, which they both smoked. It took a community to keep Bogie.

His early history was full of tragedy and death. Only fourteen months old when his mother, Philomena, died in the epidemic, he was raised by elderly grandparents who, while providing him with the necessities of life, could not adequately substitute for a dead mother and distant father. Early pictures of him standing with my mom show him to be a thin, frail little boy with a pensive face. He grew into a very thin, tall, sensitive adult whose disposition was more attuned to his sisters than to the rough-and-tumble boys with whom he went to school. I could imagine him as the frail, bookish, reserved kid on the playground, unaccomplished at sports and teased and bullied by the more aggressive males. A bit effeminate by nature in movement and personality, he grew up and lived in an early-twentieth-century Catholic town, a world in which sexuality was strictly policed, presumed heterosexual, and the word "sex" hardly uttered.

Drafted

Then, when Bogie was twenty-two years of age, a terrible thing happened that ran counter to every instinct in his being and conditioned his attitude toward the world for his remaining years. In September 1939 war was declared in Europe. The following year the United States passed a law that began drafting young men into the military during peacetime. Bogie received his papers in late 1940 and reported to duty for basic training on February 1, 1941. He went to Louisiana to train with the Army, and he hated it. His letters during this time to his sisters reflect his misery. He hated the male vulgarity, violence, drinking, and womanizing. He hated the discipline and order imposed on him, the uniforms, marching, and jingoism of the officers. Unfortunately for him, however, the Pearl Harbor attack later that year, on December 7, meant Bogie was in for the duration.

When finished with basic training, he was assigned to the Military Occupational Specialty (M.O.S.) of Aid Man, or Medic as we in the Marine Corps and Navy called them. His assignment to the medical corps is revealing. While I am sure that there were many brave Aid Men in the Army who bandaged the wounds, carried the litters, and saved the lives of thousands of soldiers during WWI, WWII, and the Vietnam War, it was also often a receptacle for misfits, in the literal sense of that word: someone who just does not know how, or is physically unable, to get with the program. Many men drafted into the service were not suited to take an active role in combat operations with a rifle and bayonet. Their personalities and physiques did not permit them to be built into killing machines. Some were conscientious objectors who volunteered to save lives and treat and heal wounds rather than search and destroy. Others were identified early in basic training as having no aptitude or desire for the military life and work. Yet here they were, drafted into the Army. What to do with them? The Medical Corps was often the answer; it certainly was for Bogie. It was also the answer for the person he mentions most often in his handwritten memoirs from this time, his close friend Peter, who was stationed with him throughout the Pacific.

When we were growing up, we knew Uncle Bogie only as the happy-go-lucky person with a "see-gar" in his mouth, a Heineken beer or Old Grandad in his hand, an easy, loud laugh and sardonic sense of humor, and a don't-give-a-damn attitude that seemed to deny his immediate circumstances. He very seldom talked of the war. We generally knew that he was an Army Aid Man who had been on Guadalcanal and still had the metal fragment from an explosion in his back. But other than decrying the stupidity of the Army and war and declaring how much he hated both, he shared few specifics with us. Then late in life he decided to examine those early years in more detail and put his memories of the war in writing; why, he also did not say.

Guadalcanal, First Blood

Here is where Bogie and I intersected in later years. I was trained in the United States Marine Corps by veterans of WWII, of Guadalcanal, Tarawa, Saipan, Iwo Jima, Okinawa, and Peleliu. During training and my four years in the Corps, I heard stories of sacrifice and death, of courage and survival. On August 7, 1942, the First Marine Division landed unopposed at Lunga Point on the north shore of the island of Guadalcanal. Only a Japanese construction crew and a few soldiers were present to defend it. The Marines' mission was to capture the Japanese airfield that was nearly finished and that, when operational, would have threatened the American supply lines to Australia where General Douglas MacArthur was putting together a force to work its way back to the Philippines and, eventually, to Japan. This was the first opportunity for the American forces to face the enemy and stop their expansion into southwestern Asia. Since the Pearl Harbor attack, the United States had been on the defensive, only able to watch as the Japanese had one victory after another. Admiral Ernest King, Commander in Chief United States Fleet (COMINCH) and Chief of Naval Operations (CNO) during World War II, wanted the U.S. forces to arrest the Japanese expansion and to defeat them at a place with strategic importance. When in the early summer of 1942, Admiral King learned of the air base being constructed on Guadalcanal, he directed the Marine Corps to seize it and develop it into one that would threaten the strategic position of the enemy. He wanted to turn the tables.

Admiral King could not have chosen a better hellhole for first battle had he intentionally determined to harass his fellow servicemen. Guadalcanal is a big hogback of an island with high, rocky ridges running east and west along its center, with many rivers and streams flowing down their sides and creating deep, jungle-covered valleys and ravines that ended in the ocean on both sides. Malaria and dysentery were endemic. Heat was intense and made boon-docking very difficult. The native Solomon islanders were known to have, at one time, killed and eaten their enemies. Kunai grass grew nearly as high as the Marines were tall and cut the skin like sharp files. Rain fell, creating ankle-deep mud and turning the bivouac area and runways into small lakes. Moisture permeated clothes that never completely dried and soon began to fray and shred. Boots fell apart, and feet were consumed with fungus. Japanese planes dropped bombs, and destroyers shelled the perimeter area nearly every day and most nights. Sleep was very difficult and punctuated by alarms and runs to fetid shelters cut from the earth and reinforced with coconut logs and sandbags.

Esprit de Corps

Guadalcanal was a bloody, murderous battle on sea and land. The waters on the north shore of the island would come to be called "Iron Bottom Sound" because of the many American, Australian, and Japanese warships that were sunk during the battles. On land, General Archer Vandergrift and his Marines fought pitched battles with the enemy during August, September, and October before the Army arrived to help. The Japanese thought that Marines were soft because of their rich American lifestyle and could not possibly stand up to an army that was highly trained in the Samurai tradition and experienced from battles in China, the Philippines, Wake Island, and the Marianas. Therefore, although surprised by the sudden appearance of the Marines on Guadalcanal, and the Americans' success in taking the airstrip and setting up a defensive perimeter, the Imperial forces believed that it would be relatively easy to move them off the island and reclaim it for the Emperor. Such hubris proved deadly, however. The United States Marine Corps had its own 172 years of tradition and *esprit de corps*. All members were first trained as infantrymen. Anyone who failed their tough boot camp was discharged and sent home. It was the mantra that we were taught in boot camp, "blood, guts, death, and destruction, the finest fighting force the world has ever known." They had training; they had pride; all of them could shoot and had qualified with the Springfield 1903 .30-06 rifle; they all were willing to die for the mission.

In August and September, two major Marine battles stand out among many skirmishes and an expanding defensive perimeter and set the stage and opportunity for the participation of the U.S. Army. In the third week of August the Japanese sent a force of nearly 916 soldiers from their base at Truk to the north shore of Guadalcanal, some twenty miles east of the Marines at what was now called Henderson Field after a pilot who had died in the Battle of Midway. The enemy force was led by an officer, a Colonel Ichiki, who thought that the field was held by just a few hundred Marines when in fact almost seventeen thousand had arrived with the First Division. Ichiki expected that his force would kill and capture the incompetent, vulnerable enemy with little trouble. The Americans were tipped off by Marine patrols and native scouts that the Japanese were making their way west along the path that paralleled the seacoast and would therefore try to assault Henderson Field across the Tenaru River that formed part of the eastern perimeter. It had a large sandbar at its mouth. The Marines emplaced their machine guns in reinforced dugouts with overlapping fields of fire and registered their artillery pieces to the area of the sandbar and farther east where the attack would likely come. In the evening of August 21, the Japanese attacked. By the next afternoon, the Marines had killed over eight hundred Japanese soldiers by rifle, machine gun, and artillery. Finally, two tanks attacked, mopping up the remaining forces while running their tracks red over the dead bodies of the enemy and firing canister shot at the few retreating soldiers. The Americans had over one hundred dead and wounded. Colonel Ichiki, shamed by the defeat, retreated east and committed suicide. It was a lesson for the Imperial staffs of the Japanese Army and Navy that the Americans were not going to be easily dislodged from their foothold on the island and that fighting them was going to entail many casualties.

From September 12 to 14, the Emperor's forces tried again to dislodge the Americans from the airfield where the Marines had now stationed fighters and bombers to attack the Japanese planes and ships. The tables were slowly starting to turn. Exploiting the hard lesson of the massacre of Colonel Ichiki's force, the enemy gathered more than two thousand soldiers under a General Kawaguchi and, coordinating with the Japanese Air Force and Navy, planned an assault on the southeastern portion of the perimeter. Here rocky ridges bordered the dense jungle. The Marines appeared vulnerable because the nearly impenetrable terrain coming down from the hogback was not considered suitable for attack and was more lightly defended when the perimeter was established. It was also only a few hundred yards from Henderson Field. Unfortunately for the Japanese, a Marine Colonel by the name of Edson also recognized the hole in the defensive perimeter and moved his Raider-Paratroop battalion onto the ridge in a strong defensive position backed up by Marine Corps artillery and a battalion of reserve troops. The Japanese attacked September 12, 1942, with a combined air, naval gunfire, and infantry assault. Three columns of enemy soldiers had been moving through the jungle for more than two weeks to get into position to attack. During this time the difficulty of negotiating the dense foliage and rugged valleys had beaten down the Japanese and had delayed their arrival. When the attack finally occurred, the Imperial soldiers were nearly exhausted from the ordeal. The battle, now known as "Blood Ridge" or "Edson's Ridge," led to a second massacre of enemy troops. The first night, the Japanese penetrated the Marine lines at various points, engaging in hand-to-hand and close-quarter fighting. Many enemy soldiers and Marines were killed and wounded, yet the line held. On the next day, Edson withdrew his forces from the forward ridge to one farther back, which shortened his lines. He then set up strong defensive positions and cleared the area in front of the lines for better and deeper fields of fire. When the Japanese attacked for the second time on the night of September 13, once again they were repelled. Almost one thousand Imperial soldiers were killed, with many others wounded. As Kawaguchi and his remaining men dragged the wounded into the jungle and made their way back to their own lines, many more died from their injuries and starvation. So many of the enemy had died that the Americans had to carve mass graves out of the ground with bulldozers, push their bodies in, and cover them with earth.

The Army, and Bogie, Arrive

The Marines fought alone on the island until October 13, 1942, some nine weeks after the first assault of the beach, when the 164th Army Infantry Regiment of the Americal Division arrived to reinforce them. This was the vanguard of a U.S. Army force that was slated to take over garrisoning and combat duties and relieve the Marine Corps 1st Division in December. Bogie's hand-written story begins here.

October 28, 1942

Peter and I sailed aboard the transport Neville. (We had been stationed on TONGATABU Island for five months and twelve days.)

October 28 to November 4, 1942

The voyage from Tongatabu to Guadalcanal took seven days. We did not cross the International Date Line.

While en route to Guadalcanal the convoy stopped at Espiritu Santo Island in the New Hebrides. We stopped there to pick up two companies of the 2nd (Marine) Raider Battalion. Warships escorted our five-ship convoy the 557 miles from Espiritu Santo to Guadalcanal.

Bogie arrived on the Transport Neville with the Army's Infantry Regiment at Aola on the north shore of Guadalcanal.

November 4, 1942

Early that morning on board the Neville, we were served a steak breakfast. We then climbed down the cargo nets and boarded landing craft which took us to shore. We landed two months and twenty-eight days after the U.S. Marines had invaded Guadalcanal.

Night of November 4–5, 1942

Rifle fire all night long by nervous soldiers. Pete and I bandaged a man mistakenly shot in the leg by a bullet fired by his buddy. I escorted and helped carry the litter to an aid station. We then carried the litter to the sick bay of a ship. While en route to the ship, he lost much blood. I used my belt as a tourniquet. Once aboard the ship, I gave his watch and wallet to a corpsman. A few days later, I learned that his watch and wallet had been stolen.

Admiral Kelly Turner, who was responsible for the transportation of the Marine and Army troops to the island, also wanted to play General and convinced Admiral Halsey, who commanded the Southwestern Pacific Area, that a back-up air base should be built on the plantation where the British Island Administrator had once had his headquarters. The order infuriated the Marines farther down the coast at Henderson Field because they needed the troops to hold and repair the current airfield, which was daily under bombardment from the sea and air. They also knew, because that British Administrator was now part of their intelligence unit, that the ground around Aola was too wet and unstable for the construction of a runway. Bogie's regiment was there to protect the engineers and construction crews. Once the Seabees found that General Vandergrift and his intelligence unit were correct, that the ground was completely unsuited, they moved the troops, including Bogie, down the coast. He describes his experience:

November 29, 1942
The 1st Battalion, 147th Infantry, departed from Aola Bay aboard landing boats. I had been stationed at Aola Bay for twenty-five days. It was a "miserable place." I had malaria and dysentery there.

We joined our Regimental Headquarters and the Third Battalion at Volinavua, Koli Point. Koli Point was located "perhaps fifteen miles" by the coastal road to the east of the Lunga perimeter.

During November and December, the thrust of the battle with the Japanese shifted to the western defense perimeter and the Matanikau

River. American Army and Marine fighters were dug in on the east bank while the Japanese had reinforced the west bank and had also established a defense in depth all the way to the western tip of Guadalcanal at Cape Esperance. Here the Japanese were bringing in thousands of new troops to strengthen their defense and to prepare a major offensive to retake Henderson Field. November and December saw numerous battles around and across the Matanikau and along the northern shore toward Point Cruz. In December, the new Army Commanding General, Patch, who took over from the Marines, decided to build-up his forces and to gather intelligence for a big push to the west in January. Bogie had continued to live at Koli Point. The following quotation is handwritten in his memoirs, possibly taken from one of his reference books:

November 29, 1942–January 20, 1943
At Koli Point Colonel Tuttle's 147th Infantry, the 9th (Marine) Defense Battalion, and the naval construction battalion had established a perimeter defense.

The Aola Force, less the 2nd Raider Battalion, built a bomber strip (Carney Field) on a grassy plain. The 147th Infantry was fully occupied as a garrison force at Koli Point, where it provided local defense....

Living conditions had not markedly improved.... Menus remained monotonously dreary: canned Vienna sausage, dehydrated potatoes, Spam, rice, string beans, watery carrotts (sic), prunes, powdered eggs. (General) Patch's soldiers and marines lived in pup tents, bitched unceasingly about the food, the mud and the rain, bragged of imaginary sexual exploits, cursed the stupidity of their commanders, reviled the U.S. Navy and (General) McArthur, scratched mosquito bites, and visited latrines frequently....

Unknown to the Americans, by the middle of January the Japanese had decided to cut their losses on the island and to perform a fighting retreat to Cape Esperance where they would be loaded on ships and evacuated. General Patch decided to move the Composite Army and Marine (CAM) force at Koli Point into the fight. Bogie describes it:

January 20, 1943
A truck convoy moved C Company from Koli Point to the Point Cruz area. I rode on top of a truck piled high with supplies. During the morning it was hot and dusty. During the afternoon it started to rain. The trucks were unloaded west of the Matanikau River. I almost stepped on a Japanese corpse. We climbed the north slopes of Hill 85 (mistakenly shown on the maps as Hill 87). Supplies had to be hand-carried up the hill. Japanese shells exploded on the trail ahead. Our objective was the ravine between Hills 86 and 77.

I was attached to C Company as an aid man.

Night of January 20–21
Peter and I shared a foxhole on a hill. All night long American and Japanese shells passed close overhead.

Many of the Japanese shells exploded on a nearby hill. It seemed that every shell would land in our foxhole! Needless to say, we did not get very much sleep that night.

Between January 20 and February 7, 1943, Bogie and his unit were part of the fighting retreat, where he experienced many skirmishes as the Americans fought the Japanese west to Cape Esperance.

January 30, 1943

The 147th Infantry left the coastal ridges and moved down to the beach. I was attached to C Company as an aid man.... During that day, I was involved in two rifle and machine gun battles. The bullets flew in every direction, but you could not locate the enemy. I was hugging the ground when a bullet grazed the underside of my left small finger. (Later, another aid man bandaged it for me. He said that now I would be eligible for a Purple Heart. I told him not to report it. Therefore I did not receive a Purple Heart.)

In the afternoon, we got caught in our own artillery barrage. I do not know how long it lasted. Shells exploded all around us. Very many of us were wounded. I bandaged at least six men.

Late that afternoon it started to rain. We were ordered to advance. Two Japanese machine guns stopped us. Four men received head wounds. Being the only aid man, I bandaged them. Eventually, we fell back.

That night, C Company returned to the high ground. In all, I bandaged about twelve men that day.

January 31, 1943

That morning we were mistakenly shot at by the 6th Marines.

During the day we were harassed by Japanese rifle fire. Of course more men were wounded.

February 1, 1943
Soldiers of the 147th (including myself) were in the strafing of the coastal strip (by the Japanese planes).

February 6, 1943
I had been stationed in the front lines for seventeen days exclusive, or eighteen days inclusive.

Either then or later, we were moved to a location about ten miles from Henderson Airfield.

March 17 to 19, 1943
I was in our tent shaving that morning. Something exploded in a brushfire just outside the tent. A fragment struck me in the "lumbar region."

I was taken by jeep to the 101st Medical Regiment Field Hospital at Henderson Field. The fragment was left in my back because it was buried "deep in the soft tissue."

Peter came to visit me in the hospital. We played hearts on my cot until I got dizzy from sitting up.

I was hospitalized for three days (from Wednesday to Friday inclusive).

May 12, 1943

The 147th Infantry sailed from Guadalcanal. I had been stationed there for six months and eight days.

While on Guadalcanal, I had several attacks of malaria and dysentery. Also, I had received two small wounds.

Aftermath

Bogie's combat experience in WWII ends here. He spent the next two years knocking around the Pacific from one island to another until at last he was returned to the States and discharged on August 27, 1945. While he would not describe or discuss his military experience, it was clear to us kids that it was a defining part of his early life. Today we would probably diagnose him with post-traumatic stress disorder. It was not just the days that he spent in combat binding wounds and carrying bodies; it was the nearly five years of a life that was so foreign to his nature.

When he returned to Delphos, Bogie first worked for his father in the soft-drink and ice business that remained from the brewery. But Father told me that he failed. He was just not prepared by experience or temperament to be an administrator of a business. The G.I. Bill was a real possibility for him because he demonstrated academic interests his whole life. But he chose not to attend college. Instead, when he received a little money after his father's death in 1947, he blew it all on a trip to Europe where he visited Rome and developed a life-long interest in classical Roman archaeology. Unfortunately, toward the end of his trip he ran out of money and did not have the means to get home. He contacted his sisters, who pooled their funds to buy him the return passage. From that trip on he devoted what few resources he had to buying expensive archaeology texts that he would study for hours. Bogie was particularly fascinated with architectural drawings of the various baths and villas and would attempt to calculate their areas, volumes, and whatever statistic he could devise. All the time he was bouncing from job to long unemployment, to job.

This drove my hard-working, conservative father nuts. He had a thing with my mother's brother, an animosity that was only slightly below the surface. Every time they were together in a room, we could feel the tension. When Mother invited him to lunch or dinner, we children held our breath between bites in case Bogie dropped some comment that would annoy the old man. Father said that we children would have to bury him.

Late in life Bogie leveraged his veteran's status into an easy clerical job with the federal government in Cleveland. He left Delphos because wealthy old Aunt Francis—who as a girl helped the grandparents care for Bogie and his sisters, who had married a successful manufacturer, and who had inherited the business when her husband died—had called him "queer" with the connotation of "strange." Bogie understood it in a completely different context, became angry at the life-long friend—one who had supported him over the years with much money and many dinners—and huffed out of town to the shore of Lake Erie, only to return to live in the area a couple of years before he died from a massive stroke, alone in his small apartment.

At the funeral home we nephews and nieces huddled about the expenses and assessed portions to each family. The cemetery plot was no problem because there was one lot left empty next to his parents and grandparents. We knew because, on a scouting expedition with him to locate it with my brothers and mother, Bogie had lain on the plot, arms outspread with a big cigar in his mouth and smile on his face, which sent his nephews into spasms of laughter and his sister into amused disbelief. At the time of Bogie's death, Delphos's Catholic Church was being renovated. The funeral was held in Ottoville just a few miles away, where the steps to the church were very high and steep. After mass, we nephews carrying the casket were surprised when it suddenly shifted to one side, causing us to mutter obscenities under our breath and laugh. It hit me on my right humerus bone and left a terrific bruise. I could hear Bogie's howls of glee in the heavens; we not only had to buy his heavy casket and carry him, but, even when dead, he was causing us much expense, mirth, and discomfort. It was a combination that encapsulated his life.

CHAPTER 4

Child Labor

Recruitment

Father had a very simple philosophy when it came to his three sons and money: if you want it, earn it. I can only remember two recurrent occasions when he would give us funds. The small movie theater downtown would have Saturday matinees for children that cost a quarter for the ticket and a nickel for a small bag of popcorn. He would give each of us thirty cents, and off we would go to see shorts and a children-friendly feature. Also, there was the fall fundraiser for the church and school. When we were very young, we would each receive a white linen bag with a red pull string full of coins to spend at the fair. These bags were used at Father's factory for holding the nuts and bolts that would be included in the disassembled poultry nests that the factory manufactured and shipped. But they were also perfect as coin purses. The fundraiser involved three days of activities in which the parishioners would participate, with three nights of wonderful Midwestern dinners served in the basement of the elementary school building with your choice of beef or chicken. It still occurs. (I recommend the chicken.) Mother was a server for many years. The gymnasium of the school was transformed with all kinds of booths for selling cakes and other baked goods, games of chance and, of course, a large bingo section.

On an afternoon before the fair, the elementary students were given the time off from academics to go to the gym and try their hand at the games that were run by the high school students and adult volunteers. It was here that we made use of our coins. In our early years, we would drop them one at a time into simple devices designed to remove money from small children. For years, Mother supervised a wall of wooden drawers that looked a bit like the safe-deposit boxes in a bank vault. Kids would put their nickel or quarter in the drawer and push it in, after which an older student working behind it would put in a small item worth a penny or dime and push the drawer back out for the retrieval of the treasure.

Other than these willing donations to the movies and the Church, however, Father was a firm believer in child labor as the sole source of a child's spending money. It was thus fortunate that from a very early age I was interested in money and how to get it. So, when David, at one of our weekly Boy Scout's meetings in February of 1959, when I had just turned twelve, offered to hire me as an assistant paperboy on his route for *The Delphos Herald*, I jumped at the opportunity. However, I soon learned that the job was bigger than I had assumed—he had one of the biggest routes in town. It began at the Nickel Plate railroad tracks and covered the eastern ends of Fifth, Fourth, and one half of Third Street for a total of 155 customers. Many of the other routes covered fewer than one hundred. Nevertheless, I signed on and prepared my green cruiser for the job, oiling the chain and sprockets, wiping down the frame, and going to the Marathon Gas Station on the corner of Main and Fifth streets to top off the air in the tires.

David was in over his head. Even though he was a year older than I, he lacked maturity and had little sense of responsibility for the route. He had a bit of a reputation as a hood at school, where he hung with a tough crowd of bullies with greased ducktails and black leather jackets. They reputedly had a great deal of success with a certain cross-section of girls and a reputation with the local police. He was raised by a poor, working, single mother and did not have the kind of supervision or family structure that I took for granted. At the age of thirteen he had already begun to smoke. As we began our route on Fifth Street, he often stopped to go under the bridge, pull out his pack of Kool Menthol cigarettes, and smoke a fag or two. He also offered me one, which I tried, but found that I did not like the taste. Father had been a smoker but had quit cold turkey a few years before because, after a night of drinking, the next morning on the way to work he had lit his first cigarette, which caused him to become terribly sick on the street. Embarrassment and the yearly cost were his motivations. To avoid potential paternal censure, I did not wish to start a habit that he had just abandoned.

It did not take long for me to learn the route. I just needed to memorize the set of houses on the streets that received the evening paper. My days thereafter were full. Up before 7 A.M., we would get ready for school, have a quick cereal breakfast, and hop into our father's car. When school finished a little before 3 P.M., I rode home on my cruiser that I had picked up at lunchtime, changed into my blue jeans, and rode to *The Delphos Herald* building only a couple of blocks away on South Main Street.

The paper had many routes in a town of ten thousand and a corresponding number of paperboys. We received our papers on a rotating schedule. If you were first on a given day, the next day you would be last and then work your way back to the front of the line, day after day. The timing of the pickup was unpredictable thanks to many variables. The heavy, lead type blocked into steel frames had to come down from the composing room and be loaded onto the printing press by Gene, the press operator, who was a large, strong man with an engaging personality. He had earlier loaded the large roll of newspaper onto the press. After the frames were set, he started the press and ran a few copies of the paper for inspection. If all looked well, he ran the press at full speed for the duration of that day's circulation. The time of year, the amount of advertising, the mechanical state of the press, and the number of runs required for an issue determined when we received our allotment of papers.

Cave Dwellers

Upon obtaining our allotments, we grabbed our paper bags and went to the dark, musty basement with a dirt floor that was illuminated only by a few bulbs. Either the floor was dirt, or it was so neglected by the mop that it seemed like dirt. There we folded each paper into a compact shape that was good for throwing from a bicycle onto our customers' porches. These times were my first experience of the group socialization of Y-chromosomes. A doctor in Delphos likened groups of young boys to packs of wild animals who ran free, undisciplined, and predatory throughout the town. While I found that a little strong and sardonic, there was a ring of truth in his words. These conversations in the cave of *The Delphos Herald* harkened back to that of prehistoric adolescents in the hills of Europe, evoking a lot of laughter and having a predominant focus on girls, food, school, friends, enemies, and competition of all kinds—anything that would give an edge of one male over another. We were not exactly competing for mates, but young sexual, aggressive energy did fill the damp spaces as we prepared for our routes. Here also is where I first met young boys from the public school in town, because the paper was "catholic" in the restricted sense of the word in that paper carriers of all faiths were welcome.

Then it was off to distribute the papers. We tied the bag around one side of our handlebars where we most easily reached the folded missiles with our dominant hand. Midwestern clapboard homes often had an open porch that was relatively close to the sidewalk and made an easy target. Dip your hand into the bag, pull out a paper, and—when in the proper relation to the porch—fling it near the front door, all the while holding onto the handlebar with the other hand to steady and guide the bicycle while pedaling down the street. Even with two people working the route, this had to be done about seventy-five to eighty times, and in all kinds of weather. In the winter it was cold and often raining or snowing with icy sidewalks and streets, while the summer was subject to late afternoon thunderstorms that crashed down onto your head and made you hunt for the shelter of the nearest porch. But many days the weather was glorious, and I was near the front in line for papers and covered the route in minimum time, all of which created a warm feeling of job-well-done.

It was not unusual to take one to two hours to give the customers their newspapers, at which time it would be early evening. Mother would have a late supper ready for me if I did not get home by a little after 5 P.M., Father's preferred time for eating, right when he got off from work for the day and before the evening news on television. Homework followed and then bed. As I said, it was a day filled with lessons for a young boy about budgeting his time, routine and responsibility on the job, teamwork, and community. We paperboys were the final part of a large team of employees needed to gather and distribute the news and advertising every day in a small town. I felt like a young Mercury on a bicycle delivering the messages of local and international news to a large segment of the community. It was nothing less than my first glimpse of, and participation in, the adult world.

Before long, much to my surprise, I had the paper route to myself. David had let the accounts get into such terrible shape that management must have forced him out of the job. Exact details of his leaving are somewhere in the fog of more than fifty years of memory, but it was clear from the beginning that he was not completely committed to the serious work and routine that such a large route entailed.

My first attempt at collecting the weekly subscription fee turned out to be a complex one. David had not made regular visits to the homes that were on a weekly pay schedule, whereby many had fallen behind in their payments and wondered where the paperboy had been. Each week the young attractive woman at the front desk, Marilyn, would give us the route books that listed the names and addresses of the customers. At the end of the week, on Friday evening and Saturday, I would knock on the door of each home and hope that someone would be there to pay me. That first week was a mess. Records of previous collections were wrong or incomplete, and the clients were complaining that I did not know what I was doing, which was true. Nevertheless, I persevered through the entire set of homes. Many had paid ahead for weeks or months so that their privacy would not be disturbed and wondered what the hell I was doing knocking on their door; I had to explain that I was new to the route, that I was sorting out the records, and that I was sorry for the inconvenience. For these I used a symbol in my book to make sure that I did not stop again. For the weekly customers, I collected what was shown in the book to be past due. That first collecting-week, when I got back to *The Delphos Herald* building after completing my rounds, I received the warmest smile from Marilyn as I dumped a huge pile of small bills and coins on the counter in front of her. When totaled, the bills came to over eighty dollars, a lot of money for a newspaper that cost twenty-five cents a week. I had done well and was rewarded with my weekly salary, that I need not divide by two, and a virtual hug from an attractive young woman. Life was good.

Reluctant Voyeur

Visiting strangers' houses while collecting for the paper often led to new, not always pleasant, situations in the life of a twelve-year-old boy. One house a little east of the railroad on the south side of Fifth Street had an enclosed porch that stank of spoiled milk and displayed an illustration of an American Civil War scene on its wall. The picture showed hundreds of emaciated and dying or dead prisoners. I could not place it as being a Union or Confederate camp. The overpowering combination of odor and image put me off each time I had to visit. Mother was scrupulous about keeping our house clean. We were lower middle class living in a small home, but she and Father were proud of what we had and were very careful to maintain the house and landscaping. This was not always the case for the households on my route, and I unfortunately got a firsthand look and smell when the door opened for my collections. A small home on Fourth Street was the worst. In the winter it would be very cold but the air would be clean and clear with a tangy sweet organic flavor. Forced air heating of the homes created a positive pressure of mixtures of hot scents in each house that, when the front door opened, would rush out the door and encapsulate me in a cloud of odors. The fragrance from this house was like a cat box that had not been cleaned for two weeks and nearly knocked me over on the porch. But I had to stand there and try not to breathe very hard until I had the money in my hand, after which I quickly turned and walked away for fresh air. The state of dress and undress of housewives and children was pretty much what one might expect in the privacy of their homes and something that I learned to see without changing the non-smiling, professional expression on my face.

And then there were the dogs. As any cyclist knows only too well, a leg going round-and-round is a tempting target for a dog. Fortunately, there were few animals that were not restrained on my route. One that did give me pause for reflection, and a little fear, was the Doberman Pinscher that was chained outside the house at a length that was just short of the sidewalk. He used to rush out at me each time I rode nearby, barking. I have always been a dog person, and my family had, at the time, a very sweet Boxer female called Duchess, so I was accustomed to large dogs that could bite. This Doberman was large, aggressive, and threatening, and I was aware that the breed was used for fighting and had a reputation for violence. I was frightened, therefore, when making my daily ride by the house, to see that the dog had gotten itself tied up in its chain and was lying in the bushes at the side of the house in distress. After finding no reply at the door, I had a decision to make. Did I play it safe and avoid the risk of getting myself bitten by that beautiful set of canine teeth and just ride away leaving the dog to suffer, or did I try to untangle the poor animal and put myself in harm's way? Our eyes met. He was barking and—not speaking Doberman—I did not know if he was asking for help or warning me off. I decided that I had to help because I could not abide suffering, human or animal, particularly when I could potentially alleviate it, even if it meant personal injury. I would heal. So I slowly walked toward the dog, talking to him the whole time and leaning close to the ground so as not to pose a threat. When I slowly reached in to begin to untangle the chain from the animal's body and legs, I found that he had suddenly relaxed and that he did not try to bite or move. Somehow, he understood that I would not harm him. In a couple of minutes, he was free of the chain, and I was petting him and checking his body for injuries. When his mistress learned of the event, she was very appreciative and gave me a nice bonus that Christmas. The dog and I continued to be friends.

The White Leather Coat

On a corner of Fourth Street, across from the public elementary school and right in the middle of my paper route, was the house of Jane, a girl in my grade at school. She had been adopted by a prominent attorney and his wife and was known to be a bit spoiled and not a little high strung. What first attracted me was the way that she walked. From the back her hips had an amazing fluid action that seemed to draw an oval in the air with each two steps. Given that I was riding by her house at least twice every day and that I was also delivering her evening paper, we soon met on the street and became friendly. In a few weeks I became smitten and noticed that she just happened to be out more when I went by and delivered the paper. Soon I was stopping at the front of her home after the papers had been delivered. We would lean against my green cruiser and talk. Communication with Jane was easy and fun, the first time that I had the opportunity to experience the joy of mutually attractive wordplay with a woman. It helped that she had a lot to say with many strong opinions. Bike conversations turned into planned meetings at the local movie theater on Friday night, where we would sit hand in hand and watch the feature and afterward slowly wander through the Delphos streets back to her house.

In the fall of 1959 Delphos had an event called "Canal Days" that provided Jane and me with a better opportunity for closeness. The Miami Erie Canal bisected the town and gave it a certain reputation in the area because it was the site of locks through which the horse and mule drawn barges moved. It was constructed in the early part of the nineteenth century to further the north-to-south transportation of goods from the Great Lakes and operated only a relatively short time before being replaced by the more efficient and economical railroads that crisscrossed the state in every direction. Nonetheless it was an engineering miracle for the time because it was largely dug and constructed by hand for nearly the length of the state. Across Canal Street from our home ran a water-filled vestige that provided us children with a playground and fishing hole when we were growing up. As an opportunity to celebrate the town, encourage people to visit and spend money, and provide entertainment for the adults and children, the city fathers restricted traffic on Main Street and recruited a company to set up a fair with rides and roustabouts who needed a shave and a bath and who ogled the young girls—and boys.

Part of the celebration was a dance for the teenagers. A parking lot next to the National Bank was set up with a disc jockey and speakers. Rock and roll music was nearing the height of its popularity. Elvis had hit the stage of the Ed Sullivan Theater just a few years before, bursting onto the scene as a cultural phenomenon, much to the disapproval of many of our parents and grandparents, who believed that this new movement verged on the sinful. Sin looked and felt fun to us. Jane and I met at the dance and spent the night moving to the music of, among many others, Paul Anka, who had just released a popular single called "Put Your Head on my Shoulder." The night was clear and cool with a suggestion of autumn, and Jane was wearing her white, waist-length leather jacket that had the smell of leather and that crinkled to the touch when it moved, one that appeared very expensive and had probably been a gift from her wealthy parents. I held her in that jacket, took the scents of her and the leather into my olfactory chambers with great pleasure, and rejoiced at the sense of her closeness and touch. Heaven should be so sweet for a boy of twelve. After the dance we made our way through the darkened streets of Delphos back toward her home and my paper route where, for the first time, I received a serious kiss from a young woman.

A Beautiful Christmas Present

That fall we continued to see each other at school, on the paper route, and in the movie theater. One of the advantages of being a young entrepreneur was having disposable income. At Christmas I decided that a nice gift for Jane was in order. On a Saturday in December after finishing my route and its collections, and with money in my pocket and the bank, I visited the local jewelry store on Main Street looking for the appropriate sign of my affection. There I found a lovely solitary green stone necklace with a sterling silver mount and chain. I admit that it was a precocious gift for a twelve-year-old. The necklace was relatively expensive and would have made any wife and mother in town happy. Future experience proved that I had an innate gift for choosing fine jewelry and art. Jane was, of course, very pleased and demonstrated her appreciation to me with smiles and affection.

Then the shit hit the fan. Our mothers were pissed off to the second power. Knowing that Mother had full access to my clothes and possessions and was likely to find my gift before I was able to give it to Jane, I had recruited my childhood buddy across the street to help me hide it in his grandmother's home that was right across the canal. When her mother saw the expensive gift, however, she naturally called my mother. I was sitting in my grandmother's home next to ours visiting with the mean old woman when, suddenly, Mother came bursting through the backdoor hell bent to rip me a new one. How dare I, a child of twelve, give such a present to a young girl? What did it mean? How dare I hide it from her? I was just a child! How embarrassed she was by the call from Jane's mother! On and on it went for what seemed like forever on the emotional rack of Mother's wrath, being stretched and broken a little more with each word. Finally, the torture passed when I agreed to take the necklace back to the jewelry store, get my money back, and stop being so serious about that young woman. (It had to stop!) I of course lied and had no intention of not seeing Jane, but at that point I was willing to risk a little sin and damnation just to make Mother shut up and leave me alone. What she and Father had not realized was that, by allowing me to get a job and some savings at such an early age, by forcing me to do it because it was the only option for getting ready money, they had thereby forced my maturation in ways that they did not anticipate. However, the die was now cast and there was no going back.

Circumstances other than my mother soon finished my budding romance. Jane began seeing a Hood in the class in front of us in school. He hung with a tough crowd, came from a poor family, and was, I believe, enamored with the idea of dating a rich girl above his station. He told me to stay away. I told him to go to hell. At the time, I had a reputation for taking no crap from other boys and was often ready for a fight when challenged, and bloody but successful when I did so. One night the Hood and his two friends made the mistake of following me into our yard with the intention of intimidation. They did not realize that my very protective and large dog with very sharp teeth was also out in the yard. Duchess angrily flew to my defense, and the three of them made tail out of the neighborhood. I then decided it was too much of a hassle, and it offended my pride, to have to beg someone to spend time with me if she was not in the mood. In fact, her moods, I found, changed almost as quickly as the weather, and when there were storms, I stood by to be hit by an emotional lightning bolt. Not wanting to repeatedly singe the delicate flower of my young male ego, I split. Also, my job and economic prospects were looking up and needed my undivided attention.

Promotion

My route continued to be enjoyable for more than a year. After establishing a routine and recruiting some extra help of my own to shorten the school-work days, I had a system and good time allocation. It soon came to the notice of my adult supervisors that I was good at organization and getting the job done. The Editor, who was also the Chief of Police in

Delphos, called me into his office for a talk. The high school student who was working in the press room was sick and had to give up his position; would I be interested in taking it? I was now thirteen years of age and was being offered a big promotion, almost an adult's job. It entailed working with Gene, the press operator, to get the papers off the press, count them out for the routes, distribute them to the paperboys, prepare the newspapers that were dispatched in the mail, and take them to the post office. Yes, I said, without a moment's hesitation. My employee who had been helping me pass the papers every day was happy to learn that he was going to have a route of his own. I moved on and up.

Of course, more responsibilities meant a steeper learning curve. I was going to be busier in more diverse ways while being directly supervised by the Editor. But I thrived on the idea of his trust in me and jumped right in with both hands and feet, literally, because the job required a great deal of manual tasks and walking. Gene was a single man who lived in an A-frame along the Auglaize River. He was large and strongly built and handled the frames of lead type with ease. When he set up the press I was often there and helped where I could. We soon became very good friends, telling stories and laughing as we each performed our tasks. The press spewed out papers at a high rate as I grabbed, counted, stacked, and sorted in the daily order of the routes. Now the paperboys looked up to me like one of the adults in the room, I was amazed to learn, because they depended on me to get them their papers and to be fair about the system of allocation. After the boys had gone to fold and pass, I took my own pile to the mail table in the corner of the press room. There lay the brown sheets of wrapping paper that had each been prepared with a name and address on a white sticker. Aligning the ends of the wraps so that about three-fourths of an inch was exposed for each one, I took the paint brush from the glue jar and ran the lumpy, smelly adhesive across the ends.

Then grabbing a single newspaper, I rolled it into a single wrap until I sealed it with the glue, after which I threw it into the hand-wheeled cart that we used for the post office. Repeatedly, I glued, wrapped, and threw, glued, wrapped, and threw, until I had exhausted the wrappers. Taking the newly wrapped newspapers to the post office, I imagined myself in a Renaissance painting as a little old man pushing a wheeled cart through the street of some European town at dusk. Only now I was a young man pushing just such a cart through the back alley along the Miami Erie Canal for three blocks in a small American town to the post office, where I directed it into the back of the building and delivered my goods. By this time, it was late afternoon or early evening, and I was very tired; so it was home to parents, late supper, homework, maybe a half hour of television, and then bed. They were busy days indeed, five days a week with a half day for Saturday's edition.

Floor Walker

During this phase of my career in the newspaper business I learned a great deal about how a paper was produced. I was given free rein in the building and took full advantage of it to satisfy my curiosity about what went on in the floors above me. My favorite was the composing room with the linotype machines that had a wonderful clacking sound, pots of molten metal, and heating devices that created a warm refuge during a cold winter day. Slugs of lead type came off the machines and were gathered by the composers, who assembled them into columns at their tables and then organized the columns into full page-frames for the press. Advertising, I learned, was what really made money for a newspaper. I had had no idea that there were employees who did nothing but go from business to business selling relatively expensive inches of ads. Our collections on the paper routes seemed paltry by comparison.

The third floor of the building was almost completely abandoned, but I found there an archaeological treasure in the form of many bound volumes of former editions of the paper. A damp, musty smell enveloped the room, and the volumes lay strewn all over in no discernible order, but I could feel the many years of history represented and was sorry that the persons responsible did not have a better sense of the paper's longevity to take better care of them. Within those old, yellowed pages were the stories of events in the lives of thousands of persons across many generations: births, marriages, deaths, legal notices, records of businesses no longer present, the whole complex of human life. Although only a thirteen-year-old child, I felt the poignancy of the room, the carelessness of its organization, the disregard of the powers-that-be for its importance, and the impotence of one so young to do anything about it. Cemeteries gave me the same feeling, all the thousands and thousands of years and days that were represented by the many bodies in the ground, now lost forever without a record other than the living who remembered them. I closed the door and sadly walked away.

Jailbait, I Wish

Marilyn, at the front desk, whom I had worked with for my collections, also became a good friend. During breaks, we often found ourselves in one of the many dark corners on the first floor of the building sitting, talking, and laughing, to the point that the Editor got quite snippy with us one day. He felt, I suppose, that we were attracted to each other, which, for my part—and to my great surprise—I found to be true even though she was at least six years older than I and had already graduated from high school. (A young man can have his dreams.) However, the Editor would have no inappropriate dreaming and flirting on his watch. His office was also on the first floor where he had probably heard us talking and giggling and made it very clear that we were to stop it on company time. And the imagined wrath-of-Mother prevented me from trying to arrange meetings with Marilyn outside of work, even if she had been willing to risk jail to spend time with me. I certainly would have welcomed the images that she could have revealed and the lessons that she could have taught.

Siren Calls

I worked at this job until August of 1960 when school was about to begin again. In September I began school football. The sport had been an early obsession for me, and I had been quite successful in the city league for young boys. Having developed faster than others my age, my size and naturally aggressive nature suited me for the violent sport, and I loved the contact, hitting other players as hard as I could with my shoulder pads. Eighth grade was the first year for organized football at our school, and I was eager to participate. The Editor was distraught and really lowered the emotional boom on me about leaving. All his arguments about more money, responsibility, keeping the job for the next five years, were for naught. I wanted to hit and be hit on the football field and gave him my notice. From this distance in time, I feel I made a mistake. Those football years were to be filled with much pain and disappointment. Unfortunately, aggressive thirteen-year-old boys are not blessed with great foresight. The Siren of football called. I followed her voice into the violent void and left my promising newspaper career behind.

CHAPTER 5

1960, Stürm Und Drang

My family experienced firsthand the postwar success that spread throughout the nation in the 1950s. The economy was booming. Ike, the five-star general who had led the United Nations to victory over the Axis powers, was in the White House, keeping the country safe from the Russians and building a huge network of freeways that would revolutionize the transportation system. The New Delphos Manufacturing Company had more orders than it could handle in a forty-hour work week and was expanding its line of galvanized metal products, sending them all over the state and country. Mother was busy taking care of our modest but comfortable home, cooking wonderful meals, and socializing with her friends in the various card clubs to which she belonged. She was an excellent player, a real sharpie and ruthless. When she managed to finagle me into a game, she took great delight in beating me with the last card thrown down on the table, a big smile on her face. I used to tease her by calling our competitions "He who plays with pain in the ass." We three boys were succeeding in school; that is, Luke and I were getting good grades. Jake was a goof-off and prankster, a real C+/- student, but he got by. We had our health, enough money to live a lower-middle-to-middle-class life in our small home, and Jake was one semester away from graduating from high school. But our Midwestern pleasure bubble was about to burst into the most trying and tempestuous emotional year of my family's life: 1960.

Beloved Aunts

First, the Grim Reaper shadowed us for a large part of it. Great Aunt Zola, my paternal grandfather's sister and one of our favorite relatives, had had a massive heart attack at Christmas, 1959, and died. In January, her sister Nell, with whom she had lived for years in Columbus and who was also elderly and had a history of cancer, came to live with us in our small home until my parents could find her a place to rent and a caretaker. Nell, who had been married and divorced, and Zola, who had never married, had no children and doted on my father from the time he was born. He, in turn, helped them with their finances and cars. As a young man, he had lived with them for a bit while he attended classes in Columbus. Nell and Zola were a part of our nuclear family. In our early childhood, it was always a treat to have them visit at Christmas. They stayed with their aunt Minnie, who was elderly and infirm but who still lived independently with her husband Harry in their home. Decorations, lights, and a tree appeared at Minnie's, followed by gatherings of our small clan with much food and merriment and us three boys running everywhere. To top it all off, Santa (Father, who had snuck out of the noisy gathering and donned a St. Nick outfit) suddenly appeared at Uncle Harry's house with a bag of presents for everyone.

Zola and Nell both worked for the State of Ohio in clerical positions, and we were occasionally allowed to visit them at work. Zoey, as we kids called her, had a wonderful sense of fun, and an easy laugh. She was tall, very thin and wore simple, elegant clothes that made her appear to walk right out of a fashion magazine from 1925. Today I believe this was largely an illusion created by her conservative nature. She was a good Republican who had lived through the Depression and had learned the value of every dollar. Rather than buying new outfits every time the fashion changed, she had taken very good care of her workday suits, dresses, and overcoats and had merely accessorized them with inexpensive jewelry and items that she found on sale. Zoey was a bit of a time capsule, and we children had the benefit of a small window into the fashions of an earlier age.

Our family often visited Zola and Nell at their townhouse in Bexley near Capital University, one of many small liberal arts colleges that dotted the state. Mother rose early and made her special Sunday chicken recipe for dinner, the meal that she prepared nearly every Lord's Day of the year. It began on Saturday when we went to the poultry store on Main Street, where the couple who owned it cleaned the chickens in the basement. It had the distinctive, but not unpleasant, odor of fresh butchered meat, cool water, old wet wood, concrete, and feathers. Mom would ask for two good fryers. The proprietor, who was a large woman with an apron tied tightly around her waist, reached into the metal cooling troughs, took a bird in each hand, and plopped them down on the large, worn cutting block in the center of the room. In a few deft strokes with a knife blade narrowed from sharpening and use, she dismembered each bird and then finished the job with a large cleaver and noisy chops. After she wrapped the chickens in heavy white paper we paid and returned home. The recipe was as simple as it was delicious, and I still use it. Mother first used salt and pepper while seasoning each piece, rolled them in flower, and browned them in hot Crisco oil in her favorite steel skillet that shined from repeated scrubbings, its handle bare, worn wood. When nice and brown on both sides, the chicken was placed in a shallow pan for baking, 350 degrees for one hour. The accompanying mashed potatoes and frozen peas were to be prepared at our destination.

We then piled into the car for the two-hour drive to Columbus. In the rear seats where we three boys sat (when we were not fighting), the wonderful scent of Mother's chicken slowly enveloped us from the nearby trunk and wet our taste buds for the meal to come. Traveling was primarily by two-lane roads through the countryside. There were no large towns between Delphos and Columbus except for Lima, which Father always tried to skirt with a detour from the main road. We entertained ourselves by counting cows, looking for interesting cars and license plates, reading advertisements on the sides of barns or the Burma Shave signs with their folksy sayings that lined the berm. But being healthy boys, we also bickered and fought until our parents' patience was exhausted, and I, being the youngest and smallest, was moved to the front seat.

We came into the city along the beautiful Scioto River on our right with very large, expensive houses on the left at the top of large swathes of sloping grass. My least favorite landmark in the whole trip was the Ohio State Penitentiary. It was a dark, hulking set of walls and buildings with black wrought-iron gates and fences and natural stone that had weathered an ugly gray color. When very young it filled me with dread, and I asked Father if I had to go there when I grew up. He said no, if I kept my nose clean and did not break the law, I would never need to go inside. I couldn't stop thinking about the wooden electric chair and the prisoners who committed capital crimes who were wired to high voltage and amperage until their innards burned and their hearts stopped. The idea terrified me.

At our destination, Nell would have homemade tapioca pudding waiting—a special dish that she knew we all loved. Each visit had a predictable form. We kids would be set loose outside when the weather was good to explore and play. The college grounds across the street were beautiful: open, wooded, well landscaped, and inviting for three young boys. Zoey and Nell's car, which sat in their garage, little used, was also a frequent target for our rough-housing and play. It was an old 1930s gray vehicle with large running boards, a shifter on the floor, and cloth seats that would emit large clouds of sweet-smelling dust when we beat them with our fists. Debbie, the girl next door, was close to Jake's age and joined in our fun. Soon dinner was on the table, where we were expected to sit with the adults like civilized people, participate nicely in the conversation, exhibit the manners our parents had taught us, and eat the wonderful Sunday fare. In the afternoon, the adults talked in the living room and watched a bit of television. At the time, many programs having to do with the history of WWII were on; I associate a very popular one hosted by Walter Cronkite with these visits. After an early supper of leftovers, we were back in the car and asleep in the darkness on the way back to Delphos.

We also dropped in at Zola and Nell's home when we were out on vacation or traveling nearby. On our way back from a two-week summer trip to Florida in 1955—Father usually took the first two weeks in August as his vacation—we stopped for the night. I had been intrigued with the alligator wrestlers whom we saw during one of the shows in the Everglades. (I believe it was a Seminole Indian vs. the gator; the Indian won.) Zola slept on the floor with us to make room for our parents, and I proceeded to relate my exploits with the gators and how I pinned one to the ground. We laughed so hard that Zola's prim, more reserved sister walked part of the way down their stairs to inform us that she and my parents could not sleep because of the racket. We were a family of seven, not five.

Therefore, it came as quite a blow to me when, on a Saturday in December 1959, I finished my paper route and went home only to find that my parents were gone, which immediately told me that something very serious had happened. Grandmother told me that they had suddenly departed for the capital because Zoey had become ill. I hopped on my bike and pedaled the short way to the shoe store where Jake worked to see if he knew anything more. It was he who gave me the bad news that our beloved aunt was dead from a sudden heart attack. Immediately I felt terrible for Father, who I knew was especially affected. He was closer to his aunts, in my opinion, than to his mother. Nell and Zola were kind, friendly, with good senses of humor. Grandmother was not. Rather she, particularly in her later years, was demanding, selfish, a hypochondriac, and jealous of Mother's marriage with her son. Losing Zola was a huge emotional blow to my stoic father. When he returned from arranging to have her remains transported home, I could sense the pain from his silence and attitude.

Gangrene

Here was the beginning of twelve grim months. Soon after Zola's death, Mother nearly became a single parent. Father had suffered for years from what the doctors had diagnosed as ulcers. In June of 1960, he and Mother took a trip to Chicago with his boss and wife. On these trips there was always a great deal of drinking. From an early age I was to learn that alcohol played an important part in Father's life. I was born only fourteen years after the end of prohibition, that great American experiment in virtue and sobriety. Stories of bootlegging and smuggling of liquor filled my childhood. The social lives of my parents and their many friends seemed to me to be centered on the bottle. This was reinforced by the barroom that Father built in the basement of our house on Sixth Street. It was very well done, with a western décor, knotty pine paneling, a pseudo-leather couch, rattan chairs, lamp bases shaped in the form of cowboy boots, a tile floor, and in the back, a complete bar with brass rail, four bar stools, a sink, cupboards, shelves stocked with liquor bottles, and an old clock fashioned from a whiskey barrel. A 33-rpm record player, gas fireplace beneath a natural stone wall, a deer's head from an animal that my grandfather had bagged, and a black and white TV filled out the room. The entry door to the bar was made from varnished pine and split in the middle so the top and bottom would open separately, as one sees in a horse's stall. My parents would entertain their friends and throw parties in the room. It wasn't long before I began to perceive the dark side of drink, however, and to understand the intentions and energies that fueled the prohibitionists' experiment.

I often wondered how much the bottle contributed to the episode in 1960, because when he returned from Chicago he quickly became very ill with stomach pains and was sent to the hospital in Lima. A crusty old WWII surgeon opened him up for exploration and found that he indeed had an ulcer that had perforated his stomach and that, even more serious, his gallbladder had burst and caused an extensive, gangrenous infection of the peritoneum. The surgeon called in Mother's sister Helen, the head nurse of the fifth floor, showed her the state of Father's abdomen, and recommended that she go to the waiting room and prepare my mother for the worst because, in his experience, my father was likely a goner. The surgeon sewed up the stomach, removed the gallbladder and the debris surrounding it, poured antibiotics into the cavity, and closed him up.

That evening, Mother returned home wearing an expression I will never forget. She sat on her usual chair in the living room with tears in her eyes and tried to explain to us the details of the procedure and how serious it had been. Brave words she gave us, but I could tell that she was blowing smoke to conceal her fear. Mother was not very good at deception and wore her emotions on her sleeve for everyone to see. When she was angry with me, I knew it; when she was proud of me, I knew it as well. This day, I could sense the thought of death that she had brought home with her but had tried to hide.

When she returned to the hospital the next day and went to Father's room, he was gone, which caused her great anxiety. Did he die during the night? Was her sister waiting to tell the worst in person? Soon she found him, tubes dangling from various places on his body and only partially covered by a hospital gown, walking down the hall from the bathroom because he did not want to use the pan, while pushing the wheeled stainless-steel tree with the saline bottle of the IV drip along with him. In a couple of days he was home and, much to the frustration and worry of Mother, returned to work at the factory.

Nonetheless, Father had changed. After he nearly died, he softened a bit; he was less easily angered and less severe toward us children. I began to feel that I could have conversations with him, not just silently, and sometimes sullenly, obeying his dictates, explicit and implicit. Yet he retained his ability to intimidate us and our cousins, who were all very cautious not to offend him. In the defense of his sons, he could be particularly fierce. This also was a harbinger of the passing of my childhood. Death and near death in 1960 made me more sensitive to the suffering and emotions of the adults around me and less obsessed with my own needs and wants. It frightened me, revealing a dark side of human life that is generally shielded from children. I was growing up.

Father's surgery and near death also meant a change of lifestyle for the family and a healthier way of eating. Because of his ulcer and abdominal troubles, the doctor prescribed a strict diet that prohibited most fried foods. A couple of years before this, he had purchased a new deep fryer that he loved to use. They were just coming on the market, and Dad loved new devices and machines. He did not do much of the food preparation in our house, but there were a few recipes in which he took great pride. One was to coat chicken pieces with batter and put them in the deep fryer. They would come out a golden brown, hot and crispy. We ate a lot of deep-fried chicken and fish, and Mother would also pan fry T-bone steaks. To cut down on the cost of meat Dad would buy a half of a butchered cow at a time and have it processed at the food locker and stored in our drawer in the locker's freezer room. When we needed some meat, one of us would go the couple of blocks across the Nickel Plate Railroad tracks with the key to the drawer and choose what Mother wished to thaw and prepare. Right after the surgery we went from fried meat and potatoes to a lot of dishes like creamed tuna fish on toast or poached eggs on toast. It seemed that anything with cream sauce on toast was good for ulcers. The deep fryer was given away. When later we resumed our Midwestern meat and potato meals, Mother broiled the steaks and meats and let the animal fats drip into the pan rather than be consumed by us. The new, non-fried food on the table was a surprise to me—and not always a pleasant one. To this day I cannot look at a piece of toast with creamed anything without a bit of psychological discomfort. However, I kept my opinions to myself and ate the food because: 1) I knew I had no choice: we ate what was put in front of us and 2) it was in Father's best interest and, ultimately, mine.

Religious Strife

Spring and summer of 1960 also churned the family with religious disharmony that echoed through my adulthood and conditioned many of my attitudes toward the supposed holy. Father always respected Mother's beliefs, and I cannot remember an argument about religion in our home—that is, until my oldest brother decided, or rather had it decided for him, to enter a Catholic seminary in Indiana in the fall of 1960 and study for the priesthood.

Jake had been a lousy student in high school. He was, however, a very successful Boy Scout. From the age of eleven he had progressed through Tenderfoot, Second and First Classes, Life, and, after twenty-one merit badges,

Eagle Scout. My parents were very proud of his achievements accomplished under the guidance of our avuncular and well-respected Scoutmaster Gerry. Jake was also a "Boy Scout" in the metaphorical sense that it is often applied: he was innocent, naïve, lacking in assertiveness, tentative with the opposite sex, completely suffused with dictates of the catechism, and subject to influence by stronger and older male figures. Jake had applied and been selected to serve as a paid staff member at the Boy Scouts Camp Lakota that summer as instructor for the axe yard. The scout executives were impressed with his character and dedication to scouting and probably saw him as a possible future recruit after graduation from college.

Jake had, however, also caught the eye and fallen under the influence of the principal of St. John's High School. Father Thomas had arrived straight out of seminary and anointment by the bishop. In his first years he tried to compensate for his inexperience by creating a long list of rules: no blue jeans on campus, shirts were to be buttoned to the neck, hair was to be cut above the collar, all students were to attend the 11:15 daily mass; the list went on. Students could either fall in line or face expulsion and attend the public school "across the tracks." He was particularly attentive to any hint of close sexuality or intimacy of students who were dating. For slow dances at the sock hops, we were required to leave enough room for the Holy Ghost. (God forbids that we have a girl's soft breasts pressed against our chest, smell the sweet scent of her neck, and have a pleasurable woody in our pants.) In the evening and on weekends Father Thomas often patrolled the town in his car and spied on the houses of couples in his school and the known necking spots in the countryside to make sure students were not snuggling and canoodling. If he found evidence of such behavior, or had it reported to him by his spies and sycophants, he would act against them and ban them from school offices and activities. He essentially had them shunned.

Father Thomas would also choose a few unattached young men from the junior or senior classes and bring them into his fold, giving them rides in his old Mercedes, playing handball with them, traveling with them to sporting events, giving them select jobs like keeping statistics at football and basketball games, and so forth. These were not necessarily the brightest students in the class, nor the richest, nor the poorest. In fact, I discerned no pattern to his choices. But once they were chosen, the probability of these young men getting a whisper from Jesus increased. It was also a covert method for gathering information about the high school students without explicitly asking his disciples to be rats; their natural conversation about school and people would give him all the evidence he needed to act against those breaking his many laws.

Jake became one of the disciples to Father Thomas, which immediately created a rivalry with our father. As a firstborn Jake had been treated by his parents and grandparents as the chosen one, a bit of the Old World's traditions creeping into the New. When Jake announced that he felt that he had a vocation to the Catholic Priesthood and wanted to attend the seminary after high school, a seismic shift threatened the foundation of our little family. Our agnostic father was incredulous and furious with the principal, suspecting that his son had been manipulated into this decision. Medical school was what Father had in mind for Jake. It was unreasonable, certainly, for a student of Jake's aptitude and ambition. But Dad's disappointment at not having gone to college himself, determination that his sons would not make the same decision, and desire for Jake to become a respected medical professional like his close physician-friends in town, clouded his judgment. Mother was caught between her husband, her first son, and the pious side of her family that included Father Bertie, the obnoxious cousin-priest, and her ultra-orthodox Aunt Laura, Bertie's mother. Arguments and anger filled the family for weeks, and Jake cowered under my father's fury and Father Thomas's bullying. Luke and I retreated from the fray and busied ourselves with school and part-time jobs.

Grandmother also piled on. Paternal grandmother Emma had a very interesting religious history. Her father was a German Jewish immigrant and tailor who had had a small shop in an even smaller town just south of Delphos, Spencerville, where she and her siblings were raised. In circumstances she left unexplained, she had been raised in the Catholic Church by her mother, though fervent she was not. (My grandmother Emma very seldom shared any personal data, not even the fact that she had been widowed before she married Evan, her first husband an Irishman who died of tuberculosis.) At no time in my childhood had I ever heard in her voice a religious conviction. Her anger at her eldest grandson's alleged vocation came, I supposed, from the favored spot that he had in her heart as the first son. Nonetheless her biting comments directed at Jake only added to the overall misery and disruption in the family.

Welcome Interval

Fortunately for Jake, shortly after high school graduation in late May, he escaped to the woods of Camp Lakota about sixty miles north of us. There he spent nine happy weeks in the axeyard teaching young scouts how not to cut off their fingers and toes or invade major arteries and veins with sharp instruments.

That summer was my own third year at the camp with our Troop 42. The first two years Jake had been Gerry's senior helper and had bunked with him in their own three-man wall tent. This year he was sharing a tent with one of the staff who oversaw the nature program. When he took me to his quarters in a clearing in the woods, I was impressed that the staff had wooden platforms in their tents so the canvas cots and sleeping bags were protected from the rain above and below. I was proud to know my brother was one of the important staff running the summer's program. Jake carried himself well among the boys and showed an assertive confidence that contrasted sharply with his timidity at home. He seemed also to have developed a strong camaraderie with the other male staff that I had not seen before. In high school he had not played any sports after failing to make the boys' basketball team as a freshman and spent his time working at a shoe store after school. His attempts to date were clumsy and unsuccessful because he did not have a natural comfort around females. Other than the two or three male friends with whom he played as a boy and then hung out with as a teenager, he was a bit of a loner, or lonely; I couldn't tell which. Now at the scout camp there appeared to be a transformation. He was in his element.

The Zen of the Axe

That summer in the axe yard Jake taught me how to take a file and a sharpening stone, support the axe at the correct angle, file the rough lips and burrs off the edge, and finish the blade with spit on the whetstone. I developed a real fondness for the feel of an axe in my hand, particularly one that was very sharp. My brother taught us the proper technique for chopping wood, which requires a rather sophisticated skill. First one must decide, given the diameter of the limb to be cut, where to make the first blows with the axe. The blade should hit at a forty-five-degree angle to the limb, and the repeated blows should be separated by enough space to remove an inverted triangle of wood between them that eventually leads to the severance of the log. When cutting a vertical trunk, we had to make sure that we knew the safest direction for it to fall when the last contact of the blade to the wood caused it to move. Of course, away from the person wielding the axe is best! This can be controlled by designing the cut so that the mass of the wood naturally causes the trunk to lean and fall in the correct direction.

I soon developed a love of working wood with an axe that has lasted to this day. Everything about it made me happy and relaxed, a real Zen experience. After that first summer, I often repaired to the woods to cut fallen logs or fell dead snags, with and without the Boy Scouts. For my graduation present from high school, Jake gave me a three-quarters axe that I used for more than twenty years until it was stolen from the back of my old Chevy Blazer. When the very sharp blade met the wood at the right angle, the force of the blow as it was transported through my arm and body provided a unique pleasure. It was a force and reaction that I could control and in which I played the central role as lever. Chop after chop, I'd watch the gap in the cut increase, perspiration forming on my forehead and running all over my body, the smell of the new dry wood as it was revealed by the axe permeating my senses, the wind blowing through the trees and cooling me through my wet T-shirt. With the blue sky full of cumulus clouds overhead, I and the woods were alone and one. When later the dark emotional clouds of depression began to move into my life, I would often grab my axe and head for the forest. An afternoon of exercise followed by a bit of daydreaming against the trunk of a live tree with luxurious foliage would usually help to dispel my funk, at least for a while.

But this was all in the future. For now, our troop enjoyed the extra attention from Jake, as someone who was one of us but also a figure of authority at the camp. During the Wednesday-night parents' visit, Jake was one of the leaders of the presentation around the huge log campfire. "Indian" dancing and costumes, singing, jokes, and skits completed the showcase for our visitors. After a fun-filled week we sadly said goodbye to Jake, broke camp, loaded our gear back into our parents' cars, and headed for home. I did not see him again until after the end of the summer camping season when the staff put away the exhibits, prepared the area for winter, and said their goodbyes.

Seminary

In mid-August the family piled into Father's new green 1960 Mercury Comet for our trip to the seminary. Its engine was tiny, 144 cubic inch displacement, that produced ninety horsepower, with a one-barrel Holley carburetor and an automatic transmission with only two gears. We sat many long, hot hours on clear vinyl seat covers, enduring the uncomfortable whining noise and vibrations the engine produced at high rpm, until we approached the southern border of Indiana and there delivered my brother to his fate. Two classmates in high school were also joining the seminary that day, and we traveled together. One classmate was the brother of a very cute girl in my class who was a hopeless flirt and tease. Words and a cute smile from her always evoked a sense of anticipation in me, only to be dampened by reality—my first of many such experiences. The third new seminarian was the middle child of another family of three boys whose father had died while the children were young and who lived on my newspaper route on Fifth Street, the main east-west artery in Delphos and part of Interstate 30. Our doctor, who delivered children at home for years, related the story of delivering one of the boys in this family. When the baby was making its way into the world, the activity caused the bed frame and mattress to collapse onto the floor with the mother and doctor following it. Luckily, he caught the new child in his hands. Baby, mother, and doctor survived.

To say that the atmosphere in our car was chilly, even in the terrible heat of late summer in a vehicle without air conditioning, is an understatement. Father expressed perplexity and anger at my brother's desire to attend the seminary throughout the drive, while Mother sat silent and sullen, knowing that defending her son would bring the wrath of her husband. She had already suffered his displeasure for months and did not wish to make the agony more acute. Luke, Jake, and I sat in the backseat, sweating on the vinyl seats, and said little. We reached the seminary in the late afternoon, with the sun casting long shadows on the countryside from the trees. The buildings, sited on a wooded campus that spread across green rolling hills, had a beautiful natural stone façade that glowed yellow from the light. There, in the perfect setting for isolating young men from the world's temptations, primarily women and booze, and teaching them how to be shepherds to the Catholic sheep, we left Jake. In retrospect, that afternoon mirrored my first day of the United States Marine Corps Platoon Leader Corps training in Quantico, Virginia, and MCRD receiving day at my later bootcamp in San Diego. The priests put the new seminarians in their uniforms, or cassocks, made them conform to a strict set of guidelines for hair length and hygiene, imposed very stern rules for talking and silence, housed them in austere dormitories, and began the indoctrination process. The purpose of the church was the same as that of the crotch, to remove the old identity and what was familiar to the young man and to replace it with an ideology of their own design. Only here, at the seminary, they were being molded into men of the spiritual arts, rather than those of professional killers.

Having dropped our victim, we four made our way home in more silence and heat. The next two months were no better in Delphos, only this time the accusations and mean words were written and sent through the post by my father and his mother rather than delivered in person. I somehow think that they were, nonetheless, not less hurtful to my timid brother who was trying to comply with the new rules and discipline of the religious order. He was caught in the worse possible situation for his personality, a vise of authoritative men, the jaws being the priests on the one side and Father on the other, both turning the handle and squeezing Jake between them. A combination of his poor academic work in high school and the barrage of angry letters took their toll. In his first Latin session the priest-instructor began speaking in the extinct language as if the students, who all had had courses in high school, should understand him. At the time mass and most of church business were conducted in Latin. Jake had terrible Latin skills. He therefore felt embarrassed by his ignorance. Four years of Latin, and he could not understand a thing.

Home

Becoming confused and depressed by his continued failures with the curriculum, his father and Emma continuing the onslaught of derogatory words and guilt, in the middle of October Jake called home and surrendered to the elders of the family. Father, the victor, joyously jumped in the car, packed him and his belongings, and brought him home. I remember the evening of his arrival by an association with a song by the Everly Brothers, "All I Have to do is Dream." Luke and I had a record player in our bedroom that played 45s, and we had a copy of that tune. As we played it over and over, Jake related to us his experience and trauma of the last seven weeks and his decision to return home. His supposed whisper from Jesus had turned into a nightmare of shouts and recriminations from his family. He had no idea what his dreams were or how to achieve them.

Now one more painful meeting remained, telling Father Thomas about the decision. The event occurred one evening shortly after Jake's return, in the rectory of the parish where my parents had been married twenty years before. My father and Father Thomas, with Jake in between, exchanged many shouts and angry words, each man blaming the other for the failure and return. With smoke still rising off my father's head, he returned home with Jake—mission accomplished, incident over. The animosity instilled in the high school's principal by this argument was to have serious consequences for my brother Luke when he graduated three years hence. It didn't help that Luke wore his hair long and played serious footsy with his girlfriend who lived at the end of Sixth Street, constantly pushing the principal's buttons. When his class put on *Bye-Bye Birdie* in their senior year, Luke was the natural choice for Birdie, the greased down, bit-of-a-hood rocker who gets "one last kiss" from the young girl star. Although an indifferent student in terms of his study habits, Luke was very smart and at the top of his class, or so we all supposed given his grades and the published honor rolls in the newspapers. When the time came to announce the valedictorian, however, Father Thomas named the chief sycophant from the class, the person who most often rode in the principal's Mercedes, laughed at his jokes, reported on fellow students, and held the clipboard and kept the statistics at the football games rather than putting his large, sorry ass on the field and helping us. Father was livid; but there was nothing he could do. Luke simply laughed and put his middle finger up at the whole thing.

In our house there was no time for mourning or celebrating. Father immediately put Jake to work at The New Delphos Manufacturing Company until he decided what to do next. Jake began weeks of drinking and carousing with his friend Charlie, on weekends and in the evenings. One night that fall I was awoken from a deep sleep—I knew no other kind as a child—by knocking on the side of the window frame by my bed and the drunken belting of "Oh My Darling, Clementine," followed by the lyrics "Roll me over in the clover, do it, do it, do it to me once again." Intoxicated to the point of falling-down, Jake had forgotten his house key and wanted me to let him in the back door. By now Mother was woken by the noise and the two of us met at the door, opened it, and caught Jake as he fell in, one of the most sloshed and happiest persons I had ever seen. Mother, furious, of course, scolded him all the way to his bed. Jake was miserable the next morning with a giant hangover. Showing no pity, Father kicked him out of bed, made him go to the factory on time, and worked him for the entire day. That evening there were angry words about direction and purpose, and strong admonitions about a repeat of the previous night's exploits. Luke and I were amused.

College

Soon the decision was made. Come hell or high water, Jake was going to be in college for the winter semester, or else. This precipitated the obligatory visits to nearby state universities in search of the right school and curriculum. The whole family went on a visit to Miami of Ohio where the son of a local scientist-astronomer and minor celebrity in Delphos was enrolled, and who offered to show Jake the campus. When we arrived at the student's fraternity house, the boys had had a party the night before that left the place in shambles, and a very large dog lay prostrate on the floor with a hangover. A great first impression.

Sometime during the drives to and from the candidate schools Father expressed his frustration with Jake's failure to articulate his life's goals, as if an eighteen-year-old who had just been torn from his first vocation would suddenly just settle on a second. At one point, however, Jake seriously surprised us and stated with determination that he wanted to become a professional Boy Scout Executive. My father, who was driving, completely and cruelly dismissed the idea, citing the profession's low pay, lack of prestige, and reputation for being juvenile, even silly. No, what Jake needed to do was to become a doctor, begin a pre-med program. Soon after this confrontation Jake meekly chose a minor state university in the northeast quadrant of Ohio, one that would accept him with his marginal high school transcript and that was about three hours' drive away. In January 1961, he began a pre-med program with an organic chemistry major.

In hindsight, this moment has always symbolized for me the importance of taking the right path when one meets a fork in the road. In my opinion, Jake's choice of Boy Scout Executive would have led to a happy and successful career with a caring woman who would have respected his choice, understood his needs and vulnerabilities, and accepted the modest lifestyle his career implied. The path that he took led to repeated rejections from medical schools, over-education in minor programs, a *curriculum vitae* that projected an unrealized competence, and forty years of professional failures, with long periods of unemployment. It also led to an unhappy marriage with a disgruntled, dominating wife who thought she had chosen a winner with large earning potential. Jake's fate was determined by the family dynamics of 1960, a hot cauldron of death, near death, argumentation, emotional turmoil, and manipulation.

In the background, there I was, a thirteen-year-old boy watching events unfold, studying my father, his techniques and attitudes. I was not to make the same mistakes. My forks would be well defined before I got to them. My paths would be clearly marked on a map. My determination to walk in my chosen direction would not be deflected. I had it all figured out. Or so I thought.

CHAPTER 6

Not a Field of Dreams

Big Fish, Tiny Pond

Summer of 1960 found me already with a reputation in the football world of Delphos. My early growth spurt, which gave me nearly my adult size by the age of twelve, was a great advantage when I began to play in little league football. The son of the owner of the local slaughterhouse and food locker, Randy, and I led the team. We won games, and one time the two of us substituted on another team and helped it win. Prognathous plastic facemasks on the helmets protected our young faces from damage, but also made us appear a bit chimp-like. I was known for the ferocity of my hitting on defense, directing my shoulder pads into the belly of the kid running toward me with the ball and hurling him backward with the full mass of my body, which gave me waves of pleasure. On offense, I took the ball and tried to run over as many of the other players who got in my way. I scored many touchdowns. I was the large, violent fish in a very small pond enjoying harassing the other guppies and tadpoles. Unfortunately, my desire to hit was not always restricted to the field. Randy was once standing with his back to me, and I decided to tackle him from the side as a surprise and joke; his ankle was badly injured. I learned a very hard lesson about violence and myself; I could injure someone, even a friend. His father was very angry, while Randy and I lost our friendship.

Big Fish, Larger Pond

I entered the eighth grade in the first week of September 1960, when we began practicing with the high school freshmen. It was the practice of the school to have a junior varsity team made up of the new players in their last year of grade school and the freshmen boys who had been practicing with the varsity since two-a-days began in mid-August. Subsequently, junior varsity would form a unit that practiced and scrimmaged separately from varsity.

That season I continued my success while playing primarily on offense and scoring touchdowns when we took on the junior varsity from other teams. Our instructor was Coach Robert Arnzen, a renowned basketball coach for our high school—known throughout the State of Ohio with strong ties to the University of Dayton. I knew him well from his summer work as Director at the municipal pool and his grooming of the baseball diamonds on the surrounding fields. He was a warm, friendly coach and directed young boys with a light-handed philosophy of teaching with firm but non-hysterical criticism when performance was not up to his expectations, or a player was goofing off. After games he went through the locker room while we were removing our sweaty, dirty uniforms and complimented his players on their good play for wins or comfort them in losses. Many times, I unwrapped tape with Coach Arnzen hovering over me, either praising my play or gently suggesting ways to improve my performance on the field. His teaching and direction were a style often portrayed in sports fiction but that, in my playing days, was seldom experienced on the field. This also was my first real experience of a situation that was to play a very important role in my life during the next ten years, that of men training men for competition or war. Coach Arnzen was probably not the best person to be the first. His firm, intelligent method imprinted me with an ideal style against which I consciously or unconsciously compared all future coaches. When varsity football began at our high school in the mid-1950s, he was the first coach and set the standard for the head football coaches that succeeded him. This year he only worked with the junior varsity.

The current head football coach had recently become engaged to my former sixth grade teacher and was in his last year at the school before leaving to take a better position in a larger program. I was in uniform and being taped for a game when he dropped by to talk. He expressed regret that legally he could not use me on the varsity team that year. Coach Zim was popular with the varsity players and appeared to me as someone for whom I would have liked to play. I told him that I also regretted that state rules restricted me to junior varsity and that I looked forward to being with him the following season. Little did I know that something quite different was waiting for me.

Male-to-male relationships are difficult to understand. Just ask any woman who shares her boyfriend, husband, or brother with his male friends how mysterious male-to-male attraction is. I say attraction deliberately because it most certainly is and can be stronger than that experienced with any woman, even when the men are heterosexual by nature and environment. Insert power—as in relationships between coach and player, drill instructor and boot, priest and congregant, teacher and student, even father and son—and the interrelationship becomes reticular in four dimensions. It becomes a thick, psycho-sexual stew in which elements of sadism, masochism, performance, failure, exhilarating success, stupendous failure, manipulation, exploitation, love, and especially hate can intermingle. The aspect of this soup that a coach chooses to emphasize determines his style as a chef. Coach Arnzen emphasized teaching, nurturing, performance, and success while guiding with a firm hand, which yielded affection and a durable love from players. The new football coach who was to replace Coach Zim in the fall of 1961 was to have a very different recipe indeed.

A Fresh Beginning

I graduated from elementary school in the spring of 1961 and prepared myself for the first year of high school. In those days, and maybe even now, the transition from eighth grade to freshman year was huge in style and content. As members of the WWII baby boom, born in 1947, my class was large for a private school in the middle of rural nowhere: 125 young bodies strong. Those former soldiers had a lot of stored sexual energy that they needed to dissipate when they returned from the war.

As a freshman I was now to experience the freedom of moving from classroom to classroom as the bell rang, learning each subject with a new instructor. During the class break students at all levels, freshmen to seniors, hustled their way to the next class. Less structure meant the need for more discipline to organize my time and performance, especially considering that between academics and athletics, I was exercising either the brain or the body (or both) for twelve to fourteen hours a day. Fortunately, discipline and organization appeared to have been hard-wired at my conception. I found the greater mix of freedom and students to be a huge relief from the stifling rigor of grade school. Finally, I was at the threshold of the adult world for which I had longed for years. In my day-to-day life I felt that I had demonstrated adult responsibility and maturity the previous two years but had been still treated like a child. Now I was ready for the big time.

A dark cloud began to form over our high school football program that summer of 1961 with the arrival of the new head coach; so, let's call him Coach Dark. My first intimation of trouble came with a conversation with Coach Arnzen at the Stadium Park, field, and pool complex. We often would hang out somewhere in the immediate area and shoot the bull. Three of us were sitting and talking about the Korean War, the third member of the group being a veteran who told of his experiences during the fight. Coach Arnzen then casually mentioned that a new person had been hired and that he had played football at Michigan State University under their famous winning coach Duffy Daugherty. At the time this meant little to me. Later it explained everything. Duffy Daugherty had the reputation of coaching by abuse and intimidation (A&I), a style that many football coaches have adopted over the years, is also practiced by the United States Marine Corps officer and enlisted training programs, particularly in their boot camps at Parris Island and San Diego, and one that I was to experience five years later. Now, training young men for war, essentially breaking down their inhibitions to kill other humans and giving them a skill set for the job, might require such a drastic technique. Training young men to push a pigskin up and down a grass field does not seem like it should require such severe measures. However, Coach Dark was hell bent on adapting his former coach's strategy for the high school football field.

I also learned that the new head coach had been a lineman while at MSU. When I met him, it became obvious because he had a short, heavy build and squat frame that would easily fill a hole and resist being moved out of it, which is how most linemen spend their time on the field. One of our U.S. presidents, Gerald Ford, played center for the other major university in Michigan, U of M. His slowness on the uptake was sardonically credited to playing too often without a helmet and thereby concussing himself into kindly, good-natured, long-term stupidity that seemed an excellent qualification for success in the United States Congress. There was nothing kind about Coach Dark, and he had the IQ of a wooden post.

Smart ass you might call me—many have over the years—but as a young person I found it highly disconcerting whenever an adult asked me to do something or tried to teach me something that I knew was flat-out wrong. Anger was my natural reaction—often very strong anger, that I had a difficult time not expressing. I was going to be hissing and spitting for the next four years.

In early August we received notification that we needed to have our physical exams and then be issued uniforms. At the end of the new extension to the elementary school building was the men's locker room for the new gymnasium where the equipment managers set up shop for the distribution of gear by year, with us freshmen going last. As a result, my helmet was the very early leather variety from the first team in the mid-fifties. It had a single gray face bar across the front that provided my larger than average nose with little protection, as I would soon discover. Shoulder pads, rib pads, hip pads, thigh pads and knee pads in the pockets of the tight pants, and a heavy jersey followed until I looked like a caricature of the monster from the Black Lagoon—but I was ready for the football field.

Small, Battered Fish, Big Pond

Two-a-day practices began shortly thereafter in the middle of August—the hottest time of the summer. On that first day we dressed in our locker room above the men's pool changing room and clattered down the wooden stairs and across the concrete of the stadium tunnel out to the practice field that was adjacent to the Miami Erie Canal. It was a two-hundred-yard stretch of grass that ran north from Stadium Street to the gravel road that formed the boundary for the park and was used by both St. John's and the public-school's team, Jefferson High School. Our first practice was from 9 to 11 A.M., the second from 2 to 4 P.M. Dry grass and earth crunched under our spiked shoes while we went through the first round of stretching and calisthenics for the practice. With my reputation as a running back I was shunted off to the side of the field with Coach Dark, who was the offensive coordinator for the team. His assistant coach, Coach Cross, also new to the program, was the line and defensive coach. Coach Arnzen worked as an assistant for the two-a-days and would thereafter coach the junior varsity beginning in September.

When playing in the little leagues I always felt and looked fleet of foot, running like a deer across the grass while bowling over everyone in my path. Now in the middle of August I found myself enervated by the heat and humidity and the heavy, close confines of my uniform and helmet. A rude awakening awaited as I lined up behind the quarterback. When I went to take the handoff, my feet felt like they were encased in cement shoes. I could hardly move and was very slow coming out of my three-point stance. Today high school athletes train year-round for their sports, many of them playing on multiple teams and never having the opportunity to get out of shape. In 1961 we did not have the facilities or the culture for such intensive work, certainly not for the first-year players on the varsity. I had not run or lifted weights before practice began; and now I was embarrassed because my reputation was much larger than my reality. That hot day in August, I was a slug in cleats.

Coach Dark did not help the situation with his innocuous patter of coach-speak that made fun of nearly everyone on the field, none of whom could live up to his expectations. Disappointment seeped from his every pore, but I immediately sensed that it was just a simple ruse that he used to try to motivate the players. Unfortunately, he combined his lame motivation techniques with the abuse of wind sprints and bleacher climbs. Getting a team in shape to play sixty minutes of football is a reasonable pursuit; using exercise to punish players for perceived poor performance—a specialty of the A&I style of coaching—verges on sadism, particularly when the temperature and the humidity are both in the eighties. Water breaks were rare; practices were long; Coach Dark's verbal insults and sophomoric comments constant. The man's incompetence had reached an apex when he decided to take the job of head coach. He neither had the social skills to work with young men nor the football skills to teach them the game. He possessed little sense of blocking technique for the offensive linemen and seemed unfamiliar with the proper way to create and execute plays for the backfield. Players saw through it all. Before long the team was decimated: the heavy bodies began to collapse from the exercise and heat, and a few of the experienced players, accustomed to the more knowledgeable and effective style of the previous coach, turned in their uniforms in frustration.

I was also experiencing the consequences of my early growth spurt and the diurnal cycle of my family's meals. Early growth was wonderful in grade school, but it often leaves one undersized, as it did me. Now I was on the field with players who were up to four years older than I and who had grown larger with age and later growth spurts. In the physical competition of blocking and tackling I was pummeled by big bodies for the first time and came out on the worse end of it. Hitting and being hit were part of the pleasures of football for me. But the repeated blows began to take a serious toll on my limbs and my psyche. Exhibiting no sympathy, Coach Dark threw the youngest, smallest, and most inexperienced players into the blocking and tackling exercises with the oldest, largest, and most experienced seniors.

After spending two exhausting hours in morning practice, I went home to eat a large, heavy meal. (Father, as a factory worker, liked to have his main meal at noon.) Afternoon practice started soon afterward, leaving a large bolus of food in my stomach that slowed my running and made me even more uncomfortable on the field. In hindsight I would have been better off with little food and lots of fluids in the morning while catching up on my calories at supper and just resting at the noon break. But Father's routine ruled our lives; I did not even consider questioning it.

We soon settled into a routine for the practices, first the stretching and calisthenics, followed by position group practices, and finally a combined practice that pitted the first offense against the first-team defense with younger players filling in on the defensive squad for the two-way players on offense. Coach Zim, the previous head coach, had taught and recruited well and had left a large, talented, and experienced group of senior players for 1961. There was the "star halfback," a red-haired, light-complexioned player who always seemed about to explode when he turned bright red from exercise. He was full of himself and treated most of the other players and coaches like they hardly existed; he was the bright sun around which everything and person in his small universe revolved. His companion at halfback was a student-farmer who had a hard time reconciling his duties in the crop field with those on the football field. For Saturday evening games he would have already been on the tractor helping his father for eight hours before he rushed to the stadium to dress for the game. At fullback was a junior, and one of the principal's sycophants, who, while large, was also a bit of a wimp and appeared to be on the verge of tears every time he had to make a block or carry the ball and be tackled hard. The next year he quit the team.

The senior linemen were a set of grizzled characters who would just as much hit you as look at you. "The Sheik" was the tight end, so named because he had lived in the Middle East with his parents for years. On the other side of the line was a tight end, Danny, who was tall with great hands that could catch a football in a hurricane. Gordo and Tim, tackles, were big and crude, their talk filled with sexual innuendo while also just plain mean. David, a guard, was a troubled kid with no father, well known to the law and the bad girls in town, who would later die in Vietnam as a member of an elite Army team. He entertained us one day by donning a pair of red women's briefs, supposedly obtained after a conquest, prancing through the locker room with a big smile on his face. Karl was my gay (a deeply hidden secret unacknowledged for many years) second cousin and would, in the future, become a renowned artist and designer. For now, he was a guard knocking defenders on their asses for the fun of it. Snarly Gene, the center, was just angry all the time. Quarterback Charlie was slightly built, a talented basketball player, and appeared to be the sensitive, emotional heart of the first-string offense and defense. They all had developed an *esprit de corps* before Coach Dark had arrived and did not adapt well to his A&I style on the field.

I continued trying to get faster and better in my running and execution of plays during practice. When the coaching staff realized that I was not going to be the emerging superstar they had anticipated, I was cross trained with the linemen for a defensive role. Coach Cross, the intelligent and sensitive new biology teacher as well as the new assistant football coach, quickly and quietly diagnosed my problems and tried to help. He knew the proper techniques for football, skillfully taught them to the players, and soon became the respected coach on the field. He put me up against Snarly Gene for one-on-one blocking drills in which we threw off the defender and tackled the ball carrier who was running up behind him. It was gut-check time for me because Snarly Gene was larger than I and had honed his superior technique during many games in the previous years. Yet never one to back down from a challenge or fight, especially when filled with fear, I used my forearm and upper body to hit him with everything I had, pushing him out of the way. I then sank my right shoulder pad into our fleet-footed junior running back, wrapping him up and pushing him to the ground, which brought a large amount of hooting and hollering from the other players and shame on the head of Snarly Gene whom I had beaten. In consequence Coach Cross double-teamed me with both Snarly Gene and The Sheik, and I got my clock cleaned big-time while vainly struggling to tackle the running back as he flew by.

Cloud Dreamer

And so it went, day after day, learning and executing the plays on offense and learning my blocking and tackling techniques for defense while answering to Coach Dark. I developed a coping mechanism that soothed my sore and tired body during the long, hot practices: I became a cloud dreamer. Cumulus clouds in Delphos are large, multicolored, varied-shaped wonders that, if studied closely, can provide a mechanism for detachment from the more stressful activities on the ground. During calisthenics, when on my back stretching and doing sit-ups and knee bends, I chose a fluffy white mass and tried to discern a pattern or shape. Monkey faces, elephants, prancing horses, animals of all kinds, a bearded Zeus, the outstretched arms of a Venus, and large anvils against which Thor fashioned his bolts populated my imagination as I stared at the sky. Dark clouds came from the west as a prelude to a summer storm. Then miraculous holes appeared, through which a column of the sun's rays descended to the ground. I interpreted these as a communication from the gods, allowing persons on earth to be illuminated by divine light and receive revelations. The color and texture of these lovely clouds alone, solid and imposing here, wispy and cotton-candy-like there, drifting slowly east against the pale blue background, fascinated and distracted me from the pain on the field and filled me with serenity. Cloud dreaming was also my first attempt at personal abstraction and wall building, using my mind to remove myself from a difficult personal circumstance, erecting a tall mental barrier near it, him, or her, and then peering back with the objectivity to see with the proper detached perspective. In the clouds I was floating somewhere above this field of sweating, dirty, violent young men. I saw it for what it was, realized its transient form, and then built tolerance and understanding. Such dreaming, abstraction, and partitioning have given me the little sanity that I have possessed over these many years and have extricated my depressed self from many a difficult space.

Scrimmage

After about ten days of summer practice, it was time for the first scrimmage with another team. On Saturday in late August, we took a school bus to one of the small neighboring towns where we played a simulated game, essentially a practice for each team under game conditions. Afterwards I felt that the scrimmage had gone well. But, when we got back onto the bus, Coach Dark had a tantrum and informed us that instead of going home exhausted when the team bus arrived in Delphos, we would have yet another practice with more wind sprints and bleacher runs. Before the bus got on the road, Coach Dark left it for a moment in order to say goodbye to the other coaching staff. This was the critical moment in the season that he lost the team's loyalty; senior members exploded in angry insults and protestations toward him. And I believe that this is what he wanted: the natural culmination of the Abuse & Intimidation style is to make players hate and fear you so much that they will do what you say. Never praise them; never show active support for them, until they will do anything not to piss you off, afraid as they are of the consequences. All the way home there was nothing but silence in the big, lumbering yellow bus. When we reached the stadium late on Saturday afternoon,

Coach Dark announced that, while we had played poorly, and while it was against his better judgment, he was going to take pity on us and not make us practice again that day. Rather than throwing cooling water on the flames of hatred, this unexpected change in plans acted as an accelerant. Now we could not trust him. His earlier scene was a mere sadistic ploy to manipulate our minds and emotions, to make us now feel good about his mercy. The die was now cast for the season; it was war.

By the first week in September my spirits began to rise with the thought that I would soon be rid of Coach Dark when the freshmen joined the new eighth graders to form a separate unit of junior varsity that would practice under Coach Arnzen. Just the year before I was hoping for a chance to play with the varsity. Now I was counting the days until I left its ranks. But then a shadow fell over my football season when Coach Dark announced that two freshmen, Tom and I, would continue to practice with the varsity, would dress for the varsity games, and would also join the junior varsity team for their competitions. This news caused my heart to sink nauseatingly into my stomach. On the surface of it, the coaching staff was paying us a compliment. The two of us had played well enough that we could help make up the practice squad and then participate in games when the score was so sufficiently in our team's favor that the first-string players came out. But this was not the whole story. So many players had become disgusted with Coach Dark and quit the team that he needed a couple of extra bodies just to have enough players against whom the first team practiced. My fate was sealed for the next nine weeks.

First Game

Our first game was the Friday after Labor Day. Beginning high school that week, I found my days very full and rigorously scheduled. I was up at 6:30 A.M. for dressing and breakfast and to school by 8:00 when homeroom would begin. Then I was off to a succession of individual classes, Mathematics, English, Latin, General Science, Religion, with a closed noon hour that included mass at the church next to the school at 11:15 and lunch in the school cafeteria. I finished by 2:40, when I headed home, changed clothes, took a short bicycle ride to the stadium, and then changed into my football uniform for practice from 4 to 6. Monday to Wednesday the first and second teams scrimmaged against each other in full pads with contact. At the end of practice, we ran wind sprints during which ranks of players would run about twenty yards at a time as fast as they could and then stop and wait for the next rank, at which point they would run back again, and again, and again, until Coach Dark decided that we had run enough. Often a set of bleacher runs at the stadium would follow, either for a set number or until once again the head coach was satisfied. On Thursday we received our game uniforms and practiced in them without the pads to run through the anticipated plays. We had Friday afternoon off to rest before the game. Many days, it was not until 6:30 or 7 in the evening that I dragged myself home, ate a light supper, studied for two to three hours, and collapsed in bed.

The first game of the season was a defensive bore. We played Van Wert High School, a town about ten miles west of us. They had been good in past seasons. The problem was that it was the first game for both teams, and neither could score. It became a battle of the defenses with luck determining which team would have more points. We finally scored one touchdown, six points, but failed to score the extra two points in the conversion. The game ended with a score of 6-0. It was a win, but Coach Dark's attitude and his distribution of wind sprints and bleacher runs made his displeasure clear.

In the second game of the season, versus another Catholic school from yet another small town close to us, the real reckoning occurred, an earthquake that triggered the eruption of Coach Dark's volcanic A&I anger. Both teams scored three touchdowns. But our opponent also scored two extra points by completing a conversion after one of the scores. We lost 18-20, which sent Coach Dark into a spasm of A&I. Monday on the practice field, he was pissed off and loaded for bear, berating us as players and telling us how bad the game was, how we never should have lost, and that we were going to pay the price. That day, that included brutal hitting during practice, he used the wind sprints as punishment for our failure to win the game, running us beyond the point of exhaustion until we were panting and swearing at him under our breath each time that we ran a set. Asshole was one of the milder epithets that we quietly directed toward him. Tuesday's and Wednesday's practices were not much better. By the time we got to Thursday's walkthrough, the entire team was posed in a wall of anger against its head coach.

8 and 1

Then we played on Friday and trounced our opponent 22-0: week 3, 26-0; and week 4, 30-0. By the first week in November the team had won eight games with the combined score of 222-24. We were winning big and demonstrating that Coach Dark had no sense of proportion, no mercy for the other team when he had them down by more points than they could possibly score in the remaining time. He left the first string in until the other side was pounded to a pulp, and there was little time left when we second-stringers, who had taken the abuse of the senior players all week in practices, could finally run a few plays in garbage time. I enjoyed the contact of those games and was always thrilled when the backup quarterback would call a play with my position receiving the ball. In my freshman year I played the fullback, the position that generally led the play and became the blocking dummy for the halfback who received the ball and ran behind him. But occasionally a play was called for the inside of the line, between guard and tackle or tackle and tight end, for which the fullback received the ball and acted as a battering ram while knocking his way through the blocking linemen and looking for daylight and the end zone. I experienced a primal thrill to the competition during a game that was qualitatively different from practice, to hearing the cheering of students, family, and friends in the stands, to feeling my pads hit those of the opposing players as I was trying to run through them, to finding room to run and pick up a first down, and to executing a textbook tackle while on defense and hearing my name called over the loudspeaker. Violence and recognition became intoxicating.

Final Game

The final game of the season was, fittingly, scheduled for Armistice Day, November 11, 1961, against our much larger and hated rival Lima Central Catholic High School. The two schools had a long history of competition, especially in basketball, in which our team excelled. The principal at the Lima school was the former principal of Delphos St. John's, who had a well-deserved reputation for salty language and trash talking and who turned these skills on our football team the week of the game. His team had had a mediocre season, but he predicted that they were still good enough to beat us, the team that had been winning by such large margins against everyone else. Local newspapers ran stories that inflamed the talk around the game and added to fans' anticipation.

By this time I had been psychologically and physically battered and bruised beyond measure by Coach Dark's practices. We had lost quarterback Charlie to a broken arm and put in his place a junior who was not quite as experienced at the position. Attrition in the practice squad had become so great that we hardly fielded eleven guys on defense to scrimmage against the first offense and often practiced with a depleted crew. We were beat up every night by the seniors and first-string players who gloried in running us over at every opportunity. One practice there was a sweep to the right side while I was playing linebacker when guard Dave and tackle Tim came out to block for our fleet halfback. I had no choice but to take the two on by myself. Even they were laughing as they came around the end and said that I would be nuts to get in their way. But I did, and paid the price with my body, falling ass over elbows as the two of them hit me high and low. In that second week of November, I was becoming shy of the contact, every day dreading the time when I had to put on the pads and head for the practice field, just longing for the end of the season when I could put this misery behind me.

Our weakness at quarterback and the larger and more numerous players of the Lima team combined to defeat us that Friday by a score of 6–20. It was a great disappointment that capped a season filled with wins without joy. Coach Dark managed to squeeze all the pleasure out of the competition and leave nothing in its place but resentment. In the bus at the end of the game, before the coaches joined us, the players were angry at the loss, angry at the season, just angry. On the following Monday I was at last happy on my ride to the stadium because I knew that I was turning in my equipment. Coach Dark stood by the equipment managers as each player piled his gear in front of them for inspection and inventory. He wore a little smirk on his face, an expression that I read as the final insult of the season, one that said, "Well, I showed you." Yes, you did, you fucking son of a bitch.

CHAPTER 7

Pool Rat

In my memory there is no time when I could not swim and did not love the water like a second home. Swimming pools, stone quarries, lakes large and small, gulfs, oceans, on top of the water and below, I have explored and enjoyed—and nearly died. Our home in Delphos was in the northwestern part and only two blocks from Stadium Park, which housed the tennis courts and football stadium where both high schools played. Attached to the stadium building that had been poured in concrete by the Works Project Administration was the center of my summer life and the beginning of my love affair with water, the Delphos Municipal Swimming Pool. It was larger than one would have guessed from the size of the town. The deep portion was rectangular and about fifteen feet deep under the one-, two-, and three-meter diving boards and became shallower as one swam away from the boards to the small concrete island that buttressed the other end. On two sides of the deep was a metal fence with open gates to the shallow areas that began at two feet of water near the walk to about four feet at the fence. Nearly every day from Memorial to Labor Day would find me at about 1:30 in the afternoon with my swimming suit rolled into its towel, walking north down the crushed stone alley that ran on the west side of our house all the way to the park. A season ticket for a child was cheap, maybe three dollars, and provided more fun for the buck, and peace and quiet for our mother, than any other activity in our small town.

I was well known to the Director of the pool, Coach Arnzen. As a young child my behavior stood out. Pool rules included no running; I ran. Dunking and harassing other children, especially the girls, was forbidden; I became adept at all rough house-play in the water. Looking over us were two lifeguards at a time, high school students from both schools who were Red Cross certified and hired each year by the Delphos Recreation Board. To discipline rowdy characters (me) they would blow their whistle, point their finger at the offender, and shout the number of minutes that we were to sit on one of the benches that circled the pool. Many an hour I sat on my backside under the scowling gaze of a lifeguard after a particularly serious offense, at least on the scale of pool offenses. In extreme cases they could ask you to leave for the day, or longer. I do not remember getting this ultimate sanction because I always knew where to draw the line with bad behavior, a trait that has served me well over the years.

Blood and Water Do Mix

Of course, the pool rules existed for a good reason. Children could be harmed. I was harmed, though I was also to blame, another pattern that would recur in my later life. My brother Luke, the middle one, was chasing me through the west sandpit, or I was chasing him; it depended on who was annoying whom. The sand pits were areas on either side of the water where once sand had been shoveled to simulate, I suppose, an ocean beach in the Middle West. Sand, however, created problems. Swimmers dragged it into the pool, locker rooms, and restrooms, and got it into their suits and hair. Also, by the end of the summer season, nearly anything might be found under the sand, partially eaten sandwiches and bananas, empty suntan lotion bottles, dead field mice, maybe a missing child. When the pool had been redesigned and rebuilt in the late 1950s, sand was removed from the pits, thus leaving sloped concrete on which to spread one's towel for sunbathing and girl watching after a dip. When I fell on such a slope, only concrete cushioned my fall backwards onto the right side of my skull, causing it to quickly burst open like a ripe melon. Anyone who has been swimming and seen an accident with lots of blood knows that the presence of water amplifies the appearance of the injury. We had just been in the pool before I fell, so the cleft in my head disgorged blood on my shoulder that quickly spread a rosy sheen all over my body. I was covered with blood-water head to toe. The other swimmers looking at me could only assume that I had been mortally wounded.

Coach Arnzen took us home in his car where Mother's initial concern quickly turned to anger that I had done something so stupid. She immediately called her older sister Helen, the nurse, who had patched up the family children numerous times before. At that early time Helen worked in town with one of the four family physicians then in Delphos, the doctor who had delivered me as an infant.

Off we went, I bitching and bleeding in the front seat. The doctor was not in. He could have been in Lima at the hospital doing his rounds, or in surgery, or delivering a baby. Therefore Helen, who was very skilled at stitching, sewed me up with ten large sutures, all the time laughing about my plight, comforting my mother with assurances about the hardness and resiliency of my noggin, and finally telling me that I would need to stay out of the water until the stitches came out or I would risk a bad infection.

My accident coincided with the opportunity for more swimming on the following weekend when my family visited Cousin Father Bertie. We children were shunted off to the pool because of a mutual antagonism between him and us. I completely ignored the warnings of my aunt and splashed with my brothers with great glee. In two days, I had a raging fever, an infection with swelling in the incision, and three popped sutures, precipitating a call to Helen. She came to our house, sat me on the toilet lid and, telling me what an ass I was, roughly cleaned out the wound and told me that she could not close it up again because it had already partially healed. Instead, she finished the job by pouring red Merthiolate antiseptic right into the gap in my skull, which caused me to shudder in severe pain. That would teach me to disobey the woman we called Kick-Ass. As I have said, she did not suffer fools gladly; rather she gladly made fools suffer.

The Yellow Swimming Suit

I was imprinted for life by a yellow swimming suit. It all started in the spring of 1962 when I decided to earn my Red Cross Lifeguard Certificate. (If you cannot obey them, then join them.) I aimed to apply for a slot at the pool for the summer of 1963. That summer a young woman who had attended my high school a couple of years earlier, and had earned her Water Safety Instructor certification, was teaching the class at the Delphos Pool. Diane was very attractive, well proportioned, and in possession of a banana-yellow one-piece swimming suit that caught my eye in its three dimensions. At the very first session I knew that I was going to enjoy this class. It included my favorite food groups: water, physical activity, and a pretty, young woman who was required to interact with me.

Technical aspects of swimming came naturally to me from an early age. But I also spent many hours in different courses and leisure swimming honing to medium-high skill the crawl, side, and breast strokes, and the flutter, scissor, and frog kicks. The physical aspects of the lifesaving course were like teaching a beaver a slightly modified way to build his dam. Under the water was also just as comfortable to me as above it, limited only by my large lung capacity. I would dive to the bottom of the pool and mimic a carp looking for food while enjoying the pressure of the water and the silence and peacefulness that it created. One skill I could not manage was floating because my body was negatively buoyant, too much young muscle and bone and too little fat. A trick I employed was to go to the deepest end of the pool, let most of the air out of my lungs, and slowly sink until I stood on the drains at the bottom while looking up and waving, a skill that came in handy during drown-proofing with the Marines during basic training. But that is a different story.

The Red Cross lifesaving handbook came along with the water exercises. Diane would gather us in the former sandpit and lay out the lesson for the day. Then it was into the water for a few laps across the pool for her to assess our ability and comfort, develop stamina, and warm us for the day's lesson. Next, she chose a class member to demonstrate the skill. We learned a series of physical skills in the water to help a swimmer in trouble, potentially saving their life, while limiting the risk of losing our own in the attempt. The first principle, which is still burned in my brain, is Reach-Throw-Row-Go. If the person is close, reach out to them with a pole or hand and pull them to safety. If a roped life buoy is present, throw it past the swimmer and pull it back to him with the rope so that he can grasp the ring and be pulled in. Of course, if the body of water is large, and a boat is available, take it to the drowning person and drag them in. Only as a last resort should you get into the water yourself and go, because trying to save a panicking, thrashing, drowning person puts two lives at risk.

In the Delphos Swimming Pool, reaching and going were emphasized because there was no need for a boat or roped life buoy. We spent most of our pool time honing our go-skills, forming pairs and alternately playing the role of saver and victim. The role of victim was hard for me. An unskilled saver would cause me to ingest a great deal of water before I was "safe." Also, the victim was required to resist the saver, act a bit like a drowning victim, to make the exercise a real test. But where did I draw the line? For years I had developed harassing and dunking skills in the water and could have easily defeated any attempt to save me. I lied with my body language, moderated my resistance, and became a good, water-logged target for saving. I did not mind doing so for Diane. She would choose at random a student to illustrate the skill before we had a go with our partner. When she chose me, I gave a perfunctory performance of drowning and, after she had grabbed ahold of me, I relaxed and enjoyed the physical intimacy of her touch.

I do not remember any of the students from that class. Diane's yellow swimming suit probably shone so brightly in the sun and my mind that its light threw into shadow any other person in the pool. After practice we were not certified in a skill without performing it on the instructor. My favorite exercise was the cross-chest carry, which required swimming to the victim as quickly as possible with crawl stroke and flutter kick. If the person was panicked it was very dangerous to come at her from the front; her first instinct was to grab ahold, which might just drown the both of you. The skill required the saver to dive just before the victim and when at her feet, take them and spin her 180 degrees so that now her back was facing you. You then worked your hands up her side, which did two things: it comforted her knowing that you were there; and it prevented her from turning back toward you. When you surfaced, you executed the cross-chest carry to transport her to safety.

Tactile heaven had just opened its doors to me. Diane jumped into the deep section of the pool beneath the diving boards and feigned drowning. I was at the opposite end of the deep and swam to her. When close, I dived, and there, to my great pleasure and anticipation, was the beautiful body in the yellow suit waiting for me. My technique was perfect. Positioned near her feet, I grabbed her ankles and spun her around. Then

I joyously worked my hands up the sides of her calves, her wonderful, shapely thighs, her well-formed backside, up the waist, and—culmination of fifteen-year-old boy fantasy—her breasts. But not lingering, not creepy or awkward was I, just a light brush with the palms and joined fingers and then we surfaced, and I threw my right arm over her chest and that yellow swimming suit and exercised the side stroke and scissor kick to transport my wonderful passenger all the way across the pool. These were some of the best twenty yards traversed in my young life, and you will forgive me if I did not swim at maximum speed. After we reached our destination and I reluctantly released her, Diane complimented me on my technique and passed me on the skill. Silently I sang "Joy to the World" with modified verse; for after all, what sweeter words can a male hear from a beautiful woman after joint physical activity?

A second skill placed me in a three-dimensional orientation with the female body for the first time, a position that was later to give me continuing pleasure in closer and modified form. It was the Tired Swimmer's Carry, used when the victim was fatigued and needed assistance but was not panicked. So once again Diane and the yellow suit were at the very deep end where she pretended exhaustion and the need for help to safety. Again, I swam quickly to her, only now the exercise called for me to woo her with soothing words to encourage her to relax and place her trust in my ability to assist, because she needed to respond to my instructions and to act accordingly. First, I swam to her back and requested that she turn and face me so that her back was now in the direction of travel. I then coaxed her to lean back and spread her legs so I could place my body between them, and she could support herself by applying gentle pressure with her legs and putting each hand on one of my shoulders. I then swam the breaststroke with the frog kick to slowly transport her across the pool. The effect of this position was to throw my face in the direct orientation of her pelvis while watching the yellow suit bob up and down as I stroked. Little did I know that swimming coupled in the Tired Swimmer's Carry was practice for the art of mature and adventuresome sex. I just knew I wanted to assume that position for a long time. Luckily my breaststroke was my weakest.

At the end of the course, I received my Red Cross lifesaving certificate and patch. Diane and the yellow suit had given me the skills necessary for the next year's application and simultaneously awakened new feelings and tactile pleasures. Thank you, Diane.

Application and Connection

How I obtained the position of lifeguard in the spring of 1963 is lost in the fog of memory. It entailed, I believe, a written application to the Delphos Recreation Board followed by an interview for those on the short list. My parents' good friend Edith was on the board that year. From her example I learned about the person who feels obliged to be part of the decision-makers in any institution to which she belongs. She and Father had gone to Delphos Jefferson High School together and had been life-long friends, along with her husband Bud, who worked for the local soybean mill. When my parents went out with friends, the two of them would invariably be members of the party, and often I heard their laughter from the barroom in our home when my parents were the hosts. Edith was a staunch Republican, active in city affairs, and a pillar of the Methodist Church, although, in our barroom, it was not unusual for us to see her sitting on one of the stools with her legs crossed and a bottle of Rolling Rock in her hand. Private pleasures are important after all, even for the devout. As a child I felt that she knew everything and everybody in town and represented the abstract noun "influence."

Did having her on the board lead to my successful application, or was I just the best candidate for the job? I never knew. When Coach Arnzen learned of my hiring he said, in my earshot, that no one knew the pool rules better than I did, having broken all of them. Appreciating even that left-handed compliment, I was thrilled to be hired. Now I would spend my days at my favorite spot in town and make a regular salary, small though it was.

Pool Set-Up

My new job at the pool turned out to be an amplification of my escape from oppressive religiosity and parochialism. Here I was going to meet and work with young people from Jefferson because the recreation board was very careful to balance the hiring. The call finally came, and I went to the pool to meet my companions for the summer and to prepare the facility for its first influx of bathers. Coach Calvin, also from Jefferson High, had replaced Coach Arnzen as the summer Director of the pool. He was our Omar Bread man when I was young and drove his delivery truck down our alley, bringing his large tray of bread and pastries to our back door, from which Mother would choose the items she desired. He summarized his experiences at our back door by offering his sympathies to my mother. It seems that we three boys were very active and loud as children, a condition that Coach Calvin likened to chaos.

Water had just filled the pool. In the winter it was pumped out because the freezing and expansion of the ice would break and crack the plumbing and concrete. This was the rural, landlocked Midwest, and our water for the pool came from wells deep in the ground. At the beginning of the season the water was very cold. Our first job was to attach the three fiberglass diving boards of varying heights to the diving platform at the south end of the deep section. Then we were given a tour of the facility and an introduction to our duties. Lifeguards, in addition to watching swimmers, were responsible for cleaning the pool, the deck, and the sandpits; maintaining the pH balance and chlorine level; and backwashing the pool when required. Pool hours were Sunday to Friday 1 to 9 P.M. and Saturdays 1 to 5. Staff were required to arrive at noon to begin the workday. Each lifeguard worked six days a week with a rotating day off. At noon we had an hour to prepare. The sandpits and deck needed to be swept and floating debris removed from the water. Trees surrounded the fence and compounded our work. Chemical balance of the water was also important because we were subject to random visits by the county health authorities, who tested the quality of the water, which, if found to be un-healthy, could lead to the closing of the facility.

Inside the WPA stadium building young women handled admissions and worked in the basket rooms. This area was divided into three sec-tions. On each side of the basket room was a dressing room, shower, and restroom, east side for women, west for men. These areas required clean-ing and disinfecting daily. I still remember the odor of chlorine and dis-infectant that permeated the locker rooms. The central basket room had corresponding women's and men's sides with wire-mesh baskets that were about two feet long and a foot wide and deep, with a stainless-steel tag and number. After entering the locker room door, the swimmer would select a basket from the pile, take it inside, change into his or her suit, and return the basket to one of the girls with the street clothes. Each basket had its numbered slot on a numbered shelf in the basket room. At the end of the day the process was reversed. The basket room and admission area also served as the central socializing area for the staff. We all had our pri-vate baskets and hung out together when the lifeguards were not on duty.

Daily Grind

At 1 P.M. the children and a few adults lined up underneath the cement arch and passageway that ran the length of the stadium. Once the admission window was open and the locker room doors unlocked, the kids would race through to the pool and plunge in. By this time, of course, we lifeguards would already be on our chairs. There were two, one at each end of the deep section and oriented in different directions, the south chair looking east and north, the north chair looking west and south. The combined areas of vision covered the swimming pool with a natural emphasis on the deep section and the diving platform. There were four lifeguards total, three fulltime, John, Jim, and I, and a fulltime employee, Mak, who divided her time between the lifeguard chair on our days off and the basket room. We rotated as well through three daily lifeguard schedules, each of which lasted eight to nine hours.

Each guard was often on a chair for two hours at a time watching screaming children having a good time splashing, diving, dunking, running, and doing many of the obnoxious behaviors that I did at the same age. At the end of the nine hours, six of them watching children, I was usually very tired and looked forward to getting home and collapsing. I have accredited my lack of children as an adult to my job as a lifeguard. After the hundreds of hours of child-like behavior I experienced at the pool, I was sated and wished for no more.

My days and weeks were busy that summer. They began at 7:30 or 8:00 A.M., when I rolled out of bed and had breakfast with Mother. In addition to my pool job, I had had a small lawn-landscaping business for years. I had, from the age of twelve, been trading my labor for dollars. I used my own green rotary mower with a one-gallon gasoline can and trimming tools to cut the lawn for three or four regular clients each week. Then in the spring and fall my clients would ask me to do planting and clean-up and irregular jobs, cleaning out eavestroughs and so forth.

Our family schedule was, as I've said, inflexibly determined by my father's work. At 11:30 A.M. the factory whistle would sound, and the men would have an hour for lunch. At about 11:35 he would come in the door, and we would sit down and eat our main meal of the day. This meant that I had twenty minutes to eat and jump on my bicycle for the pool to be there at noon. I had taken my oldest brother's three-speed Huffy English bicycle with thin tires, removed the hand brakes and derailleur, put on a pedal break and single gear, and used it for my routine transportation around town. It was light and fast; five minutes to the pool was pokey for me. In the evening we were expected to be at the table at 5:05 so that we ate before Father watched the CBS Evening News with Walter Cronkite at 5:30. During the pool and football seasons I got a family pass for evening meals because my schedule was so uncertain. Whenever I got off the chair in the evening, I jumped back on the Huffy and rode home, where Mother had a quick, light meal waiting for me. Then back on the bike and to the pool for the evening work. My workdays were a minimum of nine hours but often eleven to twelve hours in length, six days a week. Still, I was young, energetic, enjoying the labors, and eager to earn and do well.

Mak

That summer I developed a huge affection for our relief lifeguard Mak. She was a year older than I at St. John's, tall, thin, with very cute freckles on her face and body, short brown hair, and hazel eyes that I teased as being colored the tint of the sea, the depth of which I was only too eager to explore. Mak was, I believe, the oldest of a large sibship that lived just west of the Stadium Park on the corner lot. They had a St. Bernard that was often seen loping on the grassy swards that surrounded the pool. I met Mak for the first time in late May, when the four of us helped the Director set up the facilities for the season. One of the senior lifeguards, John, was in the same class as Mak, and it was clear to me that he was sweet on her, but ineffectual. John's father was a machinist at Father's factory. John's sister was in my class, and their family was also very large as well as very poor. Mak wanted no attachments and treated all boys with amused indifference.

One of my first impressions, which struck a strong physical chord in my body, was Mak's laugh. It was easy, infectious, and frequent. It had to be. This was 1963, when the women's liberation movement was just a dream and male position was secure. The male lifeguards that summer were no different, all macho football players and boys-will-be-boys. We were full-time. Mak was hired as our back-up. Therefore, she immediately had lower status in two domains. However, she adapted herself to the situation with grace and good cheer.

Mak was athletic—a bit of a tomboy—and was willing to give as well as she got. We jocks were getting in shape for the football season and running to build endurance. The stadium sat at one corner of a two-mile square that we used as a course. On the east side was a gravel road that ran north along the remains of the Miami Erie Canal and that ended at the county road near the city dump. We then turned west to State Highway 66, then south to Stadium Street, and back east to the pool. The three males had a natural competition about time and distance. Coach Arnzen, who was still employed by the Recreation Board, occasionally joined the four of us for a gabfest on the north bleachers of the stadium. We, of course, teased Mak about running. She in turn diminished our feats. She and Coach Arnzen then set up a challenge among the four of us to see who was fastest. Off Mak went, and to our great surprise, she beat our times. She laughed and laughed at us, laughter that made me want her even more, despite my small humiliation.

Subtle Intimacies

My favorite days on the chair were when one of my two male colleagues had a day off and I was guaranteed nine hours of close association with

Mak. In those periods when we were both on the chairs, we faced each other across the deep section. It was here that we bonded, at a distance. Even though we were separated by sixty feet and busy with our respective jobs, watching the customers so they did not drown or abuse one another, an intimacy grew between us. Often our eyes would meet, and small smiles were exchanged. Could it be that two bodies at a distance could send out attraction waves in a similar manner that two masses at a distance interact with gravity waves, a Mars and Venus who slightly perturb each other's bodies? Physical contact was often allowed, or sought, between us. Sun exposure and skin damage was a very real danger. We helped each other in applying sunscreen on each other's backs where we could not reach ourselves. Another custom was the carry to the north chair that was at the deep fence and surrounded by shoulder-high water. Often it was cold in the Midwestern summer, and Mak did not want to soak her brown single-piece suit by wading to the chair because a cool prevailing westerly wind would cause great discomfort until the pale, cumulus cloud-erratic sun had a chance to dry the fabric. I, of course, was more than willing to give her a lift, literally. It may have begun with an element of sophomoric gallantry, the male pubescent enthusiasm for helping an attractive woman; but it soon became, by empirical discovery, a popular ritual for both of us. For you see, to transport Mak I had to put her on my shoulders. Now this required that she stand on the pool deck while I stood in the shallow water below her, after which she would spread her legs and put my head between them by throwing a leg over each shoulder. To balance her I naturally had to hold on to her thighs, calves, and ankles. She then would grab my forehead and press her pubic symphysis against my neck. Off we went in coupled laughter to the chair where she would throw one leg on the frame and lever herself up. This was my first real experience in the art of subtle intimacy by which two people communicate messages with a discreet language, one that is tactile, not audible.

This intimacy was reinforced by our swimming together after the pool closed. That summer it was the gossip of the basket girls and other lifeguards that Mak and I would stay at the pool after closing at 9, wait until all the other employees had left and the lights had been turned off, and then plunge into the water for a swim together. By intimacy I do not mean that we were engaging in relations in the pool. Rather the closeness was much more subtle: the darkness of the sky, the warmth of the environment, the brightness of the ring of stars in the Milky Way spreading over our heads, the soft breeze rustling the trees around the fence line, and swimming together, in proximity and contact, laughing and fooling around, throwing, chasing, and stealing balls, all of this created a deep friendship in a unique time and place. There is a special comfort to warm, dark, deep water that must hold a memory of the amniotic fluid that surrounded us as infants. We dove deep after one another, grabbed hold, tussled and popped to the surface for air, like a couple of playing young seals. When exhausted by our late-night excursions we headed to the dressing rooms and shouted jokes and insults across the basket room while we dressed. It was a short walk to Mak's house. Then a short ride to mine, tired and happy.

At this distance it surprises me that the supervising adults did not question us more closely about our nocturnal activities. Maybe it was a more innocent time in which the immediate assumption did not turn dark. Or maybe it did, and people did not care. After all, we were sixteen and seventeen years of age; we would have been considered consenting adults in Great Britain where students with no university aspirations finish school at sixteen and look for training and work. An honors student and popular cheerleader-lifeguard from good Delphos families were just assumed to be doing the "right" thing. If there were suspicions, they were never given a voice.

Mak politely dismissed my attempts to take us a large step further with a smile and a chuckle. I very much wanted to take her to a movie in Lima and get a meal on the way home and cultivate a more physical closeness. I suspected that her fellow cheerleader, Julia, who was in my class and had her eye on me, had warned Mak off. Or maybe she did not fancy dating a younger student. When seventeen and a woman-senior, a sixteen-year-old-male junior can look young. What would the other seniors say? The subtle intimacies lasted that summer but had no durability in the fall, when I did begin seeing Julia. Fate had had its way, helped by a conspiracy of cheerleaders. Yet to this day I retain the feeling of closeness to Mak that developed in the pool, two bodies whose proximity and perturbation had permanence.

Our Unholy Lady of Merde

That summer I risked death twice at the pool. During my lifetime, particularly in the early years, I have had quite a few of these near-death experiences—not the seeing light and out-of-body near-death experience but the serious, dark, almost-dead kind. They have led me to question who it is that periodically strips me of my dignity and makes me perform stupid acts that lead to embarrassment and injury and the resulting near-death. For it has felt like there was an external agency at work.

Mother's Roman Catholic religion has a figure or goddess, an invisible virgin floating in the sky, the Mother of the Son in the mysterious trinity of her God who will respond kindly to prayers from her devotees. It goes variously by the name of Our Holy Lady of This-or-That. My education, scientific training and practice, combined with my agnosticism, makes me very skeptical of the existence of such a being. Virgin cults have also been part of many pre-Christian mythologies and probably date to the origin of religion itself. Nevertheless, I like the image and wish to adapt it in these pages. I imagine a figure I will call Our Unholy Lady of Merde, the invisible anti-patroness of, especially but not exclusively, young men, who works in the world through a trinity of real forces: 1) randomness or chance; 2) risk-taking; and 3) a disdain for early death. Men in their youth are particularly in her thrall because they are generally ignorant of the role of randomness in their lives, use risk-taking as an aphrodisiac, and ignore the possibility of dying.

Not the Brightest Bulb in the Sand Filter

Our Unholy Lady was certainly an agent this fateful day, directing her forces about me, when I was asked to backwash the pool's filter. The water was continuously pumped out of the pool into the filter underneath the basket room to clean it. This was a sand filter, the large bed of which was in a concrete receptacle. The water flowed into the filter on top of the bed and through the sand, cleaning it, before being pumped back into the pool. Quite a bit of sludge would accumulate in the sand and required periodic removal through backwashing. The flow of the water was reversed through the sand, then into the gutter that lined the filter, which led to the sewer. The sludge would float to the surface but would not always easily find its way into the gutter. Therefore, one of the lifeguards would stand in the sand filter and, as the sludge rose, direct a stream of water from a garden hose to push it into the gutter. The sludge took the form of a tan-colored foam that floated in an ugly ring all around the body of the cleaner.

A series of metal-mesh-screened light bulbs above the filter illuminated what we were doing in this confined place. Entrance was from three dimpled metal sheets that covered holes to the filter. The lucky person on backwash duty pulled one of the covers back, turned on the light, lowered himself in, hooked up the hose, and got to work when the pumps were reversed. Being the new guy, this gnarly task fell to me. As my attention was directed downwards, I did not notice that one of the bulbs had broken and only the filaments were left and were grounded to the metal light fixture. I was standing waist deep in water with a running hose in my hand when I backed up to get a better angle for my work and my shoulder touched the shorted metal.

The electricity from the circuit coursed through my body and shocked me so hard that it threw me across the filter room, banged my body against the west wall and, I believe, knocked me out for a time. The next thing I knew I was sitting against the wall looking up at the pool director, who was peering down from the open hole, calling my name, and asking if I was alright. Yes, but just barely. Our Unholy Lady of Merde had done her work and given me a scare. When I looked at the ceiling, I noticed the broken bulb and immediately knew what had happened. I had unthinkingly taken a risk and put myself in a situation that contained a conjunction of rare random factors, the broken, shorted bulb, the waist-deep water, and the small, enclosed concrete space. Had my head gone underwater, I would have been dead before anyone would have noticed. It is still a mystery why the electricity alone did not fry me.

Quietly amused at my near-death state, I got up, shook my head, pointed out the broken bulb to the director, and finished the backwash. At 1 P.M. I was back on duty in my chair.

Of Children and Pee

I begin with definitions for the obvious. Do bears poop in the woods? Do children pee in pools?

And now a little chemistry lesson. Chlorine is a technical advancement that allows swimming pools to maintain a healthy environment for the bathers. As a former chemistry major, I know that at room temperature gaseous chlorine is a diatomic molecule, Cl_2, that readily mixes with water, H_2O, forming hydrochloric acid, HCL, and releasing oxygen, O_2. This is part of the reason that the pH or acidity of the pool must be monitored closely so that the acid does not become too strong. But why put chlorine in a pool at all? It is because of a, literally, dirty little secret; bathers, children and adults, pee in pools. Now, Reader, don't deny it. Everyone who has swum in a pool on a regular basis has also peed in one, including myself. It is just too much trouble to get out of the warm water, chill on the way to the restroom, try to negotiate a wet swimsuit to expose the necessary equipment, stand on your bare feet next to a toilet where others have been, and use the facilities. Further, standing in cold pool water and letting the bladder do its work envelops the swimmer in a momentary feeling of warmth and pleasure. Most people do not give much thought about the content of pee in a pool; it is just a bit of water added to water.

In fact, urine is a very complex biological byproduct created by the breakdown of food. One of its main constituents is a molecule called urea: $CO(NH_2)_2$. Now this is an organic molecule, one made up of carbon, hydrogen, oxygen, and nitrogen that is very useful in the research lab as well as having many commercial applications. However, it is a human waste product that we want to remove from our pools, and we do that with chlorine. The chemistry is complex, but the bottom line is that the chlorine chemically reacts with the pee and neutralizes it. It is the absolution for the dirty little sin; should that we be washed clean so easily from all of our misdeeds.

Nearly any molecule that is beneficial to humans can also have, in the proper concentration and circumstance, a dark, even fatal, side. Chlorine protects in pools but kills in wars. During WWI, early in 1915, the

Germans decided to kill thousands of French and British by bringing hundreds of cylinders of gaseous chlorine to the front in France and then releasing the gas when the prevailing winds carried it over the British and French trenches. Chlorine is heavier than air. It crept into the trenches and settled to the bottom where it concentrated. It was noticed that the men standing and shooting out of the trenches were affected less than the war casualties who were lying on stretchers at the bottom. Masks were quickly improvised that had cloth pads to help absorb the gas. It was soon found that water, but more effectively urine, would make these pads more efficient because they reacted with the gas and neutralized it. Thereafter the soldiers urinated on their pads before they put them in their gas masks. The protection that they received was due to the same chemical reactions with water and urea that keep pools safe with chlorine. Only now war reversed the roles; water and urea were good, chlorine bad.

My German Lesson

I would soon experience this dark side of chlorine when Our Unholy Lady of Merde appeared to me for a second time at the pool. On the side of the stadium building near the west gate was the pump room that housed the mechanicals that made the pool possible. Electric motors hummed as they ran the pumps and circulated the water from the pool to the sand filter and back out again. When the water passed through the pump room it also received a continuous flow of gaseous chlorine, which was stored and delivered in large, green, heavy, oblong metal cylinders about four feet tall that stood on their flat end. Part of my job as lifeguard was to check the pressure gauge of the cylinder and, when the gas was spent, hook up a new one. This required that I shut off the valve to the cylinder, unhook the feed line with the lead washer and threaded fastener, roll out the old tank, roll in the new, hook everything back up, and open the valve. We were given instructions on how to perform our various tasks but there was little, if any, lesson about the dangers of the substance or safety precautions that we should take.

One day I was blithely on my way to the pump room during the maintenance hour when I opened the door, strode purposely in, and walked toward the chlorine pressure valve. Then I took a deep breath and inhaled a high concentration of chlorine gas. No one had noticed the leak. It filled the entire enclosed room with the same poison that was so effective in WWI. I was, as usual, in my bare feet. There was, as usual, water and grease from the pumps on the bare cement floor of the room. Had I gagged, slipped and fell and knocked my head, I would have fallen to the floor where the most concentrated gas lay, and died. Luckily, as soon as I found myself in trouble, I threw myself out the door, force exhaled the lung full of chlorine in the fresh air and breathed and breathed and breathed. My eyes teared and my nose ran, causing severe pain because chlorine reacts with the water in the body and creates hydrochloric acid. After reporting the problem to those who could do something about it, I was once again back on my chair at 1 P.M.

Farmers Don't Float

The pool closed at 5 P.M. on Saturday afternoon. In the evening it was often rented out to private groups for a pool party. One of the conditions was that a lifeguard must be present, which gave me an opportunity to make a few extra dollars by relaxing around the pool and watching the merrymakers have a good time in the water. These groups were inevitably small, engaged me personally in their party, and were generally a lot of fun. One evening I was hired by the local branch of the Future Farmers of America. Delphos was surrounded by miles and miles of farmland. Kids from the farms were bussed into the city's schools, and their schedules were determined by planting and harvesting cycles. During the busiest season, mid-May to early September, when school was out, farm children helped their parents with chores and jobs on the land. Therefore, they seldom came into town for the swimming lessons that we offered. Water was a foreign environment. Its purpose was to hydrate the animals, not to play in and about.

This evening started well. Food and drinks were usually set up in the sand pits or on the grass just outside the fence, where all the participants enjoyed a full meal before the evening swim. Then all hell broke loose. Twenty or thirty young men, current and future farmers, jumped into the pool with a ball and net to play a variation of volleyball. The city had charged them for the event, and they were unfamiliar with many of the standard rules of behavior in water. I was loathe to crack down too hard on rowdy behavior when I could see that they were unlikely to harm themselves or one another. During the evening parties, because only one of us guarded the swimmers, I usually walked and circulated among them along the pool deck that surrounded the shallow area. This also kept me dry and protected me from the cool evening breeze. It put me at a disadvantage, however, when it came to the deep section. I was farther away. But since most of the play was in the shallows, I thought it was a reasonable risk. Not! The ball was flying back and forth between the two sides; but suddenly it flew into the deep section. A young farmer who tried to catch it reacted reflexively by going backwards through the gate into the deep to retrieve it, only to disappear below the surface. I shot into the water, found him floundering, and pulled him out to the shallow area, to the great surprise and amusement of his friends. Their lack of experience in water meant they did not know one of nature's laws: farmers don't float.

CHAPTER 8

A Walk in the Woods
and to the Dam

Football Again

My wonderful summer of 1963 as a lifeguard with Mak was now over, and high school and football had descended upon me yet again in dreary monotony. Coach Dark was at his most brutal and incompetent. In his third season as head coach, he had by now alienated the boys and their parents, leaving only a small number of volunteers willing to put up with his ignorance and Abuse & Intimidation style. We played for the love of the game, imbued with the culture of small-town rural America. I had just returned from a year off, having been diagnosed with hepatitis-A at the beginning of the previous season and forbidden by my doctor to play sports. I spent that season as an assistant manager for the team, taping ankles under the supervision of Assistant Coach Cross, slopping antiseptic on cuts, and taking the game uniforms to the dry cleaners, among other chores. This season I was back in uniform playing both ways, fullback or halfback on offense and the "monster man," the wide-side linebacker, on defense. It was utter misery. In the first three games we did not score, whereas our opponents racked up a combined ninety points. It was not until the fourth game that we showed a little life on the offensive side and beat an even worse team by a score of 27-7.

I bore a guilty conscience about part of our lackluster performance. At the beginning of the season, two of our critical senior players, my cousin Philip, a guard, and Danny, the first-string quarterback, had reported to the team with long hair. Now long hair was like waving a scarlet flag in front of the bull that was our priest-principal: it made him mean and arbitrary and likely to charge the poor students and gore them with his finely sharpened rules about dress and hairstyles. Hair falling around the collar was evil, a sinful sign that these young men were potential members of the criminal class, so of course it could not be permitted on the football team. To avoid full responsibility, however, Father Thomas called a team meeting at which he essentially put us in a vise by asking the players to vote on whether these two members of the team should be allowed to play or be forced first to cut their hair. Let it be said that all the players knew the rules before the season began, including Phil and Danny. But they, and their parents, still resisted the haircuts because they thought that hair length was none of the principal's business. I was put in a moral and personal dilemma, whether to support the side of known rules that governed all the team or support my cousin. Phil had been a childhood friend and companion, the son of my mother's first cousin, Aunt Jane. Unfortunately, I chose principle over family, speaking for obedience to the rules of the team. My voice was not without some authority because I was the top scholar in the junior class and was known as a physical force as well. Phil and Danny were suspended from the team. Our inability to score a point for the first four weeks certainly resulted from the loss of their considerable talents.

October 4, a Friday, we played and won by a score of 34–20. My good friend John, who lifeguarded with me at the municipal pool that summer, was the star of the game. He was larger than I, a better, gifted athlete, and had a good head for the game. I also played well, as the following bits from Saturday's *Lima News* attests:

Delphos—Two startling scoring bursts by their opponent in the first quarter here Friday night failed to rattle Delphos, and the Blue Jays slamming overland attack stomped out a 34–20 football victory. Captain John Rupert, a 170-pound senior halfback and the muscle behind Delphos's ramrod ground game, scored four touchdowns.

Running with Rupert and tearing up the opponent's right-side defense was quick-hitter Robert Williams. The stubby, 155-pound junior flashed too much speed at early Commodore alignments and scored the Blue Jays' first touchdown...

Quarterback Bill Reinemeyer steadily drummed the crashing Rupert over tackles and fired the fleet Williams around them.

(Article continues about how it was parents' night in Delphos and the crowd had to be concerned when our opponent scored first.)

Delphos wasn't daunted. The Blue Jays hammered for 58 yards sending Williams the final 19 in three spurts, and scored at 4:10 of the first.

Stubby was I? Well I suppose having a body in the shape of a fire hydrant would lend itself to such a description. Fleet of foot was I? Flattered though I am, I can hardly own the word. My congenitally deformed foot was not built for speed, though by sheer force of will I did manage to negotiate a football field with some violent, quick grace.

Only Child

That fall found me in a new domestic circumstance: no brothers at home, only parents. I was now—for the next two years—the only child, a condition that I found most enjoyable. Small things like no competition for the second car, no sharing a bedroom, silence at night when I needed to study, and my parents' full attention made me understand that I was made for the role. Solitude was enjoyable and therefore preferable; the independence of decision and action it allowed, necessary to my well-being. It helped that my parents had great respect for these traits, and their close supervision evolved to detached admiration and trust. Father had always given me clear boundaries in which to move. Now I found that I could push the envelope beyond this or that line without precipitating a response. My parents were also becoming accustomed to, and enjoying, the absence of the routine chores of raising children. They wanted to travel, spend more time with their friends, and act like a couple with no children, like when they were first married and could concentrate on each other without distraction. Sensing this, I distracted them as little as possible.

Our next game was Friday, October 11, 1963. Mother had an unusual request. Before the game I was to go and visit Great Aunt Nell. On West Fourth Street Father had rented a small, two-bedroom house from the owner of the local lumber store where she lived with a caregiver by the name of Dora who had a congenitally defective leg that gave her a serious but manageable limp. After Nell and Dora moved in, it became my responsibility to take care of the miserable patch of lawn and bushes that surrounded the house, which had been just barely tended by the owner. Poison ivy was everywhere; the bushes were full of needles and sharp edges that scraped and cut the skin just brushing by it; and the area, while small, was difficult to negotiate with my rotary lawnmower. As much as I loved Aunt Nell, I hated that yard, the landscape from hell.

When I knocked and Dora let me into the house, Nell was sitting in one of the wingback chairs in the living room, wearing her dressing gown. She usually wore a beautiful, old-style dress tastefully accompanied by jewelry. Her attire and demeanor gave the room the feeling of fragility and sickness. I of course knew that she had not been well for some time.

Nell and I sat for an hour and chatted. Usually, she was concerned about something in the yard—this bush needed trimming, the grass was to be cut better in one spot—or she and Dora had me run an errand or make a small repair to the house or garage. But this day was different. Nell was concerned about me, about my safety and health, about the dangers of playing such a violent sport as football. It took me by surprise, because in my experience as a young boy, dealing with old relatives meant caring for them and their needs. Mother had cared for and buried my very old, twice-great Aunt Minnie and her husband Harry, also relatives on my father's side, and had the day-to-day responsibility for the care of his mother. Emma was a black hole of attention, medical services, and emotional distress, sucking them all in while letting but a few rays of light or concern escape for anyone else. I was flattered and touched by Nell's warmth and attention. I did not understand that she was communicating on two levels. On the obvious plane, Nell was expressing love for me; on the unexpressed level she was telling me that she was dying and was saying goodbye. At some point during our conversation Nell offered to pay me not to play in the game that evening. I believe the enticement was five dollars, a lot of money for someone who was born in the Nineteenth Century. We laughed about the ridiculousness of the gesture. Then I had to leave to eat something before I went to the stadium to dress for the game.

Nell went into the hospital on Sunday and was dead on Wednesday, October 16, 1963. We lost our game that Friday by a score of 8–22. Our miserable season now continued with a record of two wins over poorer teams and four bad losses.

Perfect Fall

A small compensation for Nell's imminent death and our losing season was the weather. It had been a propitious spring and summer for foliage; with the proper amount of moisture in the ground, the trees had responded by filling their branches with thick clouds of dark green leaves. The pace of autumnal cooling and freezing had triggered a perfect fall tie-dying of our deciduous woods. Middle America in mid-October of 1963 was aglow.

I naturally wanted to share the splendor of that glorious fall with Julia, whom I had just begun seeing. The day after Labor Day 1956 I first saw this beautiful girl with the jet-black hair, whose eyes, when they fell on me, instantly drew my whole attention. For the next nine years Julia and I were to progress through the grades together. But it was only at the beginning of our junior year of high school that we became close.

Julia, the daughter of the Vice President of Delphos's People's National Bank, came from an important family. Religion and family divided the town. There was the "good religion," Roman Catholicism, and everything else—just like there were the "good, old families" and everyone else. These two classifications often overlapped. I was part of the good religion and old families on Mother's side. Children of good families were suited to see and recreate with one another.

But I was a bit of a social and religious hybrid, the recipient of Protestant inclinations and blue-collar attitudes from my father. He was religiously unaffiliated and did not belong to one of the established pedigrees, his ancestors being Welsh coal miners and farmers, while he himself worked for forty-four years in a factory. A few years later, in a college German class, I would read a novel called *Abendliche Häuser*, by Eduard von Keyserling. The title, loosely translated, means "the evening of the houses" and refers to the decline of the noble families of Germany and its social consequences, one of the book's central themes. Delphos was founded primarily by German immigrants in the middle of the nineteenth century. Mother and the members of her mother's generation told stories of a time in Delphos when the social strata of families were well defined and determinative. Now, just as in the novel, these hierarchies were waning. But their echoes were still present.

Julia's family, her father's position, and her beauty undoubtedly conditioned my attitude of reverence, admiration, and fear. If she stood on a pedestal, then I stood at its base with intimidation and trepidation, particularly at the beginning. When we were freshmen, she dated one of the seniors, hardly the kind of thing to give a boy three years younger a lot of confidence.

Called Out

In the fall of my junior year, I was unhappy in high school. Julia became the perfect balm for my confused heart and mind for the next two years. Up until the end of freshman year I had been quite carefree, dating different girls, playing sports, taking my classes for granted. I had no pretenses to greatness—I was just a young boy having fun. Then a bad thing happened: I was called out as smart. From the beginning of school, I had known that I was doing well in my classes, but I did not care. Behavior was an issue. I was rowdy and prone to start fights, a pugnacious boy who took crap from no one. While I thought Coach Dark was a sadistic ass, I liked the violence of football. As a freshman, I entered a restroom that was allegedly reserved for upperclassmen, and two juniors jumped me. I went after one junior with the clear intent of badly hurting him, and the fight spilled out onto the playground, where the nuns were supervising the afternoon recess for the grade school. We ended up dirty and torn before being pulled away from each other.

From then I relieved myself when and where I wanted. I went to the sock-hops that were organized by the school, danced both slow and fast, and was invited to and attended the classmates' parties. I was popular. And then, at the last student assembly in May of 1962, I was given the medal for highest scholastic merit and achievement in the freshman class; in the small pond of 125 students, I was the number-one fish and was to stay that way until we graduated.

We had many college-bound kids who were smart. The smartest person in the class was my close friend Clint, who lived just a street apart from me. We enjoyed engaging in "smart" pursuits together: namely chess, golf, and astronomy. Our fifth-grade teacher, who talked about such things, said we were neck and neck when it came to intelligence. Only a few teachers and administrators who had access to our records knew how we had scored on the school's IQ tests. But I had learned that one of us was just a few points higher than the other. He was now gone. Clint's parents had sent him off to the seminary for high school. After he went to Jesus, we could no longer hang out in the summer because I was an occasion for sin (meaning access to girls).

This abandonment was a continuing pattern in the transition from grade school to high school. Grant, from across the street on the east side, who had been a constant companion for years—playing on the canal, swimming in the pool and quarries, hiking in the Boy Scouts—began dating a young woman whom he would eventually marry. From the fall of our freshman year, he spent his spare time with her and worked part-time at her father's printing shop. Mike, who was one of my early best friends and who had been my assistant on the paper route, also disappeared. He and I had been very close, playing basketball, hanging out at his house, where his parents had become my good friends, going to movies, riding our bicycles everywhere, and just prowling the back alleys and streets of Delphos. After he quit the paper route and I was promoted to the press-room, he joined our class's baboon troupe. These five or six solitary males regressed to a seeming third grade maturity and took on the aspect of juvenile apes on the savannah, giggling, pawing, grunting, and grooming one another. Study hall, when the monitor was out of the class and the troupe was in the corner, turned into a primate cage at the zoo with hoot-ing, hollering, and general misbehavior.

My once close male friends were gone. This began a period of pro-found loneliness and depression. Singling me out as the top student only seemed to deepen my sad, isolated, feelings and precipitated a withdrawal from the normal social life of the high school. I reduced my participation in functions to a minimum and became solitary and self-absorbed, concentrating on my jobs, sports, and studies. A tension between my need for personal privacy and a necessary social engage-ment became acute.

Now, in my junior year, I had reached my adult size, was living an independent life as the only child at home with my parents and felt like an adult in a child's world. I was also bored with most of my classes and ready to move on to college. In chemistry class I brought a novel most days. Because I had the highest score on each exam, my teacher just ignored my casual reading and went on teaching the other students. English and Latin classes were superficial and dull, taught by old nuns who should have been put out to pasture to knit booties for African chil-dren whose souls they wished to save. Religion class, taught by one of the priests, was a cruel joke, usually emphasizing the dangers of either touching ourselves or the opposite sex in an inappropriate way, or discussing the invisible virgin in the sky who cared about us on earth and would reveal herself under the right conditions, or some other such silly nonsense. My only academic salvation that year was the combination of mathematics and history, for which I developed an early passion and had exceptional teachers. I attended extra math sessions offered on Saturday mornings in which our instructor would present advanced topics to a few of the college-bound kids. On the statewide exams that were given at the local university, I scored high.

Beautiful Palliative

And then—with my lasting gratitude—there was Julia, a beautiful companion who acted as a soothing palliative. Julia shared little and asked as little from her companion; she was not a "share-your-feelings" or "what-are-you-thinking" kind of girl—just right for me. This is not to suggest that she lacked intelligence or sensitivity. She was one of those near the top of the class and probably had an entire world of emotions and aspirations lying behind those brown eyes and little smile. She, too, was private. With Julia one had the feeling that she had already identified her place in the world, having devised a general plan in which she was to lever her beauty and intelligence into the best personal and financial situation possible. For the time being, I was it, the designated smartest person in the class and a member of one of "the families" with a position of moral and physical authority in the school.

It didn't hurt too that I had a red Corvair convertible sports car that Father had recently purchased from the local Chevy dealer across the street from our house. It had a four-on-the-floor manual transmission, a red interior with a white top, and was a ton of fun to drive, even though the center of gravity appeared a little high and gave it a tendency to roll uncomfortably if I aggressively challenged a curve.

On early Sunday afternoon, October 13, 1963, after noon dinner with my family, I jumped into the Corvair and drove to Clay Street to pick up Julia for our walk along the Auglaize River. When I got to her door and knocked, I was surprised to see her dressed in a white blouse and dark slacks, attire that would be suitable for shopping at the main stores in Lima but a bit out of place for a hike. Immediately I learned that this was a new experience for her. Nonetheless we hopped into the convertible and drove to the river and parked. Along both sides of the river were margins of hardwood trees, bushes, and grasses. Between the wooded area and the river's west side, where we were, a path led north to a dam about two miles away. This day I decided to take Julia on the other side of the wooded margin because the path right next to the river was often muddy and entangled in tendrils, and I did not want to soil her clothes. So we walked on a grassy berm between the woods and a farmer's field.

Veils of Color

When we started out, my spirit soared with joy and freedom. Here I was, walking through veils of oranges, reds, browns, and yellows made iridescent by the bright sun that shone through many cumulus clouds in the sapphire sky, with a beautiful companion for whom I was developing a deep affection. A light breeze blew from the west, creating a mid-autumn rustling of dry leaves in the trees, and a moderate fall temperature surrounded us in a cocoon that permitted exercise in the absence of hot and cold. I felt released from my unhappiness with school, classes, sports, and the imminent death of a beloved relative. We continued along for about a half a mile until we happened upon a large pile of multi-colored dry leaves. My first instinct was to pick up a handful and throw them in the air in happiness, thereby trying to provoke a tussle in the leaf pile. But I didn't. My youthful inhibitions got the better of me. She looked so nice in the outfit that I was unsure whether she would react well to such a spontaneous act. Also, in the pedestal-girl policy manual, there is no paragraph dealing with wrestling in piles of dry leaves. In the hindsight of fifty years, I believe this was a mistake. This action might very well have broken down the double reserve of our new relationship and precipitated a more open, closer, physical intimacy. Intuition, right or wrong, held me back.

On the way to the dam we crossed fences and partially dried marshes. I held the fence wire up, or down, so Julia could get through and we would be on our way. When we reached the dam, we each chose a tree to sit under while we talked and enjoyed the afternoon. My inhibitions prevented me from acting on a first impulse of choosing just one tree, leaning against it, and inviting her to sit between my legs and lean back against me. While it passed through my mind, I quickly evaluated the move as too aggressive for our young relationship. I am now again unsure that this was the right choice. Later Julia proved most amenable to being held close in my arms, for hours at a time. That afternoon under the glorious sun and fall colors it was probably just as well that I did not have the additional pleasure of her body next to mine, because I might have dissolved in happiness and been absorbed by the ground.

A Waning

After lolling in the grassy area above the dam we had to start back. I knew that our glorious afternoon was waning. For the hike, I had chosen an old pair of laced street shoes. At some point during our walking the heel of one of them came detached, unbalancing my gait. I was embarrassed. It may seem a small thing but try to picture it from a teenaged perspective: I was a young man trying to impress a young woman with an activity and environment that I enjoyed, and one of my shoes fell apart. I nevertheless made light of it and managed to walk without too much trouble as we made our way back to the Corvair.

The late, fall sun and my spirits were getting low as we drove west toward Delphos. The afternoon had been a success, but now all I could think about was the imminent loss of Julia's company to be replaced by the reality of high school, more football misery with Coach Dark, and Nell's death. When we pulled up to Julia's house, I got out and walked around the car to open the door. As we slowly made our way to her front door, she thanked me for asking her to take a walk on such a beautiful day. Hesitating a little at the top of the steps, she gave me that warm look and little smile and then she was gone.

CHAPTER 9

SCUBA Ohio, Early Years

Lust for the Deep

I f I were reincarnated from a previous animal life, it must have been a Loggerhead turtle. Free diving for me was always the best part of swimming. Yes, I enjoyed being on the surface, learning strokes, taking water-safety courses, and lifeguarding at the local pool. But my real interest was below the surface, the ability to dive down deep under the water, hold my breath for a long time, and explore. From 1958 to 1961 the television show *Sea Hunt*, starring Lloyd Bridges, introduced an entire generation of viewers to the new technology of self-contained underwater breathing apparatus, or SCUBA. It had been developed by Emile Gagnon and Jacques-Yves Cousteau, who patented the invention and started a company called U.S. Divers. Every week a dramatic situation required the show's star to don his equipment and go underwater. It certainly got my attention, and I began to do research. I learned about a device called the Aqua-Lung that drew air from tanks worn on the back. A regulator with two hoses controlled the exit of compressed air from the tanks and reduced its pressure so that the diver could easily breathe. It became my desire, almost my obsession, to learn how to use one of these devices so that I could not only dive under the water but also stay there for a relatively long time. As a child, I admired the wonderful way that dolphins, seals, sea lions, and whales effortlessly move through the water and dive to great depths. Evolutionists teach that mammals in the line to humans went through an aquatic phase during evolution. Surely with SCUBA I might be able to recover some of the skills of my very early ancestors. Our origin was in the water, and I wanted to return home.

When one thinks Ohio one does not think "SCUBA." A teenager living among farmland in the 1960s was about as landlocked as they come. Yes, we had Lake Erie, but at that time, teeming with industrial waste, it was no place to practice water sports. I lived a far cry from Santa Monica, where a swimmer could jump into wonderful seawater for SCUBA, and, with enough energy and air, swim all the way to Japan. So where could a young man from Delphos go to satisfy his great desire to dive into deep bodies of water?

Stoned

Surprisingly enough, the railroads had been working on a solution since the nineteenth century. As modern industry flourished, a need arose for limestone ballast, the stone that creates the bed for the wooden ties and steel rails. The paving of roads created an even greater need for stone as a building material. Fortunately, we were blessed with limestone formations close to the surface that could be readily mined and crushed in quarries. The mine's working life depends upon the local need for the stone and the ability of the owner to purchase additional adjacent land. When the formation plays out, the economics turn bad, or no more property is available, then the mining ceases, leaving the quarry abandoned. With the high-water table, it does not take long for it to fill to the top with fresh, clear ground water that is often sixty-to-more-than-one-hundred-feet deep, a perfect environment for training and playing with SCUBA.

We explored and swam in many of the Delphos-Lima area limestone quarries as children. My uncle Don was Director for many years at a working one right outside of Delphos, where we children explored and hunted for fossils on the weekends and holidays. That is, we were allowed into the quarry on special occasions and snuck in on others because they were dangerous, and the owners were rightly concerned about liability. Our parents often took us to Long's Quarry in Lima owned and run by a SCUBA instructor, Amos Long, who had developed it as a swimming site. Quarry swimming differs significantly from pool swimming. First, there is usually no shallow area because the limestone has been carved out and the remaining walls of stone stand the height of the hole. That first step from dry land into water is a big one because you are stepping off the top of the wall. Therefore, usually only experienced swimmers frequented quarries.

The owner had created a beach by dumping sand in one area bordering the water and had anchored a floating platform he built out of fifty-gallon drums and wood about thirty yards from shore. There were also diving boards of different heights and—our favorite—the thirty-foot platform. When we climbed to the top of the platform and looked over the edge, the water appeared—and was—a long way down. But this only amplified the energy of us young boys who dared each other to perform. I first learned about the acceleration of solid bodies in a fall and the resistance of air pressure on the platform because I loved to do crazy-dives from it.

Quite different from pool water, quarry water goes through a seasonal cycle. It has a clear, greenish tint produced by the reflection of the foliage around the edge and by algae that are natural to Midwestern fresh waters. In the winter, ice forms on the surface and makes for wonderful, though dangerous, skating because if the skater breaks through with heavy clothes into deep thirty-two-degree water, the prognosis is not good. Spring brings the clearest water because the algae have not begun to multiply, but the upper Midwest does not begin to warm until April or May, and it is usually mid-June before it is comfortable to swim. A thermocline, a line between warm water at the top and cold water below, moves up and down in the quarry, depending upon the seasons, and can be detected by free diving from the surface until one feels the sudden transition of warm to cold. As the sun begins to warm the water in April, the thermal currents concentrate the warmth at the surface. As the spring and summer progress, the thermocline descends and creates ten to fifteen feet of warm water in which to swim. For the four to six weeks of August and early September, during a warm summer, the water is at its best.

The Science of Skin and SCUBA Diving

Early in 1964 when I had just turned seventeen, my neighbor Grant and I signed up for Amos Long's SCUBA course. Every Saturday night for weeks, we would drive the thirteen miles from Delphos to Lima. Allowing us to sign up for this course, in retrospect, was a large act of trust for our parents. Driving in the Midwest for sixteen- and seventeen-year-old males was itself a dangerous adventure. In addition, a historical note in *The New Science of Skin and Scuba Diving* (1970), a revised version of the course book that we used, reports that it was only in 1954 that the Council for National Cooperation in Aquatics (CNCA) met at Yale University in New Haven, Connecticut, to discuss the need to derive standards, general information, and course curricula in response to the growing interest in SCUBA in the United States. It was an entirely new field that begged for organization. What resulted was the first edition of our textbook, published in 1957. SCUBA is inherently dangerous—there are many ways to be killed while underwater--and the best protection a diver has is education, good practice, and experience. Our parents allowed us to be pioneers, trusting in our judgment; while we justified that trust in the long run, I still wonder at their decision.

The instructor ran a very tight ship. It had the atmosphere of my later military training. As "the kids," Grant and I were unusual. Adults predominated, with most persons being trained from police and sheriffs' departments because of the utility of diving in their work, pulling cars out of lakes and rivers, recovering the remains of drowning victims, etc. We started Saturday evening in the classroom with the textbook and lessons. These covered the basic requirements of skin and SCUBA, the physics of diving, medical aspects of being underwater, and the fundamentals of compressed gases. I was surprised by the rigor of the curriculum and the thoroughness with which the instructor taught it. After an hour or so of academics we headed to the locker room and the pool. If the classwork was demanding, the pool exercises turned out to be even more serious. The instructor made it clear that there was no screwing around when it came to putting compressed air tanks on our back and going underwater. We began by swimming laps. He needed assurance that his students were comfortable underwater wearing heavy equipment for long periods of time. Next, we learned how to don and use our mask, fins, and snorkel for the water exercises. Skin diving can be defined as the use of these items only, but each piece of equipment requires a skill.

The mask must fit properly and has the purpose of returning clear sight to human eyes immersed in water. Without the mask, the water impacts directly on the eye and does not allow it to focus images correctly. It might seem like an academic exercise, but losing one's mask while diving is not that uncommon. Later in my diving career, while working down a buoy chain to a wreck in the Florida Keys, a sudden swell moved the chain, which hit my mask and knocked it off my head. I watched as the mask floated away in the current until I swam out, grabbed it, put it on, and purged the sea water, before returning to the chain and the descent to the ship. Without proper training and confidence, such a scenario can lead to panic and death.

The snorkel, an underrated device, allows the skin diver to keep his/ her head directed down in the water observing the coral, fish, sunken ships, or other divers while floating and swimming at the surface and breathing normally. It turns a breathing land mammal into a breathing sea mammal. In combination with the mask, it provides the swimmer with a whole new three-dimensional submerged space to explore. It is called skin diving because the purpose of the equipment is to allow the person to free dive from the surface, swim at depth, and then return to the surface.

When used with SCUBA the snorkel provides an extra margin of safety and comfort. Before a dive, it is not uncommon to be bobbing in the water with an inflated buoyancy control device, waiting for your fellow divers to enter, when you can save air by breathing through the snorkel. After a boat dive you spend time on the surface waiting for a pickup. Air in the tank being low, the diver puts the snorkel in his mouth to breathe comfortably without swallowing a lot of water and to retain the air in the tank. Once in the Marshall Islands at Rongelap Atoll, my four diving partners and I were left by the pick-up boat because of a mechanical failure, and we bobbed in three-to-four-foot swells for at least a half an hour before a second boat was dispatched. The force of each wave caused me to grunt as it pounded my chest. Without my snorkel to prevent me from ingesting the water, I would have been in serious distress.

We Get our Fins Back

While land vertebrates may very well have first evolved in the sea and then emerged onto the land, and while there are echoes of this evolution in parts of our physiology, one vestige that is not present is an efficient organ for transportation. Is it surprising therefore that so much technology and engineering have been put into the development of fins for skin and SCUBA diving? Now, I am not talking about that first, cheap pair of fins that one buys for his child or himself to play in the water, although even these lend the user a revolutionary increase in efficiency. No, I am talking about the high-tech fins that cost hundreds of dollars and that have been developed by engineers on a computer and tested in tanks, the ones that give the owner wings on his feet for flying through an aqueous environment. These are the miracles that transform the thrashing plodder into a smoothly moving streamlined body, that return him to his evolutionary past. Try swimming a few laps in an Olympic pool using the crawl stroke and flutter kick unaided by any manmade devices. Then don a well-fitted, expensive pair of fins and swim again. It feels as if you are gliding. When free diving, the change is even more dramatic. With fins, kick over and dive headfirst into the depths. By using a scissors kick alone, you can quickly be down to twenty, thirty, forty feet or more and just as quickly return to the surface. It is not an exaggeration to say that SCUBA became possible only when an efficient set of fins was developed for pushing a diver through the water with twenty-five kilograms of mass or more on his body.

Lessons in the Water

After becoming comfortable with the basic elements of skin diving, the class turned its attention to the central theme of SCUBA. We began by learning the basics of setting up a rig. We insured that the tank was filled to the proper pressure with clean air and learned how to attach the regulator in the proper orientation. After set-up, we practiced how to put on and take off the heavy gear. Then it was into the pool to learn how to breathe underwater without dying, because many things can go wrong.

Being safe while breathing underwater requires understanding the physics of gases, how the volume of a given amount of a gas is directly related to pressure—the higher the pressure the lower the volume, and vice versa. As one descends in water, pressure increases. The volume of air one breathes each time remains constant, but the amount of air in that volume increases with depth, which means that the deeper you go, the less time it takes to exhaust the air in your tank. Most dangerous is when the diver ascends from depth. The first and most important rule in SCUBA is never to hold your breath, particularly when ascending, because the air in your lungs is going to expand and it must go somewhere. If you do not exhale it, then your lungs might burst, or large bubbles, emboli, might form in your circulatory system.

Increased pressure also means that the eighty-percent inert nitrogen in the air is increased in the dissolved gases in the bloodstream and tissues. Gaseous nitrogen is not metabolized like oxygen in the body, so it just moves in and out by diffusion. Problem is, if nitrogen is concentrated at depth and the diver comes to the surface too quickly, there is not time for the gas to leave by diffusion, and bubbles can form in the blood and tissues, causing serious damage. This condition is called the bends because, I would imagine, the resulting pain causes the diver to bend over in severe agony. The body can handle nitrogen to two absolute atmospheres. One atmosphere is the weight of the air above our heads, which is about 14.7 pounds of pressure per square inch (psi). Each thirty-three feet of water adds one more atmosphere. At a depth of thirty-three feet, the diver is experiencing 29.4 psi. Nitrogen can diffuse freely in our bodies without forming bubbles up to this limit. Therefore, a diver can have unlimited time between the surface and thirty-three feet and can, if breathing normally and not holding his breath, move freely up and down within this space with no problem. It is when diving below two atmospheres of pressure that the diver needs to consider nitrogen concentration and must plan his dive accordingly and stick with the plan. Today, sophisticated diving computers monitor the diver's progression in the water and compute the nitrogen load in the body. At the time that I took the SCUBA class we were relying on published Navy diving tables. While good general guides to safe diving, they were developed using very fit male Navy divers and did not necessarily transfer directly to the average recreational SCUBA diver who might not look anything like a Navy frogman, or, for God's sake, who might even be a woman!

The Lima YMCA swimming pool was well suited to our beginning SCUBA course because the water was deep, but not too deep, and the area was relatively confined so that the instructor could keep an eye on us as we began to adjust to life underwater. With my first experience going beneath the surface with a tank and regulator I felt a sense of claustrophobia sweep over me for just a minute, an experience I would assume is common. I had lost my lifeline of air and oxygen that I had employed for more than seventeen years and was now enclosed by water and breathing from a strange device. Taking air from an old two-stage, double-hose regulator was not like breathing from a modern two-stage, single-hose device because the U.S. Diver's regulators in 1964 were still a relatively young technology. Breathing ease was adequate but not effortless and changed with the diver's orientation and depth in the water. When water entered my mouthpiece and hoses, I had to roll on my back to allow the liquid to drain toward the regulator and then blow hard to purge.

We began by getting used to swimming laps underwater while fully equipped with mask, fins, snorkel, tank, and regulator, and performing tasks that would test our comfort and skill. The instructor threw long bolts and nuts in the deep end with many washers. We had to collect the washers, put them on a bolt, and then fix them with a nut. We had to doff and don our masks and tanks, learn how to share one tank with a second person—something called buddy breathing—and eventually put the gear in the bottom of the pool, dive in, and come to the surface fully equipped and purged. One can spend many hours learning about the gas laws, first aid, decompression and the bends, and the technology of SCUBA, but it is spending time in the water and becoming familiar and confident with the gear and the new environment that turns a student into a proficient diver.

We awaited our completion of the course and diver's certification much as we had our driver's license—with great anticipation. The many Saturday nights of classwork combined with a couple hours in the pool were mentally and physically fatiguing. By the end of the night, Grant and I poured ourselves into the bucket seats of the Corvair and drove the thirteen miles back to Delphos ready for a good night's sleep, but also pleased with our progress. The "kids" did very well. We learned the lessons, passed the written tests, and excelled at the pool exercises. I still have my tattered, green YMCA Scuba Diver certification card with the date of May 23, 1964, signed by the instructor. In the many years since, some of my happiest hours have been spent under the water in mundane and exotic places that I would have never experienced without those nights in Lima. Mid-Pacific waters I now consider as familiar and comfortable as my own home. I have swum over a pile of WWII Japanese bombs in the hold of a sunken freighter in Truk Lagoon at 190 feet. My diving partner and I have been stalked by a large whitetip shark on a coral wall in the Bismarck Sea. I have been part of a late-afternoon pageant of thousands of Big Eye fish slowly moving like nuns to vespers out of the Mili Lagoon into the open ocean to feed. Education and learning new skills, seeking opportunities and taking risks can indeed open a new world to the curious and the brave.

Bottom Feeder

The summer after my certification found me back at the Delphos Municipal Swimming Pool on the staff as a lifeguard. I was looking for any opportunity to put my new SCUBA skills to work. One of the continuing problems in the pool was the collection of trash in the deep end. Many swimmers were slobs and dropped their candy wrappers and other debris in and around the pool; this in turn was blown into the water, sank and, because the pool was sloped toward the diving boards, found their way to the deepest part. The grates at the bottom that covered the intakes to the sand filters did not allow the passage of anything but very small items. Diving without equipment and trying to remove the junk piece by piece was difficult because the water was twelve-to-fifteen-feet deep and the currents that were created by the diver's body and hands would move the debris.

The answer, my untrained engineering mind told me, was to combine SCUBA with a gasoline-operated water pump. A family of divers in town loaned me their equipment. It was a double outfit, a pair of small, thirty-cubic-feet tanks with an early U.S. Diver's two-stage double-hose regulator like the one we used in class. Smitty, who headed up the Delphos Parks maintenance crew, and for whom I would work the following year, had a gasoline-powered pump that was used to empty rooms of floodwater. A plastic hose, about the diameter that firemen used, fitted over the impeller housing for the intake with a similar fitting and hose for the exhaust water. My idea, which with some tweaking did work, was to run the intake hose to the bottom of the deep end, put on the SCUBA, start the pump and prime it to get good suction, and then dive to the bottom where I could direct the open end of the hose to the debris and suck it out of the pool. Of course, there were snags in my plan. The suction was very strong at the beginning and took up lots of the debris. But then the junk got caught in the impeller and I would lose my suction and must stop and clean the pump before the process could continue. As I say, it was a Rube-Goldberg design that sort of worked. But it gave me a wonderful justification for putting on tanks and breathing underwater once again.

The Middle Point

It was not long before I felt the need to explore deeper water. Fortunately, the best body of water for swimming and SCUBA in the area, Middle Point Quarry, lay a few miles west of Delphos. The name arose from a narrow gage trolley that connected Delphos with a small town farther away. It had been mined for limestone for many years; it seemed like a mile long and half-a-mile wide, though I never measured it. When I was young, the quarry was just filling up, and a road ran from the top near the concrete remains of the old office and crusher down into the middle part of the hole. On each side were water-filled mined areas that went even deeper. It was a center of activity for kids and adults. My parents and their friends would have picnics at the bottom of the quarry road and swim in one of the holes. Teenagers who wanted to watch the moon rise in the east while happily ensconced in the backseat of their big sedan would drive in between a couple of trees at the top to hide the vehicle and then enjoy the evening and each other.

The quarry also had a dark side that caused the family who owned the property much angst. People did stupid things and occasionally drowned. Rightly concerned about their legal liability, the owners began restricting access to this marvelous body of water. The tall, straight walls of limestone draw risk-taking males like bears to honey and encourage them to jump from great heights into the pools below, an activity that can easily go wrong in any number of ways. Members of this risk-taking clan ourselves, my friends and I used Middle Point Quarry without the sanction of its owners and at our own risk, with the occasional harassment by one of the bored sheriff's deputies who would periodically patrol the area and warn off trespassers.

Nonetheless, this quarry became the preferred venue for SCUBA. The water was clear and deep. Access was relatively easy: large uncrushed rocks at the edge of the water served as platforms for gearing-up, jumping-off, and egress. While the underwater views offered little variety, the limestone walls provided a convenient reference for orientation and made me feel like I was diving within the natural stone of a medieval castle. On the northeastern side there remained from the time of the active mine a submerged building that was made with a wood and angle iron frame covered with corrugated sheets of galvanized metal on the sides and roof. A few sheets had been lost over the years, which gave the structure a dilapidated, mysterious aspect. Swimming in and out with varying light and dark areas and with projecting sharp ends of metal throughout the building was a test of buoyancy and skill. When we were first certified in 1964, the sophisticated buoyancy control devices (BCDs) that nearly every diver wears today did not exist. We learned to establish neutral buoyancy empirically. Depending on our weight and build, the gear that we were wearing, and the depths that we intended to reach, we put lead weights on our belts to give us the maximum time in the water free from the pull of gravity and with the ability to suspend ourselves, neither rising nor falling. NASA was soon (in the 1960s) to apply this principle to training astronauts for weightless work in space. One of my favorite positions was the "Neutral Buddha," in which I would obtain neutral buoyancy, assume the Buddha position, and relax in the water while enjoying the absence of gravity, both literally and figuratively—body, time, and mind suspended.

A Stone Looks Back

SCUBA diving was such a rare skill at the time that we were asked to perform water-related tasks that required immersion. On one occasion, we helped a resident of Delphos who had had, a few years earlier, an unfortunate meeting with a brown bear. While hiking in one of the national forests, he happened upon an animal that took exception to his presence and began to chase him. Thinking that a tree might be a safe refuge, the visitor began climbing—only to discover that the bear was better at ascending branches. It quickly had him in his claws and angrily dragged him to the ground. Suffice it to say that while the hiker survived, he also served as a partial meal before the animal, fully sated and having taught the human interloper a lesson, lumbered off into the forest.

The hiker endured injuries that required many weeks in the hospital, including plastic surgeries to replace the parts that the bear had removed. One casualty of the attack was an eye that could not be repaired. He decided to visit the eye clinic at the University of Michigan Hospital, where a facility created prostheses. They took a mold of the eye socket, fashioned a false eye that conformed to the opening, and hand painted the prosthesis to match the surviving iris. As one might suspect, this process is very expensive and yields a false eye that is unique to the wearer.

So why then did he go to the Middle Point Quarry, lean over the edge, and move his head in such a manner that the prosthesis fell out of its socket into the deep water below? Only Our Unholy Lady of Merde knows. But this precipitated a panicked call to me and my new dive buddy Tom asking us if we would be willing to dive into the quarry and look for the eye. I was immediately incredulous. Quarry bottoms are covered with silt and stones of all sizes, thousands of them, many mimicking the size and shape of the prosthesis. The exact location of the eye-drop was not easily determined; finding it would be a classic needle in the haystack problem; we were looking for the one stone among thousands that would peer back at us, and that only if it had landed right side up. The cascade of small probabilities combined to make this search a likely futile one. Nonetheless, we agreed to try because any opportunity to dive is a good one.

We donned our gear and entered the approximate area where the accident occurred. When reaching the bottom, we were fortunate that the sun was shining through the water at just the right angle to illuminate the stones. That was the good news. The bad news was that, as we expected, thousands of small stones covered the quarry floor where the eye had dropped. As children, we had played marbles and valued Cat's Eyes among the best, trying to get as many as we could, and I seemed to see them everywhere. Every stone looked to me like it might be a good candidate for filling a human socket. And then fortune or dumb luck smiled on us. Tom was perusing a portion of the bottom and found an eye staring at him amid the rubble. It was the prosthesis. He held it up to me in a triumphant gesture, after which we slowly ascended to the surface. Our victim, who was waiting in anticipation at the top, was overjoyed, wiped it with his handkerchief, and popped it back into his socket.

This surreal experience taught me more about randomness, that even events with tiny probabilities occur and therefore are not to be dismissed out of hand. I would rely on this tenuous principle when I enlisted in the Marine Corps infantry in the middle of a war with the expectation that I would survive and do well. First, I would face a brush with death closer to home when Our Unholy Lady paid me another visit one early spring day.

A Blissful Death Averted

Quarries are cold. It did not take long for us to discover that SCUBA in the state's best waters at any time of the year was going to be beneath the thermocline, which meant that we needed to have better insulation. When diving, you are immersed in water and can very quickly lose heat. Physiologists tell us that isothermia for a naked human body of average weight and stature that is sitting in a room without any convective air currents is about eighty-seven degrees Fahrenheit, which is the temperature at which the body is making the same amount of heat that it is losing to the environment. A naked body in water can gain or lose heat more easily because it is encapsulated by a medium that is denser than air. When the water temperature is less than eighty-seven degrees Fahrenheit, the body loses more heat than it generates, and the lower the temperature, the higher the loss.

Mammals have a long evolutionary history in cold water that still echoes in humans' mammalian diving reflex. The reflex is most pronounced in the early years of human growth and development and is illustrated nearly every winter by news stories about a child falling through the ice and his rescue. The accounts reveal that when the body is pulled from the cold water, the child appears dead with no detectable heartbeat, his skin gray and cold. When the paramedics and hospital begin oxygen therapy and warming the body, the child soon begins to show life. Many such victims of near drownings recover completely with no cognitive impairment. This response has been derived from the ability of marine mammals to dive deeply in the cold sea, during which their body concentrates and conserves the oxygen while allowing the animal to perform its necessary tasks for hunting and survival. Infants and young humans appear able to use this evolutionary artifact most efficiently. When immersed in cold water they shut down their body's functions, slow their physiology, and then concentrate the oxygen in the vital organs, particularly the brain.

SCUBA divers cannot, however, rely on physiological responses to stay warm in cold water. They need special insulation in the form of wet or dry suits designed to minimize the transfer of heat to the water. It was not long, therefore, before I purchased a used 3/16-inch wetsuit for quarry diving. It had a hood, tunic, leggings, boots, and gloves—covering nearly every square inch of skin. Wetsuits do not completely shield the body from the water as do dry suits. Rather they are made of a porous, spongey material that becomes saturated when immersed but then retains the water. It in turn is warmed by body heat and acts as a thermal barrier to minimize heat loss by convection. Equipped now with thermal protection, I thought I was ready for the challenges of Midwestern quarries in any season.

It was, I believe, a spring break in March during my first two years at university when Tom and I decided to SCUBA dive in the small quarry at the southwest end of Delphos right next to the main railroad track where Mother and her friends used to swim as children. We had never explored it before, which made it particularly attractive because one never knows what one will find at the bottom of a quarry that has been filled with water for fifty or sixty years. It must have been a cold winter because ice still covered about half of the surface, though it was relatively thin. The water was thus very close to freezing. We both had wet suits and, while that first shock of water when we jumped in was intense (it took a minute or two to warm the water in the suit), we felt prepared for the elements. It was a beautiful late-winter day in Delphos. The trees lining the quarry had not yet begun to bud, and they thrust their bare branches straight into a blue sky with large cumulus clouds, around which the sun would periodically peek. There was no thermocline that day because the water was uniformly cold. We slowly worked our way down the east side of the quarry through the branches of old trees and large rocks. Neutrally buoyant, I felt wonderful. The sun shone through the surface, illuminating the quarry walls and debris while we descended farther and farther into its depths.

It was not long before this pleasant feeling turned into a perfectly blissful one. I felt surrounded by an aura of illuminated water, and a peace I had never felt before came over me and filled me with joy. The ecstasy was like what the saints and mystics describe as heavenly spirits suffusing their bodies. I wanted to stay there suspended in this deep peace and rapture and never move. There was only one problem: I noticed that no bubbles were coming out of the back of my regulator. I had stopped breathing. Fortunately, my mind was still working, and I remember the conversation that I had with myself: "OK, Mister, here are your options. You can continue to enjoy this wonderful feeling and not breathe, whereby you will die in blissful peace, or you can begin breathing again and live." As soon as I took a breath from my regulator, the mystical state disappeared and was replaced by a sharp feeling of cold, and I began shivering. I then swam to Tom, who was exploring nearby, and motioned to him that I needed to ascend.

At the surface I have never felt as cold as I did that day, sitting on a rock near the ice and shivering uncontrollably. In hindsight, I believe two things were happening and trying together to end my life. The first was that my wetsuit was not thick enough for ice diving. It should have been at least 1/4-inch thick but was only 3/16-inch. At depth, I had become hypothermic, and my body was beginning to shut down its systems to preserve oxygen—the mammalian diving reflex. One of the first systems to go was respiration. Second, something called nitrogen narcosis kicks in at depth. When nitrogen concentrates in the bloodstream it can have a hallucinatory effect on the diver, who then feels and does strange things. It is a bit like drinking shot after shot of alcohol as one descends while breathing compressed air. To avoid this, modern deep divers often use a different inert gas with oxygen in their tanks, like helium, or they raise the percentage of oxygen in the gas and lower the percent of nitrogen, a mixture known as nitrox. Between hypothermia and nitrogen narcosis I had one of the loveliest experiences of my life, my own occasion for spiritual rapture. I also almost died.

Our Unholy Lady of Merde loosed her forces on me big time, bringing the random, but predictable, events of ice, cold water, depth, and too little insulation together with my willingness to take the risk of the dive, which nearly dealt me her death blow. Again, I had escaped. But never again was I to feel the wonderful sense of pleasure that this near-death brought me, when I floated in that cocoon of light and warmth. It is my hope that, when the Great Architect finally decides to end my participation in the earth's plan, I will again feel it on the way out, when I finally stop breathing for the last time.

CHAPTER 10

Of Cars, Chance, and a Conjunction of Rare Events

Life is Chance

In March of 1964 I smashed my right temple into the rearview mirror of our Red Corvair one-half inch from my temporal artery. Before I explain, the circumstances surrounding my brush with death merit a brief consideration of the randomness of the universe, a subject close to my heart and profession. More than seventy years of empirical observation that lead me to embrace the power of Our Unholy Lady of Merde over the Holy Virgin also lead me to admit that, while I would like to believe that God the Father, as depicted on the Sistine Chapel's ceiling, reaches out to us poor earthlings and looks after our welfare, I cannot support the happy thought. Rather, whether one lives or dies, gets sick or stays well, marries the right person or gets dashed on the shoals of divorce, is nothing but the toss of the existential dice. Yes, we can affect and effect things on the edges—make "good" decisions, live a "good" life, work with diligence—but it comes down to whether we get the breaks and dodge the bullets that determine whether we live and prosper. We live in a world and universe that has at its heart chance and randomness; from the quantum nature of atoms to the world we see and enjoy, we live in a sea of forces, like tornadoes, hurricanes, earthquakes, and fire, and additional events, over which we have little control. Chance is everywhere, even in our biology. We begin in a sea of randomness, swim in it our whole life, and many of us die from its action.

Forty-Six Cars in a Lot

Randomness in our lives literally begins at the very beginning, when we are just eggs in our mothers and sperm in our fathers. A complicated biological process called reduction division, or meiosis, creates eggs and sperm in the ovary and the testis. Our bodies are built from many millions of individual cells. Each normal cell has chromosomes in its nucleus. Instead of discussing chromosomes and DNA, the information for life and reproduction, however, let us, in keeping with the focus of this chapter, substitute collections of cars for chromosomes and a set of wrapped packages within each of those cars for the DNA to visualize this process. Each cell's nucleus is like a car lot with forty-six vehicles made from twenty-four distinct kinds of automobile. There are twenty-two kinds in three general sizes—five large, ten medium, seven small— that are by convention numbered from 1 to 22 in descending order of size, number 1 being the biggest and 22 the smallest; then there are two additional sex cars that are medium size, the X-car, and small, the Y-car. In addition to size, each of the twenty-four kinds has unique color and trim that allow it to be easily distinguished from the others. The five largest vehicles, 1 through 5, are sport utility vehicles (SUV) such as the Chevrolet Suburban. Medium vehicles would be the size of Buick or BMW sedans, while the small cars would be compacts. The car lot consists of twenty-two pairs of cars, one pair each of the large, medium, and small cars that from the outside look identical in color and trim, plus a pair of sex cars, two X-cars for the female lot and an X-car paired with a Y-car for a male lot.

Let's say that these cars—small, medium, and large—have just arrived from the post office and are full of packages, sorted and ready for the cell to unwrap and use. While each of the twenty-four distinct kinds of cars is unique in their combination of size, color, and trim, they also distinguish themselves by having a unique set of packages (their DNA). For instance, the largest vehicle on the lot, number 1, has roughly four thousand packages that are characteristic for this kind of SUV. All human car lots will have two SUV number 1s with the same array of packages. Like the vehicles themselves, each information package is unique in its wrapping, its general shape and organization, and from the outside will look nearly identical in all persons; however, they might differ in what is contained in the packages. The result is that, with cars paired, there are two similar information packages for every unique kind in cars 1 through 22, what we might call double-packaging, but the contents of these two in each instance might be different (but not always).

In female lots, the pair of X-cars is a similar pattern to the other twenty-two sets, nearly identical cars with each having a set of X-packages. Male lots, on the other hand, have a twenty-third pair that is not symmetrical: one medium X-car and one small compact Y. Obviously, the sets of packages in the X- and Y-cars are going to be different, though not completely.

Cells of the body have a miraculous ability to duplicate themselves. They can take every car on the lot and make an identical copy of it, along with the packages in each car, after which there will be ninety-two cars. Division of the cell creates two new cells, into each of which are distributed forty-six cars that are identical to those in the original cell and with identical sets of packages. By applying this method each time a cell of the body duplicates, an identical car lot, with an identical set of DNA packages, is given to each of the many millions of cells in the body. Information is conserved from cell to cell with little or no variation, which is the objective of this conservative form of cell division. Its purpose is to give the cell a total potential for differentiation, growth, and maintenance that the body needs from conception to death.

Pre-egg and pre-sperm cells of the ovary and testis share this ability for conservative replication. However, the final time they divide they have two additional, very important talents: 1) they can exchange packages from car to car of the same kind and number; 2) they can divide twice and create four cells with car lots that each have only twenty-three different, single cars: the eggs and sperm, hence the name "reduction division." When a twenty-three male car lot in the sperm is joined to the twenty-three female car lot in the egg, the child begins as one cell with the standard human forty-six car lot and begins to grow and differentiate by the conservative duplication already discussed.

In contrast to the division of the body cells in which genetic information is conserved, the purpose of this two-tiered division is to create the largest variation possible in the distribution of packages among the cars. No one knows how this nearly miraculous mechanism evolved. Its origin is one of the ultimate questions about human and biological existence and defies human understanding with its beauty, complexity, and reliability. Yet its detail and precision are marvels and deserve their own description by extending the car analogy. The first part of the reduction division of pre-egg or pre-sperm cells begins very similarly to that of conservative replication; the cell makes an identical copy of each car for a total of ninety-two cars in the lot, four cars each numbers 1 to 22, and four sex cars. Now the differences begin. Think about the four cars of each distinct kind lining up in a row, close by one another with package handlers buzzing all around them, tossing the DNA packages back and forth. The handlers' purpose is to maintain a set of packages distinctive for each car but to exchange packages between four cars as randomly as possible.

Maybe further illustration is in order. Imagine that number 1 SUV is represented in the cell by 1A and 1B. After duplication, they are represented by 1A,1A;1B,1B; there are now four of them, two identical pairs. Now add a package that is characteristic of 1 SUV, pk1-75, the seventy-fifth package of car 1. Further, assume that the contents of the package differ slightly between the two cars. For car 1A the contents are pk1-75, the normal contents, whereas for 1B, there is a slight change in the contents, pk1-75*. Taken together, after duplication, the four cars with their packages are 1A:pk1-75, 1A:pk1-75; 1B-pk1-75*, 1B-pk1-75*. (Yes, I know, Dear Reader, that your eyes are glazing over in the complexities of the nomenclature. This is part of genetics and permutations, and I can do little about it. Try to follow as best you can. It will be worth it in the end.) The cars drive together and stop at the line where the package handlers work. After they exchange the packages among the cars, the cars might look something like this: 1A:pk1-75*, 1A:pk1-75; 1B-pk1-75, 1B-pk1-75*. All the packages are there, but now they are a different combination. Car 1A has a pk1-75* that it did not have before, and car 1B has the normal form that it did not have before. This kind of shuffling can potentially occur for each package in the cars. Each human 1 SUV holds about four thousand packages. You can begin to see how shuffling all of these would create many, many combinations across the four cars that did not exist in the original car lot. However, the creation of variation and combinations has just begun.

Now consider that this happens in a small-town setting with a Main and First streets that intersect. Main Street runs north and south. First Street runs east and west. The street east of Main on First is Library Street, which dead ends in two car lots, one north and one south of the intersection of First and Library streets. Similarly, the street west of Main on First is Church Street, which dead ends in two car lots, also north and south of the intersection of First and Church streets. The map looks like this:

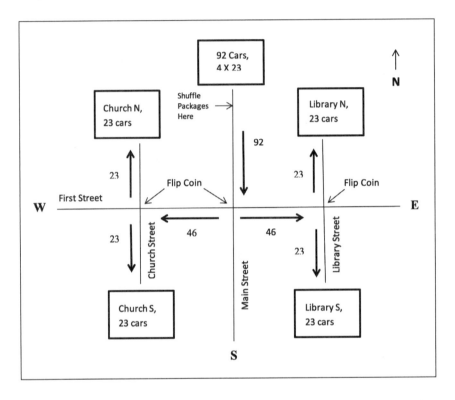

Our purpose is to distribute the four cars randomly, one each in the lots on Church and Library streets. After the shuffling of packages, the cars drive together to the intersection of Main and First, where someone flips a coin. If it is heads, then the 1A cars drive east and the 1B cars drive west, if tails then the directions are reversed. When they arrive at the next intersection, either Church or Library and First Street, there is a second coin flip. If heads, then the right car goes right to the lot and the left car goes left to its lot, if tails then the direction of the cars is reversed. The result is that each car has an equal probability of going to each of the four lots. Now extend this to all ninety-two cars, twenty-three sets of four.

The four cars, with their shuffled information, are randomly distributed among the four lots. In the end, each lot will have twenty-three cars. Each lot will also have a unique set of genetic information that has never existed before because of the shuffling of DNA packages and random distribution of cars in lots.

To return to the normal car lot of forty-six cars in a human cell, we must join the twenty-three-car lot from a male with one from a female. Geneticists who work in the field of population genetics and apply numbers to large collections of genes to describe and make sense of them have an important assumption for their mathematics called "random mating." Now this is not as it first appears. A male cannot just close his eyes or put on a blindfold, walk around the beach in Santa Monica until he finds a female body in a bikini that feels good to him, and then mate with her. She might not like the sight of this man; or she might not want to mate with a stranger; or she is saving herself for marriage; or she is just not in the mood because she does not want to get sand in her suit. Humans have, or should have, the choice of sexual mates as well as the freedom to choose the time and place, with mutual permission as the basis for the act. Further, the process of choosing does not always look as if it is random. Tall people tend to marry tall people, smart people tend to choose partners who are also above average intelligence, many people of common ethnic heritage, such as Asian Indians, arrange the partners for their children, and religions such as the Mormons and Hasidic Jews are nearly closed to sexual partners not of the faith.

Despite all this apparent non-random mating, geneticists find that random mating is a very good assumption to use to develop mathematical models because people do not generally choose a person because of their genetic background. A simple example comes from what we all know as the red blood cell type, ABO. The simplest model one can use is four types of ABO persons: O, the most common, A, B, and AB. Dear Reader, when was the last time that a potential date asked, "What is your ABO blood type?" as a condition of going out? It simply does not happen, not for the ABO gene and not for the thirty thousand other genes carried in the cells of humans. When we choose sexual partners, we do it at random with respect to their genes.

I will easily forgive you—and an author's absolution is the absolute best—if you did not follow the above detail. In summary, chance, what scientists call "stochastic variability," permeates the process of the making of eggs and sperm, the choice of genetic mate, and the conception of children. We all—those of us who are fertile—have the capacity to produce millions and millions of unique combinations of either egg or sperm, and this ability is a fundamental property of our biology. In mating, we randomly combine our unique set of genes to that of our biological partner. We assume that we are in complete control of our lives, our choice of mates, and the biological make-up of our children. In truth, chance determines it all.

Why would the Great Architect who designed earthly biological systems make chance a fundamental part of their existence? Well, while ignoring the fact that we do not know that such a designer exists, the usual explanation is that this randomness maximizes genetic variation in the species, protects it from susceptibility to disease, and provides the material for the further evolution of the organisms. However, this is begging the question. Rationalizing the existence of a phenomenon does not explain its origin; in fact, we do not know. A further observation is that, while the mechanism of shuffling packages and moving cars uses chance to do its work, that same mechanism, the egg- and sperm-making machine, is quite well designed to work the same way every time, millions of times, without error. (Well, almost without error. Packages do occasionally spontaneously change their contents in the process of making new ones when the cars duplicate; it is called a mutation and is a rare event.) No chance or randomness exists here. If our machines in our factories worked so efficiently, we would not need a quality control department. Nonetheless, chance is at the heart of our existence, origin, parental fate, and choice of mate. We are just one permutation in a universe of almost infinite possibilities.

A Chance Near-Death

Now is it any surprise that this same chance that is with us from the beginning, and that is one of the three key components of Our Unholy Lady of Merde, can also kick us in the ass and nearly kill us if the correct conjunction of random events occurs? Here I bring you back to my automobile accident in March of 1964. Our junior class in high school had a well-educated American History teacher who decided to start an evening breakout group of interested students at a volunteer's home. The purpose was to discuss in detail a chosen subject, either historical or one of contemporary interest, in more depth and with much more informality than we could achieve at school. There, we sat in rows of desks with the teacher at the front lecturing about a topic of the day, hugely formal and inhibiting to participation, particularly for those students who were a bit shy. Lounging on the couch and floor at a fellow student's home created an atmosphere of intimacy and freedom that promoted easy intercourse. The kids who were destined for college participated in these sessions, and it gave them a feeling of exclusivity along with the casualness.

I have no memory of the subject that evening. We were meeting at a student's home on the west side of town. Though a kind person, he was small, and extremely annoying, because he made everyone else's business his own. His mother, however, the hostess for the evening, was lovely. A working, single mom with an engaging, warm personality, she had gone to quite a bit of work to prepare refreshments for her son's friends and teacher.

I had driven the Corvair convertible and parked it on the street just outside the house. Father was a fanatic about his automobiles. In even my earliest memories, an image of one of his cars always hovers nearby. To him they were treasured possessions maintained like prized thoroughbreds, broken in correctly, fed the correct gas and oil, and washed often with careful wiping and pampering. Woe be it to the child who spilled a sticky liquid in one of Father's cars and failed to clean it up without a trace. His wrath could be volcanic; his icy stare could freeze you at a hundred yards if he felt some indignity had been laid on his cherished chariot. It was not enough that a carpet lining came in the trunk of his new car. He would immediately go out and get his own end-lot of carpet from the local furniture store, cut it carefully to size, and place it over the original one. This way the factory original could never get dirty and when, in two years, he traded the car in for a new one, it would appear almost as new and boost the resale value of the vehicle. When he built a new house and moved to the country in 1972, his new garage was a marvel of cleanliness, the pristine vault that held his precious automobiles. He put a coat of wax on the new concrete that made the floor shine with cleanliness. On Thanksgiving Day, I would have been completely comfortable eating my turkey dinner under the trunk of his Oldsmobile. He hung an old red and white bobber from a fishing line attached to the ceiling of the new building under the car that Mother usually drove. Its purpose was to guide her into the garage as she parked the front ornament of the hood directly under the bobber. In this way the front of the car could not touch the front wall and scratch the chrome of the bumper. Father loved my mother and was married to her for fifty-three years; but he never completely trusted her driving or care of the cars. It might have had something to do with Mother backing out of the garage of the old home on Sixth Street and hitting the side of the house. He also was super critical of my two brothers' treatment of his and their cars. To cross the old man when it came to car driving and maintenance was to tempt fate and risk domestic health and happiness.

With his interest in and thus frequent purchase of new cars, Father was well acquainted with the local car dealers. He would often travel around town in the evening to visit them, taking me along. I loved going into the showrooms where all the cars were brightly arrayed. That odor of new automobiles and rubber was like a perfume. The chrome and paint sparkled in the fluorescent lights, as primarily men looked at and talked cars. In the fall, the unveiling of the new models for the next year was staged like a mystery play. The dealers brought cars in under wraps so no one could see them until the appointed day. Then balloons and paper bunting would take over the showroom, and the new car models would appear, followed by excited customers ready to buy.

Father was a Dodge man in my earliest years. The Dodge-Chrysler dealer was tall and thin, a chain smoker with an exotic wife. He lived on the second floor of a storefront just north of the railroad tracks on Main Street in an apartment where I had often been with Dad. A steep, narrow wooden staircase rose from street level to the door of their dwelling. The two of them drank whiskey in the dealer's apartment. Soon his wife came out of her bedroom in a beautiful slip-like thing with lace at interesting places. She was also tall and reminded me of a thin, lazy cat in her movements. Even as a young boy, I noticed that her scent was wonderful and that she gave off the aura of wanting to be petted. Father told me that she usually got what she wanted. He told me things, secrets about the town. We trusted each other, him to tell me stories about people, me to keep his confidences to myself. It defined our relationship then and for the future.

In 1955 his affection for Dodge was mortally damaged by our family trip to Florida in the first two weeks of August. The first time I jumped into a wave, I swallowed a mouthful of seawater and learned what brine was. The ocean and the swimming pools held most interest for me, being a pool rat. The smell of creosote permeating the ocean pilings is still clear in my memory and nose. Unfortunately, we also experienced a lot of water inside our relatively new green Dodge. Traveling along the coastal road, we got into a tropical rainstorm, and the water began to pour into the passenger side floorboard at Mother's feet. My father was not amused. When we returned home, his friend the Dodge dealer had a hard time believing that one of his cars would be so prone to leaks. So on a subsequent trip to the Boy Scouts camp to pick up my brother, when we were again deluged inside the car during a storm, Father drove straight to the dealership, brought his friend outside to the car, and opened the passenger door for him to see the water cascade to the street. He soon traded the Dodge on the purchase of a new 1955 Oldsmobile and never bought a Chrysler product again.

In the mid-fifties Father decided that we needed a second car for Mother's convenience and for the fact that my brother Jake was to turn sixteen in April of 1958. Dad was certainly not going to turn his car over to a new driver in the family. We had already gone through a few second cars when he purchased the Corvair. Why he chose such a stylish sports car has always puzzled me—he was a conservative man. However, I sure enjoyed driving it.

Burned Image

March was typically cold with snow and slush on the ground. The temperature had dropped when the sun went down, and the slush had begun to turn to ice. We had finished the breakout history session between 8 and 9 P.M. when the students poured out of the house and into the street. Two of them, as I was getting into the Corvair, were reaching down and making snowballs in the grass in front of the house and beginning to throw them at the cars that were leaving, mine being one of the first. Immediately my mind processed the thought that these snowballs were filled with dirt and rocks that would scratch the paint on my father's car, so without fastening my seatbelt I quickly started the Corvair, shoved the gearshift into first, and pushed the accelerator down. I could feel the snowy, icy street slide under the tires. Nonetheless, I got enough of a grip to accelerate toward an intersection about fifty yards away. A quick glance confirmed that there was no stop sign, so I continued accelerating. Then the world suddenly went into slow motion. From my right, my peripheral vision picked up a black blob moving into the intersection at a right angle to me. In an image that will be burned in my mind until death, I simultaneously saw an old 1940s black iron sedan immediately in front of me. I put on the brakes and felt the car skid over the ice and snow. I realized that I was going to hit the monster broadside. It was a moment of terror with many layers: the damage or destruction of one of Father's prized cars, the recognition of possible death, my utter helplessness and vulnerability with the loose seatbelt sitting in my lap, and the terrible set of random events that created this situation. How was it that two human beings living two unrelated lives, unknown to each other, both driving cars, would share an impact that required perfect timing and coordination?

The man in the second car had been out drinking all night. When he got out of his car unhurt, empty beer bottles noisily cascaded onto the street as he drunkenly muttered protestations and indignities. He had also not seen a traffic sign as he approached the intersection because it was unsigned in both directions. Coming from my right, however, he had the right-of-way, and I did not—could not—give it to him.

I, however, was unconscious. Corvairs have their engines in the rear. In the front is just the empty space of a trunk with a relatively flimsy structure underneath the body. The collision collapsed the front of the car and made me a projectile in the car's passenger compartment, smashing my body into the steering wheel and dashboard, and forcing my right temple against the rear-view mirror. The glass broke into many sharp pieces and lacerated the right side of my face, with one cut only one-half inch from my right temporal artery. Bleeding profusely from this highly vascular area, I lay stunned and wakening in the car as the students who were following me came up to help. The same monkeys who had, by their behavior, unknowingly precipitated the event, were now trying to open the driver side door that had been crushed and jammed in the accident. The group of them finally managed to bend the door back and pull me out, by which time I was becoming aware of what was happening around me. I leaned against the wreck to maintain my balance while at my side stood Julia who held her handkerchief against my temple to staunch the flow of blood. A woman who lived in a house at the corner of the street heard the crash, came out to see what was going on, and took charge of the situation by asking me who I was, who my doctor was, and volunteering to take me for medical treatment.

The next vivid memory of that night was lying on Dr. W.'s examination table while he and his nurse Ginny assessed the damage done to my head. He had recently become our family physician and was a close friend of my father, had been a Marine and medic on Iwo Jima during WWII, and had many stories to tell about the war and his participation in it. I never completely trusted his stories, but as a tailor of bodies with needle and thread, he was very talented, and I made use of his services on a few occasions. Father and he shared interests in stamp and coin collecting, which meant that Doc was often at our house, where they would sort and grade their recent acquisitions and then share the booty. He was also particularly fond of Mother's cooking and would come for lunch, our biggest meal of the day, whenever he wanted to escape the noisy environment of his large, young family and the poor cooking of his wife.

Head Case

Doc and Ginny appeared more entertained by my condition than concerned. I was disappointed because to me it was serious. The two of them had amused smiles on their faces and made small talk about their day in the office as they prepared the suturing thread and curved needle to repair my noggin. Doc's first comment was "I think you will live." Maybe, but it was not guaranteed. Just because I had survived the crash did not mean that I would survive the wrath of Father, whose car I had just almost destroyed. To increase my anxiety, I was at fault. I felt the needle for the anesthetic poke into my forehead at three or four spots, after which numbness gripped the whole right side of my face. Ginny began using sterile gauze to clean the side of my temple and reveal the many lacerations. Then Doc began his work. About halfway through, Father arrived. He was with another doctor friend, a veterinarian who cared for our dog and who had been a life-long friend of the family. Almost shaking with fear, I looked at him in his fedora and waist-length leather jacket standing at the end of the table.

He looked at me and merely said in a gentle voice, "Are you OK?"

"Yes," I said.

Doc then told him that I was very lucky because one of the cuts almost reached my right temporal artery. That would have meant bleeding to death before I could have received proper medical treatment.

Dad then said, "W., if you can give him a ride home, I will go see to the car." Then he left.

When he dropped me off at home, he should have brought a tranquilizer for Mother. She was frantic. The host student's mother had called her and told her that I had been in a car accident and been taken away, but she could not get any more information than that. Seeing me walk into the house with the doctor was a huge relief, especially after he made a few light comments about my being just fine. Father soon returned from supervising the tow of the car to the dealership. He said nothing more, and I went to bed sore all over with a numbing pain in my head.

In the morning I woke up at the usual time, still sore from the sutures and the pummeling I had taken in the crash. Nevertheless, I had breakfast and went to school, where I received lots of concerned stares and comments about my bandaged head. I was ashamed that I had made a mistake, one that almost cost me my life, risked the life of the person I had hit, and embarrassed me in front of Julia and my schoolmates. I really, really did not want to talk about it. Besides, most of the students from the night before had seen what happened and did not need a blow-by-blow description. They had probably already spread the story to the entire class.

The incident was followed by a situation that typified the small-town nature of Delphos. By the laws of the town, I should have been cited for failing to yield the right-of-way and causing an accident and then summoned to town court to appear before the mayor, who would determine my punishment. The infraction would then have been recorded in the police and legal notices in the town's paper. However, the police chief was also the editor of *The Delphos Herald*, and I had worked for him as a paperboy and pressroom assistant for almost two years. He liked my work, and we had become friends. Father was also the secretary of the Civil Service Board. My punishment was that I had to wear my Sunday church clothes and attend a dressing down by the chief in his police office, who lectured me about what I did wrong and how important it was to clean up my act before I killed either myself or someone else. I did not go to court. The accident was not recorded in the paper.

This led to a great deal of hooting and hollering by various busy bodies in town about how Father's son was granted special favors. And it was true; I did get special treatment. My Aunt Jane was particularly annoyed. She had children who ran afoul of the law and whose transgressions were published all over the paper. She moaned for years about the injustice and the favoritism to me. I really did not give a damn what people thought and felt that my accident was partially the town's fault for leaving the intersection unsigned. It did, however, stick in the public's craw, and the occasional person let me know it. In April of that year, I pulled the curtains as stagehand for the senior students' play, *The Unsinkable Molly Brown*. One of the seniors whom I knew only little—a porcine young man who was at the top of his class but whose personality was sharp and sardonic—deliberately caught me backstage and asked whether I had been in an accident the month before. My scars were very prominent on my forehead, so this question was, to say the least, a little gratuitous. I said that yes, I had. He then commented rather pointedly that he had not seen it in the paper. My response was that no, he hadn't.

One evening, shortly after the crash, upon returning from work, Father did not park his car in its usual spot in Grandmother's garage. I happened to meet him outside. Handing me the car keys he told me Mother needed milk and I was to go to the IGA and get it. When I replied that I was in no way getting into the car and driving, he shot back, "Get in my car and get the milk!" I got back up on the horse and got the milk. It was a lesson that, while many random events must conjoin to create an accident, chance is minimized in a father's love for his son.

CHAPTER 11

Easter Sunday 1965

Save the Pagan

Year 1964, post-car-accident, did not improve much. That summer I was again a lifeguard at the pool. In July I foolishly hopped the fence surrounding the shallow area and sprained my right ankle, which ended my pool days. This was twice stupid. First, I left my chair, where I was supposed to watch for drowning or misbehaving children, to break up a fight between two young boys. I abandoned my post. Second, with my left leg already congenitally malformed and repaired, I put my other foot at risk. Now both my feet were shit. The next four weeks I was on crutches with my ankle wrapped in an ace bandage. Sitting around our house during that hot summer, with no physical activity, was one of the most depressing periods in my young life. Mother was constantly fussing about, treating me like a wounded soldier returning from battle. Being one who has never liked a hovering companion or relative, I soon became cranky. What little relief there was came from the first air conditioner that Father put in our old house on Sixth Street. Instead of mounting it in a window, he cut a hole in the side of the dining room wall and made it permanent. At least cool air was blowing over my anger.

I was also a captive audience of one for the Republican and Democratic Conventions that overlapped my sedentary period. Goldwater
was nominated for the Republicans, after which a strain of (as I perceived it) right-wing, ignorant, nationalist—"I have mine, screw you"—
politics infected the United States, one that was to be amplified by
Nixon, Reagan, the first and second Bush, and that now has gained
ascendency in the new century and culminated in the cesspool of the
Trump administration. Then, I naively thought we were on the road
to a more-educated, less-prejudiced society, only to watch as the worst
aspects of American conservatism—anonymous private and corporate
money-fueled elections, the confusion of church and state, a Supreme
Court whose conservative members apply their religious, dogmatic
(mostly Catholic) doctrine of "original intent" to the law, tax policies
that have led to the worst gap between the rich and the poor in our
history and trillion dollar deficits, a proliferation of military assault
weapons that enable mass killings, a suspicion of science, a corrosion
of the meaning of "truth" and "facts," and a selfishness that knows no
bounds—have corroded our culture and politics like an acid. Luckily,
at that time Johnson beat Goldwater in a landslide. Unluckily he soon
had us enmeshed in the Vietnam War that destroyed any hope of the
intelligent continuance of the social ideas laid out in his campaign. At
least I can say that I was a hobbled spectator at the beginning of this
latest gush of American excrescence.

As soon as I threw away my crutches, one microsecond after receiving
the Doc's OK, I began, much to the horror and disapproval of my parents,
to get ready for my last season of football. I literally went from crutches
to uniform, which meant of course that I now was out of shape and had a
gimpy left foot and a nearly healed right foot. Complicating my rehabili-
tation and preparation for the football season was a trip to the University

of Notre Dame campus that I was forced to make in the middle of pre-season practice in late August.

The previous spring I had been elected President of the school's Mission Society. This was one of two major offices for our senior class. I had representatives on my committee from the other classes, and we coordinated the begging and collecting of money from the students. We distributed cardboard boxes with a slot through the top—piggybanks for god—through which they added coins directed to Catholic Charities and its missionary work. The nuns forcing me to go were insufferable. I told them to go and pray; I wanted to practice football. After much argumentation, my parents convinced me I had no choice. The position of Student Council President was won by an experienced student who greatly desired it; he loved involving himself in school activities and being at the center of their organization. I am still not sure why I had run for Mission Society President, because I had little interest. It was, in my opinion, Catholic training in the skill of extracting money from the sheep so the shepherds could spend it, a process that over two millennia had made the church one of the wealthiest institutions in the world. How was this consistent with the vow of poverty? (I was beginning to develop the skepticism and critical faculties that would serve me well as a scientist but that are death to religious practice and belief.)

For three days at University of Notre Dame we learned how to take money from our fellow students while being shunted from chapel to chapel and service to service. That year the nuns wanted to emphasize the baptizing of pagan children, that every penny that the students put in their mission boxes went to saving the souls of those poor black babies because, of course, the all-loving God would not let an African baby who died of starvation into heaven-country without a visa from the Pope and his minions. I incurred the wrath of the nun by stating that it was more likely that the money went to the transportation, housing, gasoline, food, beer, and maintenance of the missionaries and that very little of it went to baptizing pagans. And what did that mean in any case? That the missionaries were replacing one form of superstition with another? I was beginning to believe it. I felt that the black babies would be better off maintaining, both physically and mentally, their own culture and beliefs.

That season's football season was terrible, probably the worst in the history of the school. Coach Dark had little sympathy for my lingering injury and lack of conditioning. It was testimony to his intelligence and good judgment that he immediately made me the team's punter, with my right foot just out of its bandages, because in previous years I could kick a ball in a beautiful spiral for a good many yards. Not this season. My kicks looked like ducks flying with a broken wing and went about as far. We were a skeleton group of kids. Coach Dark's reputation peeled away volunteers until, in his fourth year, very few students wanted to play for him. The team sucked. We were shit. Our archrival Lima Central Catholic beat us by more than thirty points in a deluge on a muddy field. At the end I was sore, bloody, mud- and water-soaked, and pissed. I lost my position on offense as a half-back because my feet would not carry me. I was a strong side linebacker, basically a blocking dummy, run over game after game. At the end of the season, we were 1 and 8. My only consolation was that Coach Dark was fired as the football coach but, because he was a good Catholic man with many kids, the school kept him on to teach. Of course, his incompetence made him a joke as an educator.

After turning in my uniform, November and December quickly turned into the winter and spring of 1965. In October I had received an early acceptance into The University of Michigan—known by our Ohio State's football fans as "the school up north"—U of M being the best state school in the country, in my opinion. My parents and I had driven to the university and attended an orientation course while I was on crutches. It was love at first sight, and the only college application I made. While the tuition was much higher than what my father paid for my brothers' in-state education, he was relieved that I had not insisted on Dartmouth, which had recruited me to play football, and which was insanely expensive, from a factory worker's perspective. Also, I had plans, not revealed to my parents, on joining the Marine Corps' Platoon Leader Corps the next year. My sights were set on the excitement of my future college career and military service. But first I needed to finish my Delphos period.

End and Begin

Easter Sunday, April 18, 1965: the end and a beginning were near. Graduation was in four weeks, and our high school instructors were tired of teaching. They did not intend to prepare final exams for the last six-week session, and many of us were preoccupied with practicing the school play, *The Sound of Music*. I had been cast as the evil Herr Zeller, the Nazi Gauleiter for the Austrian district in which Maria and the Captain lived. This was the last time that our class of 125 boys and girls would form a body. Soon, and it would be very soon, we would all be on our own, dispersed, never all of us to be together again. During the two following years, two of us would die in automobile crashes, and the inevitable whittling down of our ranks by the random events of accident, aging, and demographics would begin.

This was also the end of Julia and me. I had enjoyed every minute of our quiet intimacy. She had made the last two years of high school bearable. Every week I looked forward to having private time with her, seeing her smile at the door when I picked her up at her home, smelling the fresh showered scents of her hair and skin, driving with her through the dark countryside. Now she was cast as Maria in *The Sound of Music*, with her entitled first cousin as Captain von Trapp. He was one of Father Thomas's handball-playing sycophants, had a wealthy family, easy access to a car, and a disdaining attitude. He had returned from the seminary the year before, obviously more bent on sexuality and materialism than celibacy and poverty. The time spent together in rehearsal brought them close. In hindsight, however, I can recognize that his presence allowed me to make a graceful exit. My near-term plans had no place for marriage or serious romance. Still, I was conflicted, and a bit jealous. All through the last summer, fall, and early winter Julia and I had been close, very close. Holding her felt like the only comforting, tactile presence in my life in 1963-65, and I felt a strong, lingering emotional and physical attachment. Though I knew the present circumstances were best for all, I was very sorry to lose her.

In January I had turned eighteen, an adult. I could sign my own legal papers and had already begun to make my own adult decisions. And here comes the new, the beginning. August would see me as a naïve freshman; January, I would join the United States Marine Corps. Transitions were coming quickly, all part of my great design: college, military, and, assuming I survived the growing Asian war, a research and writing career.

Master Scoutmaster

While I was ready to assume my adult roles in a couple of months, in the previous two years I had begun to develop a bit of dread and regret as well. I was rooted in Delphos as firmly as any eighteen-year-old tree was in the local woods. The environment nourished me as I grew and taught me the secrets of its yearly cycles. I had enjoyed the Auglaize River, the hikes along the old railroad spur, the scents of fresh country air and mown hay, the rustle of leaves in the hardwoods, the luscious green fields of crops in the spring and summer, colors of the fall, and the brown, cold, desolation of the late fall and winter. Delphos was small, and negotiable; the people I knew and instinctively understood, and they knew me. Leaving all of this was to tear my roots from the physical and emotional soil with which I had come to be familiar, to love.

Therefore, when my former scoutmaster, Gerry, asked me if I would like to go to the river and help him cut wood for next winter, I immediately said yes. He and I had become friends in the seven years that I had been in the troop. I had not been an active member of the Boy Scouts for years, but that did not mean that I did not participate in their activities. Hiking, camping, Sunday cookouts were all enjoyable to me, so Gerry permitted me to accompany him as a "young adult leader" to help shepherd the boys. After all, I was a football player, the head of my class, a good example, soon to be a Marine. But this Easter Sunday it was just going to be the two of us. He picked me up in his old car after my family's noon dinner, and we headed out to the river and our campground.

The Catholic Church had, in the 1950s, right about the time that I joined the Boy Scouts, purchased a few acres of farmland at the junction of the Auglaize River and Route 30N, one of the major east-west truck routes, that it planned to develop as a cemetery at some future time. The old one east of the church and bordering the Pennsylvania Railroad and Father's factory was finally, after more than one hundred years of bodies, getting close to capacity. The farmer who sold the land moved his house across the highway, leaving two chicken coops, a large garage, a barn, and a huge mess of old shingles and debris. Our church-sponsored scout troop was given the responsibility of cleaning and maintaining the site in return for the right to use it as a meeting place and campground. With rotary mowers, hand scythes, and plain old sweat equity, we got the land ship-shape.

The outbuildings proved very adaptable to our purposes. The large garage conveniently housed the paper bailer that the troop used to raise money. In Delphos, a business made cellulose insulation out of recycled paper. We scoured the town for old newspapers and stored them in the garage at the campground. When we had gathered enough, we used the bailer machine to press the paper into large cardboard and wire-wrapped bails that we sold to the firm. The troop used the income to purchase military surplus equipment, like wall tents.

Acquiring insulation, plywood-panels, and a potbelly stove, we renovated the chicken coop. It became a destination for year-round hikes, storage for our wall tents and equipment, and a shelter in inclement weather. My favorites were the winter overnighters. Our normal meeting was on Wednesday evening, and we sometimes combined this with a night along the river. The troop met behind the St. John's Elementary School and then carpooled the three miles to our campsite, where we unpacked our cots and sleeping bags, set them up in the coop, and started a blazing wood and coal fire in the potbelly stove. When settled, we had our weekly troop meeting before heading outside for cold evening walks under the stars and then back again for lights-out and sleep. Scouts and cots would be jammed into the building cheek by jowl, which meant that we were heated as much by each other's radiation as by the inefficient stove. But the severity of the snow and cold outside, with the wind howling through the trees, did not inhibit the stories, laughter, and boyish horseplay that filled these evenings with warmth, intimacy, and the innocent energy of youth.

Gerry was not a scoutmaster who emphasized advancement. For this I was very grateful. We met in the hallway of the elementary school building where we did a little close order drill, and he got out the semaphore flags and taught us a couple of new letters, which I never learned. I just was not interested. After a few more business items, the meeting ended, and we dispersed. The time we spent outdoors, at the campsite, was the high point of scouting.

The campground that surrounded the outbuildings was nearly perfect in its setting. Turning in from the highway one drove north along the old driveway that ended at the barn. From the road, the land sloped east in a grassy swath to the Auglaize River. The land at the bottom of the slope was punctuated with deciduous trees of many varieties. Halfway down, on the north side of the property, between the fence for the neighboring farmer's field and near the end of the second chicken coop, we cleared a small area for a circular fire pit and our campground, which in good weather became the center of our activities. In the summer on overnight hikes, we created a circle around the fire pit with our ground cloths and sleeping bags in an orientation that was as old as the invention of fire, the descendants of cavemen reenacting the rituals of light and heat.

Waist Gunner

Gerry's stories around the campfire often took the form of his experiences in WWII. Many nights we sang songs from the era like "It's A Long Way to Tipperary." His WWII combat boots with the large, smooth leg strap and buckles were his standard attire for hikes and campouts. A pipe smoker and collector, he told us stories while running a pipe cleaner through the stem and then packing the bowl with a fragrant bolus of tobacco and lighting it with a stick from the fire. I relished the scent of that first smoke that drifted over.

Gerry was trained in the U.S. Army Air Corps as a Waist Gunner on the B17 heavy bomber developed by the Boeing Corporation in the years preceding the breakout of hostilities. It was called the Flying Fortress because it was based on the idea that a combination of a rugged structure, many well-placed guns, and a tight formation of planes would both deter the enemy from attacking and protect them when attacked. Therefore, the Army Air Corps generals thought that B17s could be used during the day, as opposed to the British flyers who bombed at night with the thought that giving daylight as an advantage to the Germans was nuts. Daylight of course meant that the enemy could see you.

"Waist" refers to the middle of the fuselage behind the wings, where two open panels, one on each side, had a fifty-caliber machine gun mounted on a post. He donned a heavy leather and fleece flak suit with boots and helmet and stood at the gun ready to shoot at any oncoming German fighter. At that altitude, the temperature was very cold—and magnified by the slipstream of the bomber. Early models of the plane left them not only exposed to the elements but with among the highest injury rates of all crew positions. The German planes were directing streams of bullets at the bombers while anti-aircraft shells or flak were bursting among the formations, throwing shrapnel in all directions and threatening to give the gunners hot metal showers. Combine all these dangers with the normal wear and tear on the planes from repeated trips over target and the possibility of mechanical failure, and it is not difficult to understand why many B17s did not return from their missions, and when they did return, why the Waist Gunners were the likely casualties.

When 25 = 7

One can only hope that Gerry and his fellow crew members did not think in numerical probabilities. When the American planes reached England in 1942 each crew member committed himself to flying twenty-five missions because that punched the ticket home. (Later in the war, that was raised to thirty-five.) That is, if he did not die first. A quick look at the Eighth Air Force numbers for individual bombing missions and losses makes ninety-percent overall probability of survival a good number. Let's say that on average nine out of ten planes returned from each mission. Every time you went out, there was a ten-percent chance that you would die or be captured. If you were shot down, not injured, and lucky enough to bail out and float to the earth, you hoped that you did not break your neck or other parts of your body, fall into a body of water and drown (or freeze if it were winter), or be shot to death before you hit the ground. The Germans were not well disposed to people who dropped five hundred-pound bombs on their heads. Now, to the average flyer in war, ninety percent would sound pretty good. He would be home with the wife and kiddies or hugging his girlfriend in the States in no time. But that was only for each mission. Let's assume that each of the twenty-five missions was independent of the others; that is, there was a constant ninety-percent chance to survive each time you went out. This is probably not true because you are assigned to the same crew and plane for each mission, the plane ages each cycle that is completed, and people learn from experience of war, which affects the likelihood that they are going to survive. Let's ignore these factors, which would affect the numbers in both directions. In order to survive twenty-five missions, you need to survive the first, then conditional on surviving it, you need to survive the second, and conditional on surviving it, you need to survive the third, and so forth twenty-five times. A simple conditional model of probability, with ten-percent chance of dying or capture each mission, looks like this: Probability of survival for 25 missions = $(1.0 - 0.10)^{25}$, or 0.9 to the 25th power. This equals about seven percent! You have a ninety-three percent chance of being shot down, dying, and/or being captured by the enemy before you complete your quota. Men like Gerry and his fellow crew members must have had some intuitive idea that this was so, that finishing was going to be tough, because they saw planes destroyed in their formations and came back to many empty beds in the barracks. One can only imagine the maelstrom of emotions and fears in a crew that had fifteen missions completed and that faced ten more. Yet every time the mission was on, they climbed into their planes and flew off again.

Gerry had taken the GI Bill after WWII and attended Ohio Northern University where he studied to become a pharmacist and then worked for one of the two drugstores in Delphos. In my early scouting years, his drugstore was at the northwest corner of Main and Second streets, right across from the post office. Inside was a soda fountain straight out of a 1930s movie set, with the tall, curving stainless steel soda dispensers and gallons of delicious ice cream. It was on the way home from the Boy Scouts meetings and was staffed by two attractive high school students, Bobbie from St. John's, and Louann from Jefferson High School. Of course, we young boys were just as interested in tasting the delights of these soda jerks' company as of the sodas themselves, two young women who were good sports and tolerated our shenanigans. I can only imagine how annoying I must have been. When the owner moved the drugstore across the street in the early sixties, the soda fountain was not moved with it. Our hangout was gone.

Cutting wood for Gerry was not recreation but necessity. I did not know his salary at the drugstore, but it did not seem the store's owner paid him much, certainly not enough to support his six young children and wife much above bare subsistence. Often, I had been in his home on north Main Street working on my Tenderfoot, Second-, and First-Class scouting and had seen firsthand the lifestyle of the family, loving but spare. I always left with an uncomfortable feeling. His wife was tall, gaunt, and spoke with a deep smoking voice. He did everything he could to economize. To save on heating, he burned wood that was free for the taking. He identified fallen limbs and dead snags at the river that had dried and that begged for cutting and burning. He owned a two-man, cross-cut saw that was very sharp and that sliced through the hard wood with just a few passes. That Easter Sunday, I was man number two.

Arboreal Primate

Cutting wood also meant an opportunity for climbing in and among trees, which I still loved to do. As a child I had looked for private spaces in the outdoors. Trees were a natural choice because they were everywhere in Delphos. They lined the streets, creeks, and rivers, and were planted as ornaments or for shade in most yards. When my mass was smaller, my center of gravity better located, and my limbs more limber, I was always looking for the ideal climbing tree. It required a lower branch that was suitable for the first lever up; higher, well-spaced branches with the appropriate strength to hold my body; and lots of forks for resting. The willow tree in our backyard was especially rigged for climbing and in the summertime had drooping limbs with leaves that formed curtained spaces. Up in a tree, with the scent of wood and new growth, hidden from outside scrutiny, looking across the roofs of houses and businesses to the church steeple and then farther out into the green countryside, was bliss.

Particularly well-suited for privacy were the lower sloping branches of large fir trees. In my grandmother's yard, there was a tall one next to the driveway that had not been cut or thinned for many years and that probably had originated as my grandparents' potted Christmas tree. Evergreens are three dimensional cones in which the branches angle up to a point. Those at the bottom are the largest and often, because of their size and weight, hang heavily with tips touching the ground. This creates a nearly perfect doughnut-shaped private space for animals and children. Evolutionists tell us that one of our early ancestors spent a great deal of time in the trees for protection, sleep, and vigilance, coming down to the ground to forage and play. It must have been another distant echo of my genetic past that led me to climb and to seek the company of trees.

Mother, of course, greatly discouraged this activity. She had seen my malformed leg when I was born, helped me through years of therapy, and did not want to repeat the experience. When she found her little monkey happily ensconced in the tree fork, ten- or twenty-feet off the ground, she was not well pleased and closely observed as the primate descended to safety. As I grew I found that physics inhibited my arboreal excursions. My early growth spurt during elementary school, which gave me my present height and weight, was a great asset on my eighth-grade football team, but it put a big crimp in my arboreal pursuits. Many tree limbs are not supposed to hold 160 pounds of weight, and attempts to lever my mature, larger frame up the tree proved more difficult.

Pole Dancer

Having been a curious child, however, and having observed the line crews for the local telephone and electricity companies, I quickly found a mechanical aid to my aging dilemma. Pole climbers are metal braces that one wears on the lower legs. They are strapped onto the leg near the knee and ankle with large leather straps and buckles. A strap of metal runs on the inside of each leg, ending at the bottom with a pointed metal projection angled inside and below the shoe or boot. A wide leather belt attaches around the waist and has a leather strap that snaps onto D-rings on either side. When one wishes to climb a pole or tree, the climber puts on the pole climbers, takes the leather strap and runs it around the trunk, and snaps the fastener in the D-ring. He then leans back on the strap and begins to move up the trunk by sinking the metal points of the braces into the wood and walking up, while moving the strap along to balance and prevent himself from falling backwards. Watching the linemen quickly make their way up and down the telephone poles, I lusted after a set of pole climbers. I therefore bought a pair, which I used that Easter Sunday.

Gerry had identified a large, dead hardwood tree close to the river-bank with many limbs already fallen to the ground. Using a cross-cut saw is easy when two experienced persons are using it. When the first person pulls, the second must relax and allow the saw to move, and then sense when it has gone the proper distance the other way before pulling it again to make the next cut. If done incorrectly, the saw warps in the cut and jerks the muscles of the puller. We took the saw and made easy work of the large limbs on the ground and piled the wood into Gerry's old car. We then set our sights on the snag that shot up from the ground about thirty to forty feet in the air. Cutting the trunk at the base would be rel-atively straightforward. Getting the remains of the tree to fall at an angle that was convenient to further cutting was a different matter. If it fell directly east, it would land in the water. We needed to secure a rope to the top of the snag and pull it into a clearing where it would be easy to finish.

I had brought my pole climbers with me; but there was a problem. I had not had the money to purchase the waist belt and climbing strap, and instead had fashioned one out of a thick piece of rope. My idea was that I put on the pole climbers, throw the rope around the trunk, secure the rope with a knot, and make my way up the tree. When near the top, I would secure a second rope that I carried with me. Gerry and I could then pull the snag in the proper direction when we had finished the cut at the base. In my mind, I had the technical aspects of this all worked out. It was simple. I had on my Marine Corps boots that my cousin Jack had purchased for me at the Quantico PX in the summer of 1962. The pole climbers fit my legs very well. I secured the waist rope, threw the end of the second rope over my shoulder, and started up the tree. On the way, I was pleased with my invention; it appeared to be working very well. The spikes on the inside of my boots dug into the old wood and allowed me to literally walk up the snag. My one issue was balance. The rope that I was cinching up with me was not moving as easily as I had envisioned. To move the rope up on the snag after I had taken a couple of steps, I had to lean into the tree to put slack in the rope, after which I pulled it up level to me again. This led to periodic moments of instability. I managed to walk my way near the top, where I was to attach the second rope. Leaning against my balancing rope, having the spikes in the tree, and beginning to reach around the snag to tie the pulling rope, I lost my balance.

There are moments in your life, when you are close to death, that clear vision prevails. I can still remember every microsecond of the fall, face up looking at the sky while the soft spring breezes rushed past my ears. I expected the worst, maybe the end, and may have even said, "Oh shit." To my great surprise, a soft mat of wet mud, leaves, twigs, and forest debris cushioned my body at the ground.

Now here is where my faith in reason and science is tested. That Easter I could have easily died at age eighteen. Luckily, I fell parallel to the ground the whole way down. Had I fallen headfirst I would have broken my neck or skull. Feet first and I would have at least broken my legs. Somewhere in between would have led to various injuries. The fall knocked the breath out of me and may have caused a moment or two of unconsciousness, but that was it. During the fall I had the sense, which was probably an illusion created by shock, that something was holding me. Not being a religious person, I find this a dangerous thought. The mythology and iconography of angels have always fascinated me, especially their origin and persistence across cultures. As a child, we were told by the church that each person has a guardian angel with them. It did not take me long to dismiss this idea when I saw reports of people dying in grotesque accidents, or six million of them being sent to gas chambers and crematoria.

Where were all the angels when those people needed them? Yet here in my experience was a sensation of being held and protected and landing from a terrible fall with no injuries. How could it be explained? Was it chance? Probably, but I like to imagine it was the intercession of Our Unholy Lady of Merde, who must have a black sense of humor. She did not wish to see me dead or injured, just wanted to emphasize the stupidity of my climbing the tree with improper equipment, leaving me shocked and embarrassed. Once again, the trinity of her forces, chance, risk-taking, and a disdain for early death, almost sent me to the grave or hospital.

When I opened my eyes, Gerry was standing over me with a very worried expression on his face. He first asked if I was hurt. Moving my various limbs suggested that I was not. He then said something to the effect of "Thank God, because if you had been injured, Father Thomas would be very angry with me!" That he would first think of the Director of the class play and my role as the Nazi Gauleiter Herr Zeller in *The Sound of Music* immediately struck me as very funny and absurd. Then again, I am not convinced that even pretend Nazis are deserving of life, while I was hoping that in this next performance, I captured the entitled Captain and sent him to Bremerhaven and the German Navy and taken Maria for myself—minus the annoying children. After all, I had a history of attraction for nuns. I had a lot to live for.

CHAPTER 12

Transitions

Having more than fifty years of hindsight on which to draw, I can say that all my transitions were difficult, but the ones from St. John's and Delphos to The University of Michigan and young adulthood were the worst. I probably was not alone. The year 1965 reflected cultural changes that were like the receding water preceding a social tsunami that would consume many generations. Elvis Presley and the Beatles replaced our parents' music with rock 'n' roll, permuting Lawrence Welk into the Rolling Stones. The sexually inhibited fifties were turning into the "sex with all at all times" of the sixties and seventies, the HIV tragedy of the eighties and nineties, and the hook-up culture of contemporary America. Now, instead of only cutting grass, more people began to smoke it. Overt, Jim Crow racism was being replaced by a subtler, more lingering form; soon parts of major American cities would be engulfed in the flames of racial frustration and hate that smolder well into the twenty-first century.

In the second semester of my senior year, at the beginning of these impending storms, however, I had other more immediate concerns. It all began after Christmas break. Suddenly the faculty's and seniors' attitudes changed. For the former, benign neglect replaced a compulsive need to supervise and teach. Curricula became more perfunctory and exams less frequent. The senior play proved a distraction for those who produced, directed, and starred in it. Nearly all of us going to college already knew where we were to matriculate in the fall and were making plans for summer orientation trips. I was overwhelmed with projects before and after graduation. In addition to having a supporting role in the class play, I was to meet a new friend, interview for my summer job with Parks and Recreation, and prepare my valedictory address at graduation.

Sarah

A very attractive distraction came into my life that spring, though one from an unexpected location. The senior classes of Ohio's high schools participated in a program to recognize the students with the best knowledge of current events. The winners traveled for three days to Cincinnati, on the banks of the Ohio River, where they learned more about the present state of the nation and politics, attended seminars, and generally rubbed elbows with their peers. Predictably, the valedictorian, and Mary, the salutatorian, were chosen to represent the school. We were driven to the event with a married couple who served as chaperons and two representatives from Delphos Jefferson High School, also the top students in their class. Climbing into the car, I sat down next to a lovely young woman with long blond hair and a very sweet scent. She looked like a young Shirley Jones just off the set of the movie *Carousel*, and I soon learned that her name was Sarah.

The four of us students happily chatted away, completely ignoring the adults assigned to protect our virtue. Sarah immediately began to tell me, with a mirthful smirk, details about my life on West Sixth Street that only someone who was familiar with me and my family would know—the variety of dog that we had, the way I worked in the yard and washed the car, the model of the car that I drove, who my parents were, my part as Herr Zeller in the school play, and so forth. The more she spoke, the more puzzled and confused I became. Finally, she took pity on me, sort of, by suggesting what a myopic doofus I was by not recognizing her. She also lived on West Sixth Street, at the end of the next block, just eight houses away! Impossible, I said! No, it was a fact. And to pour more salt into the wounds of my embarrassment, she related that she often walked along the sidewalk by our house, occasionally even seeing me and my family working outside.

To be fair, there were extenuating circumstances. First, she was from the public school in town, and we Catholics were not encouraged to socialize with its students (an understatement to be sure). Second, Sarah was a bit of a nomad, caused by her mother's divorce and remarriage and other family circumstances that remained unexplained but seemed a little dark. She lived with her grandmother on West Sixth Street during the school year but with her mother and other relatives in the summer and on breaks. Later, in high school she worked in Van Wert, thirteen miles west of Delphos. Sarah was also a bit sad and quite solitary—she did not socialize with her peers in the normal way. The combination of her beauty and brains also isolated her; many young men were intimidated, while her female classmates were jealous and put off by her taciturn manner.

I, on the other hand, was immediately smitten and motivated to learn more about her. During the three days at the conference, we four students hung out together while attending the sessions. Mary and Sarah shared a sardonic sense of humor that made them immediate friends and made me the butt of their teasing and jokes, which tickled more than offended. By the time we traveled back to Delphos I had managed to arrange a first date on Palm Sunday evening, April 11, 1965. This choice of day would turn out to be a dark omen for us and our future together.

Near the appointed time that evening I jumped in the Corvair and drove the short distance to Sarah's grandmother's house. Nervous, I got out of the car. I had been seeing Julia for nearly two years. She and I had become very comfortable with the other and picking her up at her house caused me nothing but the joy of anticipation. Now that she was spending time with her entitled first cousin, I was exploring new, exotic territory and was unsure of myself.

I walked onto the open porch where I knocked on the old screen door that rattled in its frame. And there she was, even more beautiful than I had remembered. Her blond hair was falling over her shoulders and down her back. She was dressed in a button-down blouse that revealed her pale skin with just a suggestion of cleavage and a skirt that fell a little above the knee, simple and elegant. Her lips, subtly tinted, formed the smile that I had first enjoyed in the car. As she walked past her scent gently embraced me. I inhaled deeply in its wake and felt a stirring in my body. This was the first indication of what I was soon to learn, that Sarah was a mature, intelligent, confident, sexual person, and—though we were the same chronological age of eighteen—well ahead of my development. Also, for the first time in my life I was to spend time with a woman who could, and did, puncture the inflated balloon of my masculinity and demand a relationship of equal power. She was the whole package. But was I ready and able to receive and unwrap it?

I opened the passenger door and helped Sarah settle into the Corvair's red bucket seat. Intimacy was immediately established. It was a compact sports car in every sense of the word. We sat very close to each other, with only the arm of the four-speed manual gear shifter separating us. Third and fourth gear, however, were especially pleasurable because they occasionally allowed a fleeting brush of her leg. We had no set purpose that evening but to enjoy the spring countryside, talk while

I drove, and possibly stop in the next town for something to eat and drink. I set out northwest of Delphos on the two-lane rural roads that crisscrossed the farm fields interspersed with stands of hardwood in early leaf and creeks and rivers full of spring rains and late-winter melt.

Conversation was a bit stilted because it was a first date, but we managed to grow more comfortable with familiar subjects such as high school and common friends. I learned that Sarah knew quite a lot about Julia and me, while I knew nothing about her previous friends. During the drive she also told me about a review that she had written for *The Delphos Herald* about our school play last year, *The Unsinkable Molly Brown*. I remembered it because I had worked on the stage crew for the production, had attended each of the rehearsals and performances, and still had the songs bouncing between my ears like squirrels in a wall. The male lead for Leadville Johnny Brown, a neighbor and friend of mine, croaked his songs more than sang them, and Sarah had said so in her article. Our principal, who was also the director of the play, was livid when he read it and wrote an angry letter to the editor, something about these were just young people trying to do their best and that strong criticism was not, therefore, justified. The fact that the review had been written by a female non-Catholic student from, as he always referred to Delphos Jefferson, "the school across the tracks", intensified his anger. I did not know that I had asked the radical author on a date; the discovery delighted me. She had revealed the true nature of the director-priest as a pious, Catholic, We/They prelate, the universal feature of all conservative religions to divide the world into the chosen-saved and everyone else, which feature greatly contributed to my future rejection of such institutions. My admiration for and attraction to the passenger next to me were growing with every story and laugh.

We were so wrapped up in the intimacy of the car and our new friendship that we, or at least I, the driver, failed to see what was happening in the sky around us. It didn't help that it was already dark, the sun having set just before 7 P.M., right about the time I was at Sarah's home. Also, her hair and clothes were so well done that I had the convertible top up and secured with latches at each corner of the windshield frame. With the top up, it was a little like sitting in a small tent. Corvairs were, like most autos today, unibody construction, which means that there was no frame that ran along the bottom of the car. The various metal pieces were stamped out with a large hydraulic press and then welded together. The body was a bit like a metal eggshell on four wheels. Being a convertible, this also meant that it lacked the usual strong metal posts welded in a frame that separated the front and rear portions of the car and gave it strength. Critics categorized this car with an air-cooled flat-six boxer engine in the rear as "unsafe at any speed." Still, I loved the car and loved driving it, safe or not. But General Motors did not have an F-4 tornado in mind when designing it.

When we first noticed the weather taking an eerie turn, we were on a curved road that paralleled a creek with a swimming hole that my mother and her friends frequented as young adults. It was also not too distant from the Delphos Golf Course, built on farmland a few years before. Suddenly the darkness intensified, rain began, and the wind picked up. Sensing that this was not a common spring thunderstorm, I pulled over to the side of the road onto a grass berm and turned off the engine. Then all hell broke loose. Torrential rain poured down on the cloth top, causing a cacophony in the cab and reducing visibility to zero. The soon ferocious wind treated the unibody car like a toy. It violently moved in three dimensions, yawing, pitching, and rolling. If our some-two-hundred-and-fifty pounds of mass had not anchored it to the ground, I am convinced that it would have rolled into the creek. It was as if a giant's hand had reached down from the sky, grabbed our car, and shaken it.

Sarah and I looked at each other, and I could see the fear in her eyes. Later she told me that all she wanted at that instant was for me to reach over and hold her as tightly as possible. While that would have brought joy mixed with fear, I was busy processing what to do. If we stayed in the car, we risked being swept away by the tornado and killed in the impact when we hit the ground. As light as the Corvair was, it would probably fly well. I did not know how close the funnel was. Immediate action for a tornado when caught in the country is to get out of the car and lie flat in the deepest hole or depression that one can find, usually the drainage ditches that parallel the road. But that would have meant leaving the tenuous safety of the car and exposing ourselves to the elements outside. I also assumed that the ditches were already filled with water, and we were as likely to drown in them as to survive. What I feared on that day—the day that celebrated Jesus's ride into Jerusalem on an ass—was that our asses were going to be swept away in a storm of biblical proportions. In the end I decided that we should remain belted in our bucket seats and hope for the best. This was yet another time that I gave myself up to Our Unholy Lady of Merde to determine my, and Sarah's, fate.

After what seemed like an hour of brutal buffeting, noise, and rain, but was only a few minutes, the weather began to ease and, finally, a calm such as I had never experienced in the countryside descended on the car. I started up the Corvair and pointed it back toward Delphos. When we approached the village, I saw that there were no lights on anywhere, no streetlamps, no traffic lights, no curtained windows with light behind them, nothing. Also, virtually no cars were on the streets. This being a Sunday night in a small town, that by itself was not unusual. But it was like Delphos had been abandoned. I took the road on the west side by the quarry. A police car approached and stopped opposite us. The officer rolled down his window and said that we had better seek shelter because the weather service had issued a tornado warning and that large cells of bad weather were on their way. Well no shit, I thought to myself. I drove back to Sarah's house, where we checked on her grandmother and I ensured they had a basement to stay in should another storm come. I was hugely disappointed, to say the least. The first date was going swimmingly until the vengeful weather gods decided to intervene. But still, there would be other times with Sarah, many other times. And some would also prove to be a bit stormy, in the figurative sense of the word.

When I arrived back at our house, my father and two brothers were milling around outside looking at the sky. They were waiting for the tornadoes. Mother had gone to our old Aunt Feff's house to be with her. She had a basement that had been partially renovated into a recreation room where she entertained guests. The two of them were safe and comfortable. We sat on the back steps of my grandmother's house and watched the rolling clouds. It was much like the parting of the Red Sea in the movie *The Ten Commandments* with the clouds moving at a very fast clip, west to east. Then we saw it. Suddenly emerging from the chaotic black mass, a funnel made it three-quarters of the way to the ground, right over our heads. It was one of the scariest things I have ever seen, literally like a monster with a club in his hand, ready to clobber the earth and everything in its path. Luckily for us, it did not descend in Delphos but waited until it was a few miles east before it again began slicing through farmhouses, woods, and villages.

Next morning, we learned through our transistor radios that the damage had been extensive all around us, but Delphos and its immediate area had escaped the worst. That evening many people died and had been injured in a swath about 450 miles long. Power was out for three days. Grandmother had a two-place gas burner in her basement where Mother made pot meals for us, like chili and soups of various kinds. We boys wanted to volunteer in the clean-up efforts that were going on east and west of town, but Father said no, that the emergency people had things well in hand, and that we would probably just be a nuisance.

The next time I asked a girl out on a date for the first time, I decided that I would first check the weather report.

Of Grass, Maggots, and Tampons

At about the same time that tornadoes blew through our neighborhood, I began my job as assistant to the Parks Manager of Delphos. I had a long history with Midwestern grass. Not the kind you smoke, mind you, but the kind that you fertilize, roll, weed, cut, trim, and rake in torrents of perspiration. Midwesterners seemed obsessed with the yards. The grass always had to be groomed—not too long, not too short—especially on Sundays when the landscaping would be noticed by neighbors and churchgoers. In April, when the temperature moderated and the sun shined more frequently, mowing machines appeared from the back of garages and the first pull of the rope starter stretched the muscles in the operator's arm until the sputter of that one-cylinder engine represented the beginning of another five-month season.

Mowing was my job. Our family compound consisted of two homes—one for us and one, on the corner, for my grandmother—and lots of grass. My earliest memories have me behind mowers, both reel and rotary, inhaling flying cuttings, dust, and debris while learning every square meter by heart. Maple trees lined the streets, divided from the houses by cement sidewalks. In between were long, rectangular swathes that needed careful attention because the trunks obstructed a straight run with the machine. Then the larger areas adjacent to the homes required endless overlapping lanes, back and forth until the job was done. Of course, especially in the spring, five days later the damn stuff would have again grown tall enough to get Father's attention, and the process would start all over. When I got a little older, I "requisitioned" one of my family's rotary mowers for my own use and started a small business with a few regular customers for whom I also did some planting and landscaping. If I were to have such an intimate relationship with grass, I might as well be paid for it.

It was a natural transition, in the winter of 1965, I was interviewed and hired as Assistant to the Parks Manager. The Recreation Board of Delphos already had a history on me because of my work at the city pool. In our family, after high school graduation, Father immediately put us in The New Delphos Manufacturing Company to work the summer before college. But this year was different. My older brother Luke, home from his sophomore year in June, was scheduled to work there. It was not fair to the other college-age kids that he hired every year, Father lectured me, to have employed *two* of his sons. Therefore I, having the lowest seniority in the family, had to fend for myself.

The job description appeared attractive. It was to help the Parks Manager—Smitty, as he was known to the locals—maintain the three parks in our small town. I knew him a little because he was the stepfather of my Scoutmaster and had the reputation as a town character. "A bit of a rough cob" summed up Smitty. He was small, wiry, and smoked cigarettes in quick succession. His voice, at least an octave below normal, was as gruff as his attitude, while his body fat had to be negative ten percent, all muscle and strength. Further, he did not suffer fools or young punks. My first thought was, hooray, I will be out of doors all season and be able to get a nice suntan for the third summer in a row. But my second quick thought was that I needed to toe the line if I didn't want my supervisor kicking me in the ass for goofing off.

The park topography was large and complicated for a town of about ten thousand souls that was 1.2 miles wide east to west and 1.7 miles long north to south. On the north end was Stadium Park, one I knew intimately from my lifeguard years and because it was only two blocks from our home. It had a football stadium, swimming pool, cement basketball court, swing sets and teeter totters, macadam tennis courts, picnic tables, baseball-softball diamonds, and a large area with goalposts where the local football teams practiced in the late summer and fall and that seconded as the outfield during baseball season. In the middle of town was a small park that I had not even seen in the first eighteen years of my life. It was merely a bit of green space with a few amenities for playing children. On the south end of Delphos was Waterworks Park named for the municipal facility that treated and distributed its water. It was smaller than its sister park at the north end, wedged between homes, state highway Route 66, and The Fruehauf plant that assembled trailers for semi-trucks. Its open gazebos and picnic tables meant it was devoted primarily to municipal and private parties on the weekend and holidays. On one corner near the street was a ball diamond that had seen better days: it was not maintained with the same care as those on the north end of town. Grass was growing where groomed dirt should be, and rust covered the metal fencing and much of the supports on the dugout.

When I first reported for the job on a sunny spring afternoon and officially met Boss Smitty at Stadium Park, I thought I knew the general outlines of my tasks. Grass was everywhere between and around the facilities, thousands of square yards of it. Obviously, I assumed, my job would be chief turf tender. However, I was quickly disabused of this notion. Smitty took me to the locked hurricane-fenced area near an aerator where water, having been being pumped from the ground in one of the town's wells, spilled over a set of wooden baffles to atomize it and allow oxygen to perfuse it. Here he introduced me to my new ride for the next four months. It was a red McCormick Farmall Cub tractor that looked just like the tractors that I had seen my whole life in the fields around Delphos but was about half the size. Two large wheels and tires in the back surrounded the metal seat, steering wheel, throttle, shift lever, and clutch and brake pedals with two much smaller wheels and tires in the front. Attached underneath was the housing for the largest rotary mower I had ever seen, probably five feet wide and four feet long, that could be moved down for mowing and up for travel with a large lever near the steering mechanism. Behind the tractor was a two-wheel open trailer with a metal bed and wooden sides with a hitch and chains. Paired and filled with shovels and rakes, the tractor and trailer became my primary tools.

The job was much more complicated than I had first thought. Yes, grass was a primary focus. But I was also responsible for monitoring and emptying the trash cans in the parks, cleaning the restrooms, performing the maintenance on the backstops and dugouts of baseball diamonds, removing rust and flaked paint and repainting, trimming any bushes and trees that got in the way of recreation, and generally keeping all three parks attractive and in good order.

Mowing grass with the Farmall tractor combined many of the things that I enjoyed doing, like driving a machine that responded well to the steering wheel and throttle, even though its aesthetics were the antithesis of the sports car in which I normally traveled. It also allowed me to share a little style with the farmers in our area because, after all, it was a tractor, a machine associated with country roads and fields, blue bib overalls, cow dung, and long, plowed furrows. True, while mowing, I had to keep the speed down. But on the road I pushed the throttle to full bore and zipped along the streets of Delphos. I had to be careful, however. When just beginning, I had gone a little fast around a corner at the Stadium Park just as a Delphos policeman passed on Pool Road. The officer stopped me, screwing up his face like a prune as he lectured me like the errant schoolboy I was. After that, I watched my back when I pushed the throttle forward.

Mowing grass was always a bit of a Zen experience for me. It forces one to concentrate on the job, to go slow, evaluate spaces, design patterns of coverage, and spend hours alone in contemplative pleasure. I was outside, the sun warming my body, bleaching my hair, and coloring my skin, the wind blowing against my face and through my hair. The scents of freshly cut blades mixed with twigs, dirt, the sweet smell of burnt fuel, the steady sound of the engine, the monochromatic music of the blades in the rotary mower, all underneath leafy hardwood trees, huge cumulus clouds, and the moisture-laden blue sky of a Midwest spring and summer created a meditative environment as rich as any enjoyed by Tibetan monks.

I established a regular schedule for each park and mowed them in succession, Stadium, Central, and Waterworks. This required that I take along in the trailer a small, hand-pushed, rotary mower and hand tools for trimming in areas that were too small for the tractor. Central Park was my least favorite. Though it was the smallest, it had the poorest design and required much handwork. Nonetheless, my tractor and I were happily back and forth across town many times in those months. As a result, the park lawns were neat and trim, easily passing frequent close inspections by Smitty and members of the Recreation Board.

One of my jobs was to empty the fifty-gallon steel-barrel trash cans that dotted all three parks. This duty has always held a special meaning in my life and raised for me in later years an interesting philosophical query: Does the job define the person who is performing it? Or are the two variables independent of each other? Let's take as an example one profession, though I believe it is true of many others. If one considers modern faculties at universities, a human subspecies with which I am all too familiar, the answer seems inescapable. They are what they do. For the majority there is little to no psychological separation between them and their work. Suddenly denied that crutch, they stumble into disorientation, loneliness, and depression. Criticize their research and peer-reviewed papers, and they feel it as a personal attack. They wear the professional acknowledgments of completed dissertation, research and publication, and academic promotion as a second skin that is permanently bonded to their bodies, impossible to remove without serious damage. As an academic, educated at two of the best universities, Michigan in the U.S. and Cambridge in England, and having enjoyed the fruits of promotion and publication, I can relate to this tendency. And yet I have always been able to find a space separate from my professional work. Why, you ask? Because I emptied trash cans in the summer of 1965. I was a part-time garbage man.

When a child, Delphos had a simple waste-management system. A matrix of alleys bisected rows of homes; there, families had garbage cans where they would dump their waste. A man with a wooden prosthetic leg, called Peggy, drove through the alleys where he and his helpers emptied the cans into the back of his stake truck and took the load to the dump just north of town. I occasionally went to the auto junkyard—the location of Peggy's office as well as his home—with Father when he paid the garbage bill in cash. It was not unusual that, while sitting in the car and waiting, I would see rats the size of toy poodles scurrying around the yard between the derelict cars and parts. The junkyard was in the southwest corner of Delphos, called Marbletown, where the poorest of the poor lived in ramshackle homes. If Delphos society were to be viewed as a multi-story house socially stratified from the bottom with the elite living on the top floor, this was the old, disused coalbin in the dark basement corner.

Here I was, age eighteen, valedictorian of my senior class, and member of one of the families on the first floor of the status house, performing my own waste management duties in the park. Monday was the worst day. On the weekends many families and organizations had celebrations in the parks. They always included food and drink, the remnant of which ended up in the garbage cans. If there were more than fifty gallons at a time, it would be waiting for me on the ground at the can's base.

This was my first close experience with maggots of the common house fly. Larvae of many species of fly are remarkable creatures that serve a real purpose. One species is known for its ability to clean wounds. Another has anti-bacterial properties. Forgive me, however, for not being enamored of that of the common house fly, whose primary purpose is the breakdown of carrion and biological waste, and that inhabits as one of its favorite environments the summer weekend garbage can. Food left in a sun-warmed, open fifty-gallon metal barrel can, in twenty-four hours, produce thousands of maggots. They begin to consume the waste and produce a noxious liquor that drips to the bottom just waiting for the Monday attendant (me). At the time, there were no fifty-gallon plastic bags lining the cans. To empty them I merely tipped them into the two-wheel trailer behind the tractor and moved on to the next one. It was foul work indeed. The maggots crawled and squirmed through the trash while the liquid remains of putrefaction ran out the back of the trailer.

But the fun did not stop there. I also had to clean the bathrooms. Many persons use public toilets differently than they do their own. Or at least I hope so, or else I would not use their facilities. Littering the floor with paper towels, stuffing various non-organic matter down the commode that needs to be pulled out, deliberately damaging the plumbing and porcelain, writing offensive messages on the wall and doors, vomiting all over the place: all of this and more faces anyone responsible for cleaning locations of public excretion. After a while I began to look at every human being as nothing more than a contributor to the total cubic meters of urine and the metric tons of poop generated every day. It immediately raised the question in my mind: where did it all go? It is such a necessary biological process and disposal that nevertheless remains hidden from sight and discussion in our culture. Only the worker bees in the field of human waste disposal and facilities directly confront it. I found the women's restrooms, surprisingly, more littered and carelessly used than the men's. Also, having only brothers and a very conservative Mother who never mentioned the word menstruation, I had only an intellectual understanding about the process and its aftermath in the bathroom. endometrium sure as hell looks like blood, which it partially is; and my first experience in dealing with it was a bit of a shock. Luckily my stomach is not easily upset, so I was able to keep the men's and women's public facilities up to snuff. I just put my lucky clothespin on my nose, my rubber gloves on my hands, and got to work. When the trailer was full, I headed for the dump, where I shoveled out the waste and went back to the Stadium Park to wash everything, including myself, with a hose.

To this day, seeing an empty wrapper on the ground at a public place or a dirty, littered public toilet gives me a tiny pain in the chest. I developed a deep appreciation for the dignity of the work that the waste management personnel of our towns and cities perform. But the main lesson was this: I was not what I did. I was not inherently garbage because I collected and disposed of garbage. Our moral person and integrity are derived from different sources—family, education, experience, and conscience—and not solely the function of occupation. The two are independent variables. I learned this at the town dump. If only more of my academic colleagues had emptied garbage cans as youths, faculty meetings, departmental receptions, national gatherings of the discipline, and promotion and tenure committees would have been a lot more enjoyable.

Graduation

Those final weeks of school were painful. Neither the senior students nor the teachers really gave a damn anymore, but we had to keep up the appearances of learning and caring. That is, until the nun who ran my home room began jawing with me. I don't even remember what the issue was. We disagreed, she insisted that she was right, and I did not back down. She got very angry, and I told her to go to hell, after which the witch tromped to the principal's office in her ugly black shoes to complain of my insolence and I was summoned to the chief executioner's lair for my punishment. He merely told me that we had only a few weeks yet to suffer together and asked me to please back off until then. I agreed, and we were done.

As the top student in the class, I was required to give the valedictory address. This precipitated a months' long battle with my English teacher, Sister Mary Annoying, who suffered from palsy and moved her head rhythmically from side to side when she addressed me, desperately demanding my own sympathetic motions in response. It took all my strength to hold my head still. First, I had to decide what I was going to say, choose a topic. Even at eighteen years of age I was wary of the wisdom of young people and would have rather run my fingernails across the chalkboards than have spent any time listening to the philosophy and advice of one of my fellow travelers in high school. So how was I to perform such a duty? It was not the public speaking that concerned me. I had developed a good speaking voice and was comfortable enough in my own skin to get up in front of four- or five-hundred people and talk. It was the subject. What could I possibly say that would be of interest to so many persons and that would somehow cap our twelve years in school?

The exact inspirations for my talk are lost in the mists of time. However, I early developed a deep interest in Ernest Hemingway and his short stories and novels. Part of my fascination was his death. He had put a shotgun in his mouth and killed himself in 1961. Given that his violent ending and prominence as a writer were widely covered in the news, Mother and I had discussed him and his novels. She avidly read and gave me the habit at a young age and was a little concerned about the sexuality in Hemingway's work and its influence on an impressionable young boy; but she did not stop me from exploring his short stories and longer novels. After his Michigan fishing adventures, I picked up *For Whom the Bell Tolls* and found myself immersed in a world of war, masculine expression, bravery, individual action, and romance. I knew nothing about the Spanish Civil War but soon learned that it was the rehearsal for WWII, a cauldron of competing democratic, fascist, and communist forces. To me the book was about the potential of individual action, and it could very well have been part of my inspiration for the valedictory address.

I titled that address *Intrepid Individualism*. Looking back on it more than fifty years later (I still have the original copy with handwritten changes that I used on graduation night), I cringe not only at that title but also at the speech's romanticizing of "rugged individualism," its repeated use of the term "men" to stand for both men and women, and its still quite Catholic sense of absolute right and wrong. But it does end on a note that I like to think has inspired my actions since, helping and educating, learning and creating throughout my career and my life. The last line advocates, "Dare to be a conscientious oddball and add a little color to your life." My life has had quite a bit of color, some of it tending toward the darker shades at times—many of those yet to be described—but color, nonetheless.

Last Good Look

By high school graduation day, Smitty and I had become fast friends, so I invited him to the ceremony. He, the supervisor of the waterworks at

Stadium Park, and I would often stand around and shoot the bull. They would smoke and tease me about women while relating their successes, stories that I did not believe. I just smiled and nodded my head. Smitty was always up for an adventure. On one occasion that summer, he asked me if I had ever been to the top of the water tower. I had not, because climbing it was illegal and very dangerous. Throughout the Midwest the water tower was a fixture of most towns, often the first structure that one noticed when approaching because it projected above the trees and buildings and announced the town's name. Pumping the water and storing it in the tank exploited the force of gravity to move the liquid through the city's pipes.

Delphos's water tower had to be three to four hundred feet tall. A metal ladder ran up the side of one of the supports. Up the rungs Smitty and I climbed until we got to a metal walkway with a rail that circled the base of the tank. A second ladder took us to the top, where we sat near the red light that warned planes at night. The view was fantastic. I could see forever, in all directions, all over Delphos and far into the country. It was a beautiful summer day with a light breeze and many cumulus clouds. I was intoxicated by the height and the perspective, one that I had not experienced before. Smitty and I just sat up there for a half hour or more talking about the town and our lives in it. It was my last good look at a place where I had lived happily for eighteen years. The town had been a chrysalis in which I had slowly developed and from which I was soon to break free. I would fly into many dangerous winds and storms. But my life in Delphos gave me the compass and strength that would get me through.

CHAPTER 13

Flesh Eater

Freshman Again

I entered the University of Michigan in August 1965. The first trimester was filled with much work and a chronic case of home sickness. It had felt as if I had been torn body and soul from my native soil and was threatened with withering and dying in an environment with many foreign features. First, the undergraduate portion of the school was three times larger than Delphos, a huge metropolis in the perspective of a country boy. Second, many students intimidated me, top students from everywhere, the wealthy and preternaturally sophisticated from fancy private schools back east, upperclassmen disdainful of freshmen, and young women who exuded confidence, assertiveness, and sexual maturity. The first time a student asked where I had prepped, I knew I was being asked about my preparation; but for what, I could not tell. The idea that wealthy families sent their offspring to private schools where they received entitled chips on their shoulders and names that they could drop at mixers and cocktail parties was unknown to me, much less the identities of the schools.

I was staying in a dormitory on the east side of campus where a Pilot Program was in its first year, begun with the intent of creating a small, liberal arts-like space within a large university. We were boys, primarily freshman and sophomores. At least here I found a few other persons just as young and unsure as I; and the atmosphere was as sophomoric and male as one would expect. I compensated by losing myself in my studies. First semester German and Chemistry were hard. I had declared Chemistry as a major, not because I was particularly interested in the subject, but because Jake had graduated with a chemistry degree. My ignorance of the subjects available to me was nearly complete. In hindsight, I would have loved mechanical or computer engineering. I now rebuild old cars, learn how mechanisms work, and fix or rehabilitate them, and have been designing and executing computer algorithms for forty years. These were not in my knowledge base as options. So, Chemistry it was.

I also had to learn how to live closely with another person. As a lesson, it did not go well. The roommate to whom I had been assigned was a hybrid of honey-bear and pig. For the previous two years I had lived with my parents as an only child, in my own bedroom, and was accustomed to the privacy and the ability to organize my space to my liking. I lived alone and studied quietly alone. Roommate was a devoutly Catholic, Italian American, momma's boy from Detroit, tall, heavy set, more than slightly effeminate in speech and manners. In his honey-bear mode, he was social and outgoing, going from room to room in the dorm where he and the other students would spend hours in bull sessions. Not in our room. I made it very clear that it was not to be the center of anything except my living and studies, and his, if he chose. In his pig mode, he was insufferable. He hardly ever made his bed. Clothes, when removed, immediately landed on the floor and stayed there until Friday afternoon, when he stuffed them in a laundry sack and took them home to Momma, who washed and ironed them. Everything—books, papers, old drinking containers, food leftovers, nick-knacks, shoes—was in a state of chaos on his side. He just spread his large, pudgy frame across his unkempt bed like a Roman emperor and ignored it all. When I noticed that it was creeping across to me, I took a roll of masking tape and put a line down the middle of the room with instructions that nothing should cross it that belonged to him. I was the roommate from hell, and in personality and interests, the antithesis of everything he believed and stood for. Second semester he was living with a Marine Corps Platoon Leader Candidate preparing for his first training. Toward the end of our eight months together Roommate informed me that he had joined the Jesuits and was to begin his seminary training in the fall of 1966. I often think that my being such a mean bastard drove this poor young man into the priesthood, where he could shelter himself from people like me. Unfortunately for him, the Jesuits have the reputation of being the Pope's intellectual mean bastards, so he probably had a bit of a surprise.

It was not all work. I played intramural sports for our dormitory house and attended football games. Michigan has always been a football powerhouse, and the main rival of Father's favorite team, *The* Ohio State University. Football Saturdays in fall were wonderful. We all had season tickets as part of our tuition. The band played and marched to the west side dorm where students and fans congregated and followed it through the streets to the football stadium. The crisp air, the trees in full color, people waving from their porches, alumni tailgating on the lawns, music blaring out in all directions, we gaily made our way to the game where we spent four hours shouting, cheering, jeering, and encouraging our players on the field. It is the largest stadium in the country, seating more than one hundred thousand fans, and sold out for every home game. Being among all these cheering, happy people and stirred by the adrenaline of the game was indeed an intoxicant. Afterwards we made our tired way downtown for pizza and Coke while enjoying the street party that inevitably ensued. Good days, those.

Plinking

By the end of the first semester, when my parents came to get me for the break, I had done quite well, having earned three As and a B. My brothers were also home. Jake was in graduate school in a chemistry program while applying to numerous medical schools. After months of study and academics, both of us needed some time in the country. We therefore decided to head for Camp Lakota for a little plinking. It was located on the Auglaize River just south of the city of Defiance, Ohio. To get there one could drive, or, more adventurously, put a canoe in the river just east of Delphos and paddle north for a couple of days.

One of our favorite half days at scout camp was the rifle range. It was like the ones I later experienced in the Marine Corps with stations for the scouts and targets stapled on backboards at a prescribed distance all backed up by the "butts," a large hill that prevented the bullets from killing a cow or a farmer in a distant field. Guns and young boys seemed normal in rural areas. We might as well have had .22-caliber rifles in our cribs at birth. The Scouts trained us on gun safety and use. The range was necessarily regimented, and the range director brooked no misbehavior. Bolt action single shot .22-caliber rifles stood in their case behind the shooting area. Each scout would choose one and take his station, after which there was a safety lecture and a description of how and when to load the gun. No pointing of rifles at others, only at the ground, in the air, or down range; no loading a round in the chamber without instruction; no shooting without the proper order; when the "cease firing" order was given, all scouts must unload their weapons, leave the bolts open, and place them on the deck. All of this was to prevent injury and death.

Nonetheless we had much fun. Competition was keen and a great deal of trash-talking and boasting occurred. I had confidence in my skills and excelled at the sport. My eyes at the time were better than 20/20, and I could line up the sights of the gun with the center of the bullseye with little difficultly. Breathe in, sight-in, slowly let out my breath while squeezing the trigger and then "bang!" another .22-inch piece of lead would perforate the black center of my target paper. My cluster of target holes often formed a circle that was a couple of inches in diameter at the relatively short distances that we used. Outside the Scouts we all had our own .22-caliber guns, rifles, and pistols, and twelve- and twenty-gage shotguns. It was common for us to grab our weapons and head to the river for a little target practice and plinking. An old, rusted Campbell's soup can at thirty yards was the perfect target.

It was thus a natural act of family bonding that my Eagle Scout brother Jake and I decided to go to Camp Lakota, explore the grounds, and do a little target practice. Ranger Denny, who lived with his family on the grounds, was a very good friend of Jake because the two of them had worked together for four summers and his daughter had had a crush on my oldest brother. Part of the trip was devoted to sitting around and shooting the bull with Denny and sampling a few of his special recipes. He had designed and built his own meat-smoker from a retired refrigerator and was adept at cooking game. He also told us about his plans for a new privy lagoon. Each year, after the season was over, Denny had to clean out the two-hole, outside toilets that dotted the camp, a process called honey-dipping the privies. He decided that he was going to create his own organic disposal system and had identified a certain species of water plant that would filter the honey. In later years, I had the opportunity to see the lagoon myself and admire its design, technical efficiency, and the proliferation of flowering water plants that did the work. The Ranger was a bit of a rural renaissance man.

From Well to Unwell

After our chat with Denny, Jake and I took off into the Lakota woods to shoot. We chose our target, set it up where there was a backstop, and took turns trying our luck. When we finished, I took the clip out of the pistol, a Ruger that reproduced the look and action of the German Lugar WWII 9mm pistol in a .22-caliber and pulled back the bolt to make sure that it was unloaded and safe, and then put the clip into the pocket of my button-down shirt.

Off we went to explore more parts of the campground when, suddenly, we came across an old, open well. Someone, probably the farmer who sold the land to the local council, had dug this for water or disposal but never covered it. Of course, what young male is not attracted to a large hole in the ground? I walked over to the edge and peered in. At the bottom, some five feet from the surface, I could see the top of an old, rusted fifty-gallon drum, the kind that was used to deliver oil and gasoline. Just as I was about to pull back from the edge, the gun clip that was sitting loosely in my shirt pocket fell out and splashed into the dark, murky water.

My first thought was "*oh shit*" because the pistol and the clip belonged to my father. Now while I loved him and appreciated everything that he had done to raise me and allow me to thrive, he was a severe man who at times scared the hell out of his sons and their cousins and friends. He was also not opposed to corporal punishment. No time-out or sitting in the corner or "let's talk this through" nonsense for him. When we were young, he fashioned a paddle out of 3/8-inch plywood that lived in our kitchen's corner. It was not often that we felt its sting; but feel it we did when the sin was serious enough, like the evening we three boys barricaded ourselves in the back bedroom and threw shoes and projectiles at the babysitter until she broke down and cried. Even though we were sure to be in bed by the time our parents returned from their night out, little angels sound asleep, each one of us got a sound crack or two.

I needed to get that clip out of the well. A gesture like this was, by this time in my life, completely unnecessary. I had graduated from high school at the top of my class and had just finished my first semester with a 3.75 grade point average. Father was pleased with me. Losing a clip from his pistol would have been a minor inconvenience, one easily remedied by buying a new one. Yet that early conditioning led me to ease myself down into the well, with the help of my brother, and stand on top of the fifty-gallon drum. The first thing I noticed was that the top of the drum was partially rusted away. I rolled up my right shirt sleeve, steadied myself on the drum with my left hand, slowly knelt on the cold metal, and dipped my right hand and arm into the water up to my shoulder. When I began to explore the dark liquid, I noticed that I was not alone. Cold December air had masked the scent of rotting animal flesh. Someone had used the hole for the disposal of dead bodies. I could not make out the exact species or parts of species that surrounded my arm, but there they were. Soon I determined that the water was much deeper than the length of my arm. Trying to retrieve the clip was hopeless. I worked my way up and out of the well, only to be followed down by my brother, who also convinced himself that we had no chance. We called it a day and made our way home while looking forward to a quiet Christmas with the family.

Let the Feast Begin

A couple of days later I developed a fever and began to feel a severe fatigue and disorientation as my right arm swelled up to twice its normal size, turned the color of green olives, and throbbed with pain like a base drum. My parents took me to Dr. W. who diagnosed a case of the flesh-eating bacteria and who shot me up with many, many units of penicillin. The examination revealed that I had a small lesion at the top of my arm, near the shoulder. A bacterium, probably from the Lancefield Group-A Streptococcus family, had invaded my body and begun to eat it. In medical texts it is called necrotizing fasciitis, which means that the skin and tissues below it rot and peel away. But first the tissue, after swelling and turning dark, develops very large blisters that crack open and ooze a disgusting thick liquid. My arm began to melt. I have never been so sick in my life. And I could do nothing but endure the pain and symptoms and watch my arm being eaten by millions or billions of hungry bacteria.

Mommy and Mummy

Mother bought rolls of gauze and wrapped my arm like a mummy. Soon the gauze turned dark from suppuration and needed to be changed. My life turned into a series of wraps and disgusting unwraps that revealed the terrible open sores that brought on more trips to the doctor for yet more shots of penicillin. And I stunk. I was a putrefying body carrying an aura of decay and death, like a dead muskrat that had been in its trap too long. My noxious odor drove my brothers to keep their distance and voice loud complaints. When I sat down with the family at Christmas dinner the mixture of scents from the food and my arm must have been a wonder to the senses.

I should have been in the hospital. The mortality rate for necrotizing fasciitis is between twenty-four and thirty-four percent, which means I was at considerable risk of dying. But this was rural medicine in the mid-1960s: shoot up the poor bugger with antibiotics and hope for the best. It might be a blessing that I was not hospitalized because the specter of my arm was so awful, I would not have wanted to display it to the surgeons who would have had a ready answer for my problem, starting at the shoulder. The minimal surgical treatment would have been to open my arm along its length and have the surgeon clean out the dead tissue, a process called debriding. Infections this serious, however, can spread to the entire body, which then becomes septic. Combine the disease with streptococcal toxic shock syndrome (STSS), and the mortality rate climbs to sixty percent. To stop the spread, amputation is often necessary. To a carpenter with a hammer, everything looks like a nail; to a surgeon with a scalpel, my disgusting appendage would have presented an irresistible opportunity to demonstrate his wisdom and skill.

Our Unholy Lady of Merde had once again appeared with her trinity of compatriots: 1) I took the risk of climbing into a well that, 2) by chance, contained deadly streptococcal organisms and 3) whereby I again disregarded the possibility of young death.

Julia

After about three weeks of being an invalid, my arm began to heal by going from deeply disturbing, dripping, stinking, and disgusting to merely disgusting. My wraps had to be changed less often, the pain eased, and I began to feel better, so much so that I called Julia and asked whether I could come over and see her. It was also her first semester, at a small Catholic woman's college, near and affiliated with The University of Notre Dame, and I wanted to see how she had done. In retrospect, I cannot believe that I did that.

We had not parted well the previous spring when she developed a fondness for her entitled cousin and I had discovered Sarah. Imagine, me full of some of the most fearsome bacteria on earth and I carry them to her house. We sat on the couch in her living room by the big picture window where we had so often snuggled. Her parents were very regular in their habit of going to bed at 10:00. We timed our return from dates for 10:15, when we would turn on the color TV, turn down the lights, and curl up for two or three hours. She worked part-time for her father at the bank, so she was usually tired, which meant that I held her close as she snoozed. Holding her gave me some of the quietest, most peaceful, and happiest times of my high school years. But now we sat on that couch as strangers in uncomfortable conversation. I was still sick and disgusting, although I had worn a fresh white, long-sleeved shirt to hide my wrappings. I understood that her first term at college had not been a big success. No "in sickness and in health and till death do we part," I left her home that afternoon for the last time.

When I returned to college at the beginning of January, penicillin had killed most of the hungry bugs, and my immune system had taken care of the rest. It took many weeks for the tissue on my right arm to recover and take on the form and texture of normal skin. For years, near the site of the lesion on my upper arm, the epidermis was rough and scarred.

I suppose the lesson I learned was, if you want to feel well, stay out of one.

CHAPTER 14

Har-Thar Harry

I t was the voice coming across the dark, oil-soaked hardwood floors of the can department that first caught your attention. Then the ready smile, the gapped, tobacco-stained teeth, half missing, the small, angular face with pearl-white skin and shiny blue eyes, as he slapped you on the back and shifted the large lump of tobacco in his cheek. Uncle Harry was reported to have been the distant cousin of the nineteenth-century-style owner and president of The New Delphos Manufacturing Company, but I never did get the biological connection, nor why we young college guys, working that summer of 1966, called him Uncle. His greeting was so loud and distinctive that now, more than fifty years later, I can still hear it reverberating in my head and see the blue denim overalls with the broad shoulder straps that he invariably wore to work. I also find it odd that at this distance I should think of Harry. He was unremarkable by contemporary standards, had no fame, fortune, or position, and lived in a Midwestern cultural and geographical backwater during a time that Nineteenth-Century America was grudgingly giving up her dominance and yielding to the twentieth, but with only partial success. Yet he stands out to me as emblematic of a time and place.

WWI

At the time of this writing, it is now more than one hundred years since World War I began. Harry had been born in the previous century, on May 22, 1895, and had, at the age of twenty-two, been drafted into the U.S. Army near the beginning of America's participation in the European conflict. He talked about his experiences with the usual set pieces that veterans develop to block the actual horror of their experience or to fill in the absent memories. Grandmother Emma was born in 1884 and told me about going to the train station on the Pennsylvania Line and watching the Delphos boys shipping off to training and foreign war. Harry represented for me the adventure of the country boy, torn from his comfortable, poor, rural roots, sent to a strange state to train in the practices of killing human beings--the Germans, from the land of Goethe and Beethoven, those cultured Europeans with the Prussian military culture, whose many emigrant men and women founded the town of Delphos— with methods that he could hardly have imagined as a youth. For Harry, guns were for squirrels and pheasants, not humans. He was transferred from training to the American Expeditionary Forces (AEF) on August 22, 1918, with orders for the battlefront. He then was put on yet another train, sent to the port, loaded on his first ocean-going ship, and transported to France. France—could anyone conceive of a more jarring contrast, thousands upon thousands of American country boys in General Jack Pershing's army being dropped into the City of Light, the center of European culture and style? It must have seemed to the natives as the invasion of the boobs: naïve, awkward young men with more knowledge of butchering pigs than of European geography and manners. And when I looked at Harry, the contrast was stark. How could this gentle soul with the kind face and demeanor kill anyone in France? How could he possibly understand the cultural and political dynamics of the war and his role in it? He was just a cog on a small wheel in the big American military machine. He had no choice and little freedom. It was a situation that I would later understand only too well.

Harry was only exposed to the carnage of WWI for a short time. He was attached to the 155th Army Infantry Regiment that was part of the 39th Infantry Division. Before they were fully trained and incorporated into the lines, the war ended on November 11, 1918. His regiment was to participate in the big American push of 1919 to help the Allies win the war. Luckily, Germany and Austria decided on an armistice that saved Harry and his fellow soldiers from the trenches and what would have been a bloody fight to the Rhine and beyond. He advanced in rank quickly, making Corporal on September 1, 1918, and Sergeant on May 27, 1919. The next month he was honorably discharged from the service.

Returning, he went to work for the factory and had been there ever since. From the time that I was a child I had known Harry because my parents often took me to his home in the summer. Along with the professionals on the farms, many amateurs turned their hand to gardens, including Harry, who was known for the beefsteak tomatoes that he raised in his backyard on Fifth Street. These were the largest, firmest, juiciest, reddest, plumpest, and most delicious fruit that I had as a child. He would proudly take us for a tour of his plants and there, on stakes about three feet high, would be the vines dripping the large fruit in various colors of ripeness from the deepest green to yellow, to orange, and then to a mature red that would hurt the eyes in the bright summer sun. Laughing and leaping through the rows of maturing vegetables like a young child in a candy store, Harry would choose the choicest items of each variety and hand them to Father and Mother.

Therefore, when I was new in the factory, when I felt strange, out of place, and uncomfortable with the new work, Harry was a familiar face.

He sensed my discomfort and offered a smile and friendly greeting. At this time, he was in his early seventies and mostly retired, but came in to perform a few jobs that he had mastered and that none of the younger guys did better, like pounding irons. He also liked to talk; and I liked to listen.

It was Harry that reinforced my awareness of overlapping generations and the connections that they produce. In my adult profession, I have worked in the discipline of Human Genetics, one aspect of which uses mathematical models to track the movement of genetic material from one generation to the next. To simplify the math, I treat generations as discrete, in which persons are born and die at constant, arbitrary times. This is not, however, how generations work; they overlap, and each person represents one or many generations, depending upon age. Older persons connect us to earlier times. All human experience can be represented by a reticular network of overlapping generations, ages, and connections. Harry was my connection to WWI and the living representative of the men who fought and died there; my uncle Bogie was the living representative of WWII; now I am a living representative of the Vietnam War for those born in the last forty years whose concept of 1968 is just as distant as 1917 was for me. Harry, Bogie, and I were all contemporaries in 1966 whose generations overlapped and revealed the constancy of war and young men's role in it.

The Can

The purpose of the can department was to make many and varied cans. One-gallon, two-gallon, and five-gallon gasoline cans, Penguin Pal coolers for water and picnics: all were fashioned out of galvanized metal, iron that had been coated with tin and zinc. For the gas cans, the tops and bottoms arrived from the press room, where they had been formed in large hydraulic machines that pushed the metal into dyes, forming the correct size and shape. The sides of the can were flat, rectangular pieces bent at the edges and then joined and crimped, forming a cylinder. A small ninety-degree edge was rolled on the top and bottom of the cylinder that, when matched to the top and bottom with a similar edge, could be crimped and rolled together, forming the can.

The crimped joints, top, bottom, and side, were not leak proof and needed to be soldered: that is, sealed with a hot metal in the spaces of the crimps so a liquid would not leak through the cracks. Using a technique from the early Industrial Revolution, the scene was filled with the mist of molten solder with heat radiating from every surface. For the end seams, there were ceramic, circular chucks that rotated on an iron rod with a hot gas flame blowing against it, the circumference of the chuck just the right size to fit inside the end seams and hold the can. The operator took the can, and set it on the chuck, and allowed it to turn long enough to heat to the melting temperature of the solder, which came off large spools as long, thick, spaghetti-like threads. As the end of the thread was held on the end seam of the hot can, the solder would melt into the empty spaces and make it watertight. There were two hot chucks on each side of the line with two air-cooled chucks in between. It was a ballet of precise movement of hands and feet to solder the bottom seam, cool the can in one of the middle chucks, then turn it end for end and solder the top before moving it into a large, air-cooled space down the line. Four cans would be in process at once, and the operator had to move them on a relatively fixed schedule to heat the seam to the proper temperature but not overheat the metal and turn it to scrap.

I was put on the solder line and soon learned that I would never dance with the New York Ballet, because my movement and coordination stunk. I left the cans for too long on the hot chucks, creating circles of white, pasty residue on the metal. Even with gloves and long-sleeved shirts, I burned my hands and arms. The crimping of the end seams left a 3/8-inch edge on the top and bottom and was the only leverage for moving them. After using the tips of my fingers to pick them up, I developed bruising underneath my fingernails, which after a while, caused them to fall off, leaving my hands a sore mess. Operators standing at the chucks dealt with very high heat, loud air from blowers, and the scent of melting tin-lead-based solder and hot metal. How many grams of toxic heavy metal I consumed in two summers, I will never know, although it might have worked to my favor over the years. Perhaps I too am galvanized inside, and it is the partial secret of my longevity.

Pounding Irons

Harry's role came with the side seams of the cans, in a couple of aspects. To melt the solder in these, soldering irons were heated in gas furnaces to red-hot temp. The irons had a large wooden handle attached to a metal rod that was in turn attached to the working end, the soldering iron, a sloping block of metal. The worker would take a can, and with a small brush put a coating of acid in the side seam to neutralize any oil present. He then melted the solder in the seam with the tip of the iron by holding a rod of solder against the heated end while simultaneously moving it down the seam. Seam after seam, can after can, hundreds, thousands of them, day after day, and year after year, he worked.

But my most vivid memory of Harry was in his job pounding the soldering irons, which he normally did on weekends in order not to interfere with production. The irons, after many cycles of heating and use, got distorted, lost their sharp edges and points, and needed to be reformed. My two brothers and I often accompanied Father on the Sunday inspections of the factory. He checked the heating system and the pressure in the water lines for the automatic sprinkler system and walked the floors to see that everything was well. We often saw Harry at the gas furnace with a large pile of used irons to rehabilitate. He heated them until they glowed the color of an Arizona sunset and then took a ball peen hammer and pounded them back into the wanted shape for soldering. To dress them further, he used large files of various grades to smooth each face of the iron until it was ready to take on the next thousand side seams. And all the while he smiled, talked affectionately to my father (whom he had known as a child when my grandfather Evan was superintendent), and moved the tobacco lump from cheek to cheek, the dark liquid creeping around the gaps in his remaining teeth.

This must have been in the years 1960 to 1967, or even earlier. Harry was still doing the hard, physical work of a younger man. Work at the factory for the men and women on the line—stacking and cutting the metal, working the presses, painting the cans, loading the trucks and boxcars—was work with an uppercase "W": hard, sweaty, muscle-stretching, back-bending effort that took a physical toll, even on us youngsters. Each evening I was exhausted and sore. Each morning I awoke with muscles complaining and temperament flagging for the anticipated workday. Here was Harry, seventy-one years old, having spent most of his adult life in The New Delphos Manufacturing Company, still pounding irons with a smile.

The Recipe

One of Harry's great pleasures was chewing tobacco, a habit straight out of the previous century and one that the factory tolerated for many years by furnishing the departments with convenient shiny brass spittoons into which each chewer, in theory, deposited his contribution when the spirit came over him or his mouth swelled full. Harry had his own recipe. It began with a foil pouch of a fresh, fragrant, shredded chewing tobacco, to which he added crushed peppermints, the circular ones about an inch in diameter with pink stripes, and followed these with small lengths of black licorice, the long, braided strands purchased at Grant's or Woolworth's, the five-and-dime stores on Main Street. After moistening the mixture with a little water, he sat it on the sill of one of the large windows facing south toward the double tracks of the Pennsylvania Railroad that ran next to the building where the can department was housed. Harry allowed the sweet mixture to age for a few days to join the flavors before he dug into the pouch, formed a large plug, and stuffed it into the side of his mouth, leading to a huge smile of pleasure and satisfaction. I myself was never tempted to try the concoction. As a boy, Jake, following the example of men at the shop, had given me a plug to chew behind the brick incinerator in our backyard. It precipitated waves of nausea and explosive, oral elimination. I had no desire to repeat the experience.

A factory legend, related by Jake, claimed that a thief was suspected of stealing from Uncle Harry's stash on the south sill. To teach the unknown miscreant a lesson, the men of Harry's department hatched a plot during break time. A fifteen-minute break, begun and ended by the factory horn in the middle of the morning and afternoon shifts, found the gang in the second story head sitting on the toilets (sometimes using them) and on upturned buckets. Here they smoked, joked, teased the younger guys, and generally shot the bull. (During these sessions, I learned a great deal about the supposed WWII exploits of many of the men, as well as the details of their sexual fantasies and alleged experiences at the hands of the South Lima prostitutes.) When they found out that Harry was being robbed, this group, by means of the Socratic method in the bathroom, came to a solution. They used their pocketknives, which nearly everyone carried, to shave hair from their legs and chests that they then added to a trap-pouch on the south sill, in the same location that Harry normally stored his supply. Very soon after, the thievery stopped.

Demon Whiskey

We all have our demons, devils that hex and haunt our lives causing us to do and say things that, while impelled by some dark energy from the depths, work very much against our wellbeing and mental peace. Whiskey was Harry's demon. It ruled his life and behavior like a mad king, causing him to stay at the Eagles Bar until he was completely sotted, then race though Main Street on foot, loudly addressing pedestrians as he went, shouting in that baritone to any who had the misfortune to be close. And then our home telephone would ring, the instrument over which Father maintained absolute authority and dominance, logging long-distance calls by the second in a small loose-leaf book and questioning the necessity of all incoming and outgoing conversations.

As superintendent and secretary of the Delphos Civil Service Board, Father had the connections with the police to become "in loco parentis" to the men who worked for him. When bad behavior ensued involving alcohol, the police often called him to intervene. Such intervention meant talking the offender down from his drunken rage or picking him off the floor of the local drinking establishment, or off the street, as the crisis would dictate. Father then escorted him back to his wife and home, where he slept it off and returned to work the next morning without having bothered the police blotter with nuisance entries that required official time and money, not to mention a humiliating article in *The Delphos Herald* police report.

Uncle Harry was often the subject of this late evening rescue. Dad would hop into his Chevrolet or Oldsmobile and drive to the site of the incident. One night he had to go into the Eagles and talk Harry into getting into the car and going home. Harry always greeted my father very solicitously, whether drunk or not, and on this occasion quietly followed him out and jumped into the passenger seat. Talking all the time on the short drive to his house, Harry was soon inside with his wife, safe and sound. A more cooperative and congenial alcoholic one could hardly imagine. Father was soon at home again when the telephone rang with Harry's wife on the other end. It seems that when Dad was in the front, getting into his car as Harry's wife offered her appreciation for the help, Harry was climbing out the rear window of the bedroom and making a beeline back to the drinking establishment. The cycle of life continued.

Piecework, Labor, Capital

Harry not only offered me a fuller picture of men's struggle with whiskey and the understandable but misguided policies of prohibition that still echoed through my childhood; he also furnished part of my early adult understanding of the relationship between the working man and capital. This was symbolized by the contrast between Harry and the President-owner of the company. The two shared a last name and at some time in the past a common ancestor. There could not, however, be a greater social and financial divide between them. Instead of denim overalls with wide shoulder straps, the President wore dark, pin-striped suits with a vest and a pocket watch. Instead of pounding irons, he sat at a beautiful roll-top desk in the office building on the corner that stood separate from the factory buildings. It was two stories with pale-yellow brick, large windows that punctuated both floors, a full basement—not much different from the many early-century homes in Delphos. It was paneled in dark oak with oak benches in the entryway and oak and rolling leather chairs in the offices. Smelling of wood oil and floor polish, it always appeared in stark contrast to the factory floor, an isolated island of sweet-smelling women and self-important, Midwestern industry and values. The President also held a similar position at the People's National Bank on Main Street, as well as being a prominent Mason and member of the Chamber of Commerce. Nothing much happened of importance in Delphos, particularly where money was involved, without some knowledge or direct participation by the President and his only son, who was Vice-President.

True to the ethic of Nineteenth-Century capitalism, there was no workers' union while the owner and his son never generated a dollar at the factory that they did not hold close to their bosoms and release with great reluctance. Only when necessary, would they parse out a few coins to their employees. But only a few. Salaries were very low for a plant that size and the wealth that it generated. Father's salary was particularly low for all the responsibilities that he carried. On the floor of the factory, the Victorian practice of piecework prevailed; a man or woman was constantly trying to reach a target number of parts per hour—a number that the President and his men-in-suits set in the office—in order to make an adequate wage.

Piecework was particularly dangerous in the press room, where the operators of these machines put all their manual digits at risk with each strike of the die, and where shortcuts were a heavy temptation to beat the rate. Many workers there were short of digits, literally. My great uncle Roxie, who was the foreman of the press room and who had worked at the plant since 1914, lost the same finger on three occasions, knuckle, by knuckle, by knuckle. When the insurance company complained that the factory had turned in a claim on three occasions for the loss of the same finger, Father had to explain to them that by doing piecework Roxie had lost his finger piece-by-piece.

During my two summers in the factory, I came to hate the idea of piecework. One of my jobs was to use a spot-welder to attach ears to the top of gasoline cans before assembly. An ear on each side would hold the wire and wood handle by which the can could be carried. I put the ear on the bottom piece of the welder, held the top of the can in the proper orientation, and then tripped the switch with my foot, which brought down the top arm of the machine. When contact was made, the large jolt of electricity heated the two parts and bonded them. I then rotated the top 180 degrees and attached an ear on the other side, hundreds if not thousands of times, in the most mind-numbing exercise I have ever experienced. I felt completely manipulated and abused by the people in the office who set the rates for the machines, who could maximize the owner's profits and productivity by increasing the number of ears per hour that I needed to weld, thus giving him even more dollars. And there was no appeal by the workers for fairness because there was no union or organized representation from the ranks.

At the People's National Bank at the end of an exhausting week, my paycheck would read about ninety-six dollars after taxes. Five and a half days of grueling work for about eighteen dollars a day. And the irony of it all was that I gave the owner his money back in the bank so he could lend it and make even more money! Management-enforced worker productivity it was, in all its glory. Want the squirrel to run faster in the wheel for the same number of acorns? Merely speed up the wheel. At the end of the summer, if someone had asked me to storm the barricades of capitalism and create a workers' revolution, I would have been more than a little amenable; the experience has conditioned my attitude toward labor and capital to this day.

Blue Collar Iron

Yet I was the lucky one. Soon that summer of 1966 I was to leave the factory for six weeks to train with the Marine Corps. At the end of August I was back for my second year at Michigan. I did not experience the deadening monotony of factory labor until the next summer when I was back again, but just for four months. Harry had been there his whole life and had no opportunity for higher education. Other than his experiences in the Army, he had lived as a small-town manual laborer with little chance of advancement. Nevertheless, it was Harry who helped heat and pound me into the blue-collar hardness and shape that, even with future academic degrees, honors, and publications, became a permanent part of my person, one part of a multiple personality suite that I have always prized.

CHAPTER 15

First Marines

Motivation

W hy did a freshman honors student with a hidden bum leg join the United States Marine Corps in January of 1966 at the beginning of a grim war in Southeast Asia? In retrospect, that is a damn good question, one my dearly beloved mother frequently asked me in later years, usually with anger still shooting out of her blue eyes. The program was called the Platoon Leader Corps (PLC), the Marines' equivalent of the Army and Navy's Reserve Officers Training Corps (ROTC). In the summer between freshman and sophomore years of college, and again between junior and senior years, officer candidates would go to Marine Corps Base Quantico, Virginia, to undergo their basic training. If both summers were satisfactorily executed, candidates would be commissioned upon graduation and attend a further six to eight months of officer training at Quantico. They then entered regular service as a shave-tail second lieutenant, the lowest of the low of officers' ranks.

My first thought was that I wanted to fly jets, drive muscle cars, and date hot women, the lifestyle of the prototypical fighter pilot who becomes intoxicated by risk and lives 24/7 with elevated levels of scotch and adrenalin in the blood. My first cousin, Jack, who had taken that route nine years before, qualifying as a fighter pilot, served as my inspiration. My eyesight through my third year of high school was better than 20/20. Standing at the football practice field a half mile or more from the Catholic church, with the four faces of its clock in each of the four directions of the compass, I could resolve the hands and tell the time. Then in my fourth year my eyesight took a sudden plunge to 20/40 and has remained there since. My PLC physical indicated that I was not a candidate for the flight program and would need to settle on a different military occupational specialty (MOS). With flight school not an option, the most probable one at the time was infantry, leading a platoon of four squads of enlisted Marine grunts through the boonies of Vietnam looking for the Viet Cong or North Vietnamese Army, engaging them in firefights, and killing them.

What in the hell *was* I thinking? Motivation comes from disparate sources. Congenitally I was pugnacious, always looking to pick a fight and maintain some standard of masculine honor; I enjoyed the violence of football. My testosterone levels must have been high from early on because I matured quickly in grade school and developed my secondary sexual characteristics before my fellow males. The male culture of the time was to reject all aspects of perceived weakness and project only the strong and manly, with a smattering of the violent. World War II and Korea were very recent and contributed to a culture of war participation for young men. The draft also presented the real possibility that my services could be demanded in a time and way not of my choosing. These factors must have played some role in my decision.

But one lingering circumstance from four years before overrides all these, my perceived failure of manliness, sprinkled with cowardice, in my sophomore year of high school. As has already been related in these pages, Coach Dark was at his very worst in my freshman year of football when I was forced to play with the varsity in addition to the junior varsity of eighth graders and freshmen. Serving as a tackle dummy for the upper-classmen at practice left me beaten down and shy of contact at the end of the season. In the spring, driving back from Lima with Father, I tried to explain my feelings to him. He was empathetic and said the decision to play in the coming season was my own and that he would support me whatever I did. It was shortly thereafter that I began to develop pains in my side. Dr. W.'s partner diagnosed me with hepatitis A and restricted me from any sports for a year, including of course, football. In my sopho-more year I took the job of assistant manager for the team and spent the season passing out salt tablets, mending small wounds, wrapping ankles, filling water jugs, getting the game uniforms cleaned, and performing any additional necessary services. However, in the back of my mind was the nagging suspicion that I was sandbagging, that I had trumped up this fake illness as a pretext so as not to subject myself to another season of Coach Dark's Abuse and Intimidation style.

That summer, 1962, our family—minus Jake, who was working at the factory and watching over our home and Grandmother—took a trip to Virginia to visit Jack who was recovering from a plane crash. Immedi-ately before he was to earn his wings, he had been in his Grumman F9F Panther burning off fuel before landing. It happed at a low altitude over a large ranch in Texas near the Gulf of Mexico, where he was returning to his aircraft carrier, when an actuator rod that attached his flight controls to the elevator snapped and rolled the plane into an inverted position with the canopy and his head facing down instead of up. Just before the Panther hit the ground, Jack managed to snap-roll it right side up. Instead of exploding, it belly-flopped and bounced again in the air. When he felt the plane hit and rise, he pulled his ejection lever, and he, his canopy, and his Martin-Baker ejection seat went flying into the air, propelled by the artillery shell under his backside. Although his parachute deployed, he was close to the ground and hit it with a great velocity. The combination of the ejection and landing compressed his spine and caused serious injuries to his lower vertebrae. His flying career was over. The damage to his body prevented him from passing a flight physical, and the Marines decided to give him an honorable medical discharge. When we visited, Jack was stationed at Quantico, Virginia, waiting for his papers to be processed.

Here was the first time that I had been face to face with the uniformed United States Marine Corps. Sharply tailored young officers walked everywhere on the base and platoons of candidates marched and trained in their green fatigues. I very much wanted a pair of Marine Corps boon dockers for hiking. These were black leather, high-top boots that Marines wore with their utility uniforms. Jack took us to the post exchange and purchased a pair for me after I had found my size. Then he took us on a tour of the base. The obstacle course immediately caught my attention, a children's playground for adults with walls to climb over, ropes to climb up, and telephone poles in every architectural design imaginable to challenge the physical strength and agility of the candidate to get up, over, and through. Watching these young men training to put themselves in harm's way, even risk death, for a larger cause, I felt the ache of regret and the fear of cowardice and failure. They trained as a team, groups of candidates running between obstacles and helping each other finish the course. And now I had let down my fellow players on the football team because I was not willing to risk the A&I style of Coach Dark but instead sandbagged my way out of a year of football. My heart sank in shame; I made a promise to myself then and there, in the middle of the woods of Quantico, Virginia, that never again would I face a severe or dangerous challenge and shrink from it. Hence, in January of 1966, at the beginning of a war, I joined the Marine Corps.

Shaping Up

I was scheduled to leave for my PLC training in early June. The University of Michigan was on the trimester schedule. Finals finished at the end of April, when my parents came and took me and my dormitory impedimenta home for the summer. Freshman year had been a great success, culminating in my receiving a freshman prize for high academic achievement at a ceremony while Mother and Father beamed. They were less enthusiastic about the Marine Corps.

I had been drafted for work in the factory that summer; in this I had little choice. It was a matter of pride that Father's college-educated sons worked as regular employees along with the men and women who had been there for years. We also were put in the lowest-of-the-low jobs to begin, bailing scrap iron, degreasing cans, counting nuts and bolts, etc. This would be my first factory summer. My first day on the job, the morning after my return from school, I was assigned to the loading dock with Forman Gilbert, a tall, heavily built man in denim overalls with a permanent frown and temperament to match. I loaded and unloaded the semi-trailers that pulled up to the dock and the railroad cars on the spur next to the building. In between I packed the various galvanized metal products into heavy cardboard boxes, stenciling the side with information about the contents, ticking them off on the inventory sheets and invoices, and preparing them for shipment. It was good work, the mindlessness of it a relief from school.

Father, however, was annoyed. He took exception to my leaving for six weeks in the middle of the summer to attend the PLCs. I believe that one factor was a loss of face caused by his son interrupting the important factory work for military training, which, having not been a soldier himself, he did not understand. He also interpreted this time away as a vacation for me, like working on the eastern shore at a taffy stand or as an ice cream vendor while ogling the bikini-clad college girls on the beach, summer jobs that some of my friends had taken. Further, I believe he felt that my entering the service was completely unnecessary. He had supervised the correction of my congenitally deformed foot for more than three years and knew that, if I had gone to the local orthopedic surgeon in Lima, I could have easily obtained medical documentation that, when submitted to the draft board, would with high probability have classified me 4-F at an induction physical—physically unfit for military service. Or maybe he just feared for the life of his son in Vietnam, should I go there.

I, on the other hand, was completely preoccupied with doing my best at the factory and preparing for the rigorous physical challenge that I knew was in front of me. Since early football years I had jogged and kept myself in good shape. Jogging I could do; it was slow and steady. We had mandatory physical activity classes as freshmen. One of them involved a great deal of running on the track. My problem was always my fucking clubfoot. It was merely adequate. My running speed and endurance never equaled my classmates' or, eventually, the other candidates'. My left Achilles tendon was foreshortened and easily irritated by boots. Complicating the issue was my physical build, which can only be described as a fireplug: stout for my height, five foot eight inches (in the morning) with quite short legs. Pound for pound I had little body fat, was negatively buoyant, and quite strong. But propelling my body with asymmetric lower limbs had always been problematic.

After I had signed up and been accepted, the Marines began to send me information. One of the brochures was in frequently-asked-questions format.[1] Question 10 under Part II – Summer Training read, *"What physical conditioning is required prior to reporting and during the training period?"* The answer had five exercises that we were expected to perform in the physical fitness test given at the beginning and end of the session: (1) Pull-ups – 6; (2) Squat thrusts – 29; (3) Push-ups – 27; (4) Sit-ups (2 minutes) – 47; (5) 300-yard Shuttle Run (1 minute). But the best was yet to come:

> Candidates are required to successfully complete the Marine Corps Physical Readiness test which simulates physical requirements imposed by combat conditions. This test, taken while wearing combat equipment, includes climbing uphill, casualty evacuation, rope climb, advance by fire and maneuver and a three-mile forced march.[2]

Holy shit! Combat equipment meant full utilities: blouse, trousers, T-shirt, skivvies, and belt.[3] In addition, I must wear combat boots, field marching pack, M14 rifle, and steel helmet. I had to get ready.

My pre-PLC weekdays took on a routine pattern. I woke at 6:30, had a light breakfast, and drove to the factory with a neighbor. Morning break was 9:30 for fifteen minutes. At 11:30 it was home, where Mother would have our main meal waiting. At 12:30 the workday resumed with another fifteen-minute break in the middle and then a whistle at 5 P.M., the end of the factory day. After a quick supper with the family, I donned my running gear: short cotton gym shorts, light T-shirt, and tennis shoes

---

1 PLC Answers, Information for the Platoon Leader Classes United States Marine Corp. NAVMC 5926 (Revised) 1 Aug 1965, pp. 4, 5.

2 Ibid., p. 5.

3 In the 1960s the Secretary of Defense, Robert McNamara, standardized utility uniforms for all services in a monochromatic dark green design as an economy measure.

and socks. This was before jogging was trendy, before Nike, Adidas, New Balance, and the other shoes engineered for comfortable exercise. I used "tennis shoes," a generic term for canvas shoes of various kinds, not particularly designed for the purpose to which I was adapting them. I just had to tolerate a series of blisters and sores on my feet. Late in the training I began to exercise with the combat boots that I had gotten in 1962 to get used to their feel.

My running path was a three-mile course in the countryside that I had used for years. From Sixth Street I went north down the alley for three blocks to Stadium Park and our city pool, then take the stone road along the canal into the country, and cut west on a road that skirted the town dump to the main highway, from where I headed back south again to the iron bridge that crossed the creek, then east again on the pool road and home. After it opened, I varied the routine by ending my run with a plunge in the pool. Sarah's grandmother, who lived near our home, was usually swinging on her porch when I ran by. Jogging was so unusual in 1966 that she complained to Sarah about my attire, saying she did not like seeing me run by her house in my underwear, and requesting that I please in future be properly clothed. At home, exhausted, I decompressed on our back steps, took a shower in the basement, and collapsed in bed to prepare for another day. Cold or hot, rain or shine, wind or not, tired or not, I would exercise, motivated by the knowledge of what lie before me.

In between, I tried to squeeze a bit of a social life with Sarah. This summer she was living with her mother in Lima and working odd hours. I had a path through the countryside over which, at a high rate of speed, I could be at her front door in seventeen minutes. An occasional dinner, movie, and/or cuddle along a river was all that we shared, given our busy schedules. It was a casual relationship with no emotional drama. Perfect for me, and, it seemed, her.

Reception Day

Monday, June 13, 1966—the infamous Marine Corps reception day—dawned sunny and hot in Delphos. In the next few years, I was to experience two of these, long travel followed by the reception at the airport, arrival at the base and organization in ranks, haircut, issuance of uniforms and gear, assignment of housing, racks, and locker, and only after all of this was done, sleep. The whole purpose of reception day was to create in the new trainee a sense of psychological stress and disorientation and to create a brutal transition from civilian life to the Marine Corps officer candidate or boot.

My parents and I drove eighty miles south to the Dayton Airport, where I was to catch my first commercial plane flight, UA #710 to Washington, D.C., at 9:40 A.M. to arrive at National Airport at 1:02 P.M. Leaving my parents at the gate door I walked out onto the tarmac and up the stairs to the four-engine propeller plane that was to take me east.

Excitement and anticipation overtook me as I found my assigned seat. The last time I had flown it was with Father's boss, who was in the Army Air Force Reserve. He flew artillery spotter planes during the battle of Okinawa and in Korea and had to get in his flight hours. Knowing my interest in planes he asked me if I wanted to go up with him one Sunday afternoon. After eating a large dinner, I drove with him to the small airport at Lima, and we climbed into the small, single-engine plane with four seats. After he took off, I became very hot in my winter coat while the plane rolled up and down. My head spun, my stomach rebelled, and I filled a vomit sack.

I dreaded the shame of getting sick one more time on the larger plane in front of all my fellow passengers and the very cute flight attendants. Not to worry. When we took off, I found the flying very pleasurable. What really roiled my brain was the anticipation of the military training that I was about to face. In short, I was scared. The physical demands seemed large. Would I be able to cope? And now I was on my own. There was no one to back me up if I got into trouble. It was the second time that I experienced the existential loneliness that was to become my inseparable companion in the coming years. It hit me that first week of college classes as a freshman. Now I was facing something potentially much more serious, a challenge tinged with the excitement of the unknown with the single-minded determination to succeed, or literally die trying.

I arrived on time at National Airport, met with a sign that led me to the bus to Quantico Base. We were met on base by the officers and NCOs who were to become so familiar in the next six weeks, the ones who were to yell at us, harass us, encourage us, teach us, abuse us, and stretch our coping abilities to the maximum. We lined up in ranks and were marched to the administration building, where we received our orders and were assigned to our training company and platoon. My first mistake was not to stand at attention when I approached the desk of the officer but to lean on the front of it with my hands. "Do not lean on my desk, Candidate, and stand at attention! Where in the hell do you think you are, still in sloppy civilian life?" (I paraphrase because in the fog of fifty years, the exact admonition issuing from his mouth is lost. Nonetheless, the effect of his words is still real and strong in my memory.)

We were then hustled, marching and running, to the building where we received our new clothing and first Marine Corps haircut. It took just a minute or two for each of our heads to be shaved at the three or four stations that had been set up. Then we were hustled to the tables with the piles of utility tunics, trousers, covers, belts, underwear, socks, and combat boots. Here we stripped out of the civilian garb and donned a complete set of utilities, bombarded with shouted instructions about how to properly tuck in the tunic, center the belt, blouse the trousers at the top of the boots, and look like a Marine. Civilian clothes would not see the light of day for several weeks. We thus began our transformation. They removed our personal style and substituted the uniform hair and clothing to emphasize that each of us was no longer an individual but a part of a team, a larger organization of men who would work together to perform the mission, without question, without complaint, by following the orders of our superiors and keeping our mouths shut until asked to speak.

Then it was more running and hustling to where the gear was to be issued. Each of us had been given an Individual Memorandum Receipt that listed the items that we could receive. For the PLCs, we received just the minimum gear for our training. Even so, it was a daunting array and heavy. After the issue, we were hustled to our assigned Quonset hut. These metal half cylinders were manufactured out of rolled, corrugated galvanized metal and anchored to a cement slab. During WWII thousands of the quickly constructed barracks were built for the draftees and enlisted men, and many survived the following years because of their robust construction and functional design. Along both walls were lines of metal bunkbeds with thin mattresses. We each were assigned a rack and shown how to use our sheets and blankets to make it up the Marine Corps way with hospital corners at forty-five degrees and the blanket so tight that a coin would bounce when dropped on it. We each had one wall and one footlocker to store our clothing and gear. Our NCOs told us where everything went. Every item had its place and was subject to inspection at any time.

Then it was time to hustle over to the armory and pick up my new constant mate for the next couple of weeks that would be closer to us and receive more attention than a new bride. All Marines are "grunts," or infantryman. All other military occupation specialties in the service were subordinate to this first one. The primary weapon of the Marine Corps grunt-in-training was, in that era, the M14 7.62mm NATO, semi-automatic assault rifle, which was the second generation of semi-automatic infantry rifle for the Marines after the M1 30'06 of WWII. I was issued serial number 48781 with the appropriate equipment and cleaning gear. It was clear from day one that the M14 was to be our most cherished item. We learned to field strip it, clean and oil it, carry it on marches, shoot it for familiarization, and use it on the marching field, or the grinder, where our platoon performed close-order drill and practiced the manual of arms.

After the armory we marched back to the Quonset hut and secured our weapons. Sometime amid this activity, we marched to the chow hall and had our first meal as PLCs. Each rank would go single file through the line, each candidate holding his metal tray to be filled by the enlisted Marine behind the counter. Dinner was not leisurely. We were constantly being harassed to shut the fuck up, eat quickly, and get back out in formation.

By the time the officers and NCOs finished with us, it was late, and we were standing in front of our racks for the final inspection of the evening. That night and every night, an instructor would walk up and down the hut with us standing in our skivvies, the so-called skivvy check, before lights-out and hit-the-rack. After traveling eight hundred miles by plane and bus and being forced into transition from civilian to candidate Marine, I found myself at the end of reception day replacing anticipation with exhaustion and a deep need to sleep, which I did soon after my shaved head hit the pillow. As my consciousness faded, I could hear my mind complaining. Six weeks of this! Fuck a duck! What have you done to me!

Training Days

Our days soon took on a familiar pattern. At 4:45 A.M. we were rousted out of the rack, dressed for physical training, and went in formation to the PT area, where calisthenics would begin. For two hours, we performed organized exercises of all kinds, sit-ups, jumping-jacks, push-ups, pull-ups, squat-thrusts, knee-bends, etc. under the scrutinizing eye of the training officers and NCOs to watch for candidates who were unable to perform the required sets or who were dogging it, something that brought much criticism and humiliation. Creating the stress of performance, they discovered who could, and who could not, perform to Marine Corps standards. Those who did not stack up quietly disappeared from our ranks. I suppose one of the reasons that we were not allowed to make our own return plane reservations was that the Marines were going to make them for us if we failed the course before it was finished.

We also ran in formation. The "running" was more what we would call jogging today. In the formation of the platoon, one of the NCOs would shout out regular calls and cajole us to keep our formation while we slowly jogged along for a mile or more. We had two uniforms for exercise. The first was what we candidates called our Mickey Mouse outfit: bright yellow T-shirt with red lettering, red cotton gym shorts, with a red ball cap and tennis shoes. No problem running in Mickey Mouse gear. However, our second outfit was combat boots, utility trousers, white T-shirt, and Marine Corps utility cap. Running miles in combat boots put a great deal of stress on the toes, ankles, and leg muscles. By the end of the two hours I felt like I had just completed a normal workday rather than a pre-breakfast warm-up. After returning to the huts in formation we had a very short time to shower, shave, don our uniform of the day, and form up again in front of the Quonset before marching to breakfast.

The heat determined the day's activities and their timing. In Virginia in June, it is hot. Flags of different colors flew to tell the instructors just what kind of physical exertion was allowed. Mornings after chow it was still relatively cool, which meant additional physical challenges and exercises. One such was a pugil stick fight. A pugil stick is a wooden bar with heavily cylindrical pads that extend past the end of the bar at both ends. It simulated the M14 rifle and gave the candidate practice in killing in hand-to-hand combat; the bayonet at one end was used to thrust and slash, while the butt of the weapon was used to smash the body and head of the enemy, who also had a rifle with a bayonet.

We were taught the various moves with the rifle that would disable or kill an opponent. Then we suited up in helmets and gloves with the pugil sticks to practice what we had just learned. Two by two we entered the ring; the other candidates stood around shouting and encouraging while the two opponents beat the shit out of each other. My first experience in the pugil ring was with a stocky football player from Cleveland who at first kicked my ass. Then I quickly learned that I had to bring major adrenalin, muscle, and attitude to this exercise if I was not to end up a pummeled pile on the ground. I began to hit back with everything I had and managed to land a few powerful blows of my own, my anger at his first attack having risen very high. Finally, the whistle blew, and we parted to make room for two more combatants.

Often the morning session was a run through the obstacle course. It was one of my favorites, thanks to my childhood tendency for climbing like a monkey in trees. It also did not put undue strain on my foot and leg. I enjoyed clambering up and over the wooden walls, climbing the multistoried towers, running along logs, and climbing the thick ropes. Especially the ropes made me feel accomplished because we used our feet to climb them. I soon mastered the technique of folding the rope around my leg and under my boot while holding it tight with my second foot; this maneuver served as a lever to push me higher until I got to the top. Coming down was always worse for me because gravity-assist put a great deal of force on my arms, and the legs could only offer partial support with the rope sliding past the boots.

On another morning, we found ourselves on our belly cradling our rifles in our arms to keep them off the ground while we crawled under barbed wire that was strung over us at a height of about eighteen inches. Firing over our heads was a machine gun. I do not remember if it was firing blanks or not, but the sound of the gun firing terrified us enough as we made our way through the dirt. "Keep your fucking asses down, Marines, or you die!" shouted the instructors who stood on the edge of the field with rocks in their hand. When they saw a candidate who was not keeping down, they would sling a rock at his steel helmet and ring his bell as a reminder to lower his ass and noggin. One of the rocks found me. I literally ate dirt after that. I became a lizard with an M14, I slithered so low. They also set off explosions as we crawled our way under the wire to the end. No shrapnel in the charges, of course, but they sure did scare the crap out of one when they went off nearby.

Grunts hike! The Marine Corps is infamous for training their candidates and boots by hiking. Early on we received instructions on how to make up our field marching packs and gear to hike. I learned to hate that son of bitch of a heavy rock on my back. We put nearly everything that we had been issued in the pack along with the heavy entrenching tool that was fastened to the outside. We also wore the steel helmet and a webbed belt that held a canvas-covered canteen full of water and a bayonet in its scabbard. We were in full utilities and skivvies with belt and combat boots. Finishing the well-equipped grunt was the heavy M14 rifle slung over the shoulder. When it was all properly donned, the whole assembly probably weighed forty or more pounds.

We hiked in the same platoon formation in which we marched and ran. I could never understand, and early on learned to resent, the Marine

Corps' method of placing candidates in ranks. And never did I envy tall men more and hate my early growth spurt that left me height-challenged. Tallest men were at the front, with descending height as the rank went to the rear. I was always near the end of the rank. Those up front were well over six foot, with long strides and weights of over two hundred pounds. To them a forty-pound set of gear was a relatively small proportion of their mass. We smaller-sized men had shorter strides, while the field marching pack was a much larger proportion of our weight. As the hike progressed, we were always trying to catch up to the pace of the men in front of us, and the strain on our bodies was much worse. Viewed from the top it must have looked like the action of a slinky toy closing and opening, the men at the back running to close the ranks under the cajoling and yelling of the instructors and then allowing them to expand again as fatigue set in and we shorter folks with the smaller steps fell back. And then there was my fucking clubfoot. Nonetheless, I had made my commitment; I would pass out or die before I would drop out.

Early in the training we took our very first conditioning hike in the Marine Corps and fell out in front of the Quonset hut in full military gear for inspection. Then it was off to the Virginia boonies that surrounded Camp Upshur in every direction. The first hike was modest, maybe five miles, to check out the candidates and their reaction to the exercise and to accustom them to wearing the full Marine apparatus. The joking, laughing, encouragement, and overall camaraderie of my fellow candidates helped. We had to be careful because the officers and NCOs would get pissed if they heard what they perceived as too much chatter. Nonetheless we managed to communicate and exchange funny observations, like about how the officers' field marching packs looked so much lighter than ours and how much more mobile the officers themselves appeared. We suspected that they stuffed their packs with crumpled newspapers that gave them the look of bulk but were very light. There was no question however that they were all in good shape, marching step for step with us with ease, even when they were traversing the columns back to front and front to back to encourage us on our way.

Hiking had always been a pleasure. Despite the heavy gear, my foot, harassment by our trainers, and the tall candidates in front of the ranks, I found I could maintain the pace; it was a joy to be in the woods. Following the candidate in front of me, taking in the scent of the trees and forest, gazing up at the cumulus-laden blue sky, and feeling a sense of accomplishment helped me find a rhythm that I felt I could maintain indefinitely, or at least while the instructors pushed us. Of course, they always had surprises. Near the end of the first hike they marched the battalion through a shallow creek, water flying everywhere, slippery rocks and mud underneath our boots, followed by dust settling on us and our gear on the other side.

When we returned to the Quonset hut and stood in formation, we were given only minutes to peel off our dirty gear and clothes, clean our rifles, and hurry back in formation for inspection. The instructors often stressed the candidates, purposefully, in this and other ways. PLC training was the most psychologically challenging environment that I have ever faced. "The Word," as they called the instructions, was always changing, usually under a time constraint, deliberately to pile stress upon stress. We were the rats in the Marine Corps Virginia maze with doors opening randomly here, closing randomly there, as our trainers observed our ability to negotiate the paths and our reactions, noting them in the training log. When they found a rat unable to negotiate his path, they removed him.

After the cooler morning exercises and our second meal, we were marched in the early afternoon to the large metal buildings that acted as our classrooms. Inside we sat with our pens and small Marine Corps exercise books at long tables on folding chairs positioned every couple of feet. Unfortunately, all elements that foster sleep were present. We had been up since 04:45, exercising most of the morning, and had just had a meal. Now we were sitting between metal walls and under a metal roof. The sun beat down on the building with no air conditioning, creating an ambient temperature of about eighty-five degrees Fahrenheit. All the while, we listened to an instructor talking about Marine Corps history, field stripping an M14 rifle, small unit infantry tactics, orienteering, the uniform code of military justice, and many other such stimulating topics that could put a college student into a deep slumber. Knowing that this was true, the instructors brought in very long bamboo poles, like those used for old fishing rods. When they observed a candidate's head nodding off to sleep, the rod would slap the head and shoulders awake again. It is amazing the wakening effect of bamboo under the correct conditions.

The Grinder

By late in the afternoon the temperature would begin to moderate, the sun falling near the tree line in the west. Then for a couple of hours we'd head to the grinder, which was a large macadam-surfaced lot carved out of the forest for marching large formations of men with rifles. Our platoon was turned over to an African American Marine non-commissioned officer and Vietnam veteran, a sergeant drill instructor, assigned to teach us how to perform close-order drill and the manual of arms. Here again, as with hiking, we took our place in each of the four squads of about ten men, each by height, tallest candidates in front.

I had not come in close contact with a black man, particularly one who could order me around. In Delphos we were segregated, not the southern pot-bellied sheriff with a nightstick, hangman's rope, and packs of angry German Shepherds segregated, but the upper-Midwest rural segregation that used attitude and small-town xenophobia to exclude outsiders, especially those with dark skin and African heritage. The only African American I had seen growing up was Simonize Sam, a man who would come to Delphos only in daylight to wash, wax, and detail the cars of the wealthy families. Sam knew the times of the setting sun through the seasons by long experience and was sure to be gone before dusk. In my eighteen years of maturing in Delphos I cannot remember one black person, never mind a family, walking down our Main Street and shopping in our stores. It just was not done. No laws were on the books to prevent it. Restaurants and bars were open to everyone. Thousands of black people lived just thirteen miles away in Lima; but they knew better. The invisible signs of white hostility and exclusion were clearly exhibited on the streets that led into town.

Let's call him Sergeant March, because I do not remember his name, just as I do not remember those of the white officers who trained us. Here he was, in the middle of the Virginia boonies, with a whole platoon of smart-ass college candidates of European heritage who wanted to be Marine Corps officers, and, sometime in the future, maybe, take him into battle. The contempt for us literally ran out of both sides of his mouth and onto the ground.

He was a bit of a social miracle. The Civil Rights Act was just two years old; the Voting Rights Act passed just the year before. For years, African Americans had been joining the enlisted ranks of the Marine Corps in large numbers because of the opportunity to escape poverty and discrimination, advance through the ranks, and retire after twenty years with a nice pension. There was an irony and tension in this. Many of the officers in the USMC came from southern states, where Jim Crow laws and prejudices were very strong. Yet many of the men that they led and depended upon were the same black persons with whom legally they could not share a meal in their hometown. By 1966 many black men had risen to high rank as non-commissioned officers and a smattering of African Americans were becoming officers.

Sergeant March had a wonderful accent, a soft southern patois, and an ability to create syntax that delighted our ears. We were the "doofus fucks who didn't know shit" about his Corps. We were good mostly "for standing our skinny asses on the grinder with our thumbs up our asses not knowing whether to turn right or left." "Fucking" became a member of many compound phrases. We were "fucking unbelievable," "fucking candidates," could not put one "fucking foot" in front of another without "fucking falling on our asses." "It was right face, Candidate, not left-fuck-ing-face," he would scream when one of us turned the wrong way.

We practiced for hours in close order drill, marching in step at the correct amount of distance in front, back, and between each candidate in the ranks. Right face! Left face! About face! Forward march! Halt! Each platoon sergeant designed his own "Jody call" to accompany the march-ing men he was leading. This was usually some form of a chant that was uttered by the sergeant in rhythm with the marching men; something like "hoyda, hoyda, hoyda, hoyda." Hour after hour we marched up and down the grinder to the sound of Sergeant March's Jody call while perfecting our close-order drill.

Then we stopped and executed the manual of arms with the M14. Right-shoulder arms! Left-shoulder arms! Port arms! Order arms! Present arms! We practiced moving the rifle around our bodies in synchroni-zation, each of the forty men in the platoon simultaneously executing the skill. After we learned the basics, we combined the two skills and performed the manual of arms while marching. The whole purpose, of course, was to build cohesion among the candidates, to execute orders in synchronization while keeping our mouths shut, to lose our individuality to the enforced repetitive movements of the group. This was training that went exactly counter to our college experiences. Going to class and studying, we were primarily alone, individual, private, moving in a rhythm that we each described. We had choice. Now here, to survive the training, our first consideration was the squad and platoon, the group, the mission. We had no choice, only orders to obey. Ultimately this learned discipline and sacrificing of self to group was to be transferred directly to the construction of combat teams and tactics to kill the enemy.

It was not all physical and classroom training. Occasionally they took us for field trips in what we called, out of the hearing of the officers, our cattle cars, articulated trailers with benches and screened windows hooked to a tractor. One trip was to a naval airport near Washington where we were introduced to the new F4 Phantom fighter. It took off down the runway and, right at the end, pulled up to a ninety-degree angle and shot straight into the air, much to our amazement. We also visited the rifle range and had familiarization with weapons. On these trips we were treated with a courtesy that I never experienced later as an enlisted man. There was that patina of entitlement of the officer that even then, in PLC training, was being inculcated by subtle special treatments.

Final Hike

Toward the end of the training there was a final conditioning hike, and it was a bitch. This time the battalion took a forced march, again in full combat gear. It was the middle of the summer, and hot, probably eighty-five to ninety degrees with high humidity. The hike tested the conditioning and training that we had been doing for more than four weeks. It was fucking miserable. We were loaded down with our gear, sweating profusely through our heavy utilities, and we short candidates in the back were periodically again running our asses off to keep up with the giants. It was not a good sign that the battalion was followed by trucks. On their beds were "shit-cans," large corrugated-metal garbage cans with no lids, filled with ice water. When one of the candidates passed out from the heat, the officers and sergeants would pick him up and throw him in the back of the truck, where enlisted men would dunk him in the ice water until he regained consciousness. After being shocked awake, he joined the other overcome candidates on the truck bed and rode the rest of the way.

At about mile twenty I was hurting. My legs felt like I was carrying cement blocks in the bottom of my boots. Breathing was difficult and running to catch up to the tall candidates leading the platoon was costing me every ounce of energy that I could muster from my failing body. Every one of us was nearly done. Doubt about our ability to finish this bastard of a hike snuck into each of our minds. The number of men in the back of the trucks had grown larger. On and on we went, seemingly forever. The trees on both sides of the road leading into the endless Virginian forests were oppressive, seemingly channeling us into this narrow strip of suffering that stretched out in front.

Particularly affected was a candidate in the rear, close to me. He did not belong in the training. Let's call him Candidate Doe. His father was General Doe, an officer in the Marine Corps. He was here because his father's rank had given him no choice; he was merely fulfilling family expectations. He and I were in the same Quonset hut and had become friends during the training. What struck me most about him was his sensitivity. A poet, an artist, a minister, a family counselor, a doctor devoting his practice to the poor, these professions I could have imagined for Doe; but a Marine Corps officer, there was no fucking way. It was apparent to me from the beginning that he was a gentle misfit, had too much fat, and was not in the best shape, even after the previous weeks' physical training.

Now I looked over at him, blond with pale skin that had become a deep red while pain suffused his face. His body was slightly bent forward at the waist under the weight of his pack. He was stumbling in his gait, and I could see that he was shortly to be a candidate for the shit-can. Then a horror occurred. The battalion took a hard right through a clearing in the forest, and there directly in front of us was a small Virginia mountain that was narrow and steep, like an aircraft carrier deck that had been tilted up at a thirty-five-degree angle with a steep drop off on both sides. The lead officers shouted at us to "charge that hill." I saw the perfect psychological design in this tactic. Take the candidates to their furthest point of physical stress and then lay one last, enormous effort on top of that. Exhaust the rat in the maze; then release the cat to chase the rodent up the hill. Immediately my only goal was to show those fuckers that they were not going to break me. This rat would not be manipulated to failure. I would get to the top.

Part of the way up, I noticed in my peripheral vision that Doe suddenly disappeared. At first, I thought I was hallucinating. But when, exhausted, I topped out, he was gone. I later learned that he had stumbled to the edge of the hill and fallen over the side. When the staff got to him at the bottom, he could not see. Candidate Doe had gone hysterically blind, what fifty years later, in a more politically correct climate, is called a "conversion disorder" and given the medical carbuncle of a name "functional neurological symptom disorder." The body converts stress into a biological dysfunction. Immediately I felt a pang of guilt that I did not help in some way. But each of us was so burdened with the gear and exhausted by the exercise that carrying an additional candidate up the hill would have been impossible. And I had no opportunity. Doe just disappeared before I could act.

That night we had our first experience setting up a defensive perimeter for the battalion. We combined our shelter half with another candidate to form a complete pup tent with the lines and tent pegs that had been issued to us, went through the chow line with the mess kit and cup, and cleaned all the gear and rifles. When we had been in camp for an hour or so and had begun the routine of settling in, most of us had recovered our strength and attitudes and were ready to throw the bullshit and laugh with one another while cursing and swearing about the fucking conditioning hike that the officers and NCOs had just put us through. At least those of us who made it without the shit-can dunk were relieved and happy.

Then the watches were assigned. Unfortunately, I got chosen for the 2 to 4 A.M. watch, which, for me, was the worst possible. First, I was exhausted and craved the opportunity to close my eyes and fall into pleasant unconsciousness. Second, for me sleep had always been a much-needed escape from life, the sleep of the dead, and I embraced that death every night. This training had been a bitch. From 4:45 A.M. to 9:00 P.M. we were stressed to the maximum, physically and psychologically. When I hit the rack at night, I just closed my eyes and went someplace else. I knew not where. That was not even important. Maybe it was to the land of my dead relatives, because I certainly dreamed of them often. Just to run away into oblivion for eight hours was a necessary tonic for my day. This night I was going to be denied it at a time when I needed it most. Worse, my sleep was interrupted. Shaken out of a deep slumber at 2 A.M. to pick up my weapon and stare into the Virginia forest for two hours was painful. My eyelids were so heavy, my body so sore and fatigued. But the worst thing that a Marine can do is to fall asleep while on duty in the defense perimeter of the battalion. In a combat situation, all the men are sleeping primarily because they think that you have their asses covered, that if there was an infiltration or attack, you would sound the alarm and begin the resistance. Also, the supervising officers were making the rounds all night to ensure that we were awake and alert. That alone kept me alert, particularly because they made snarky comments to us as they walked by.

The next day, when we returned to Camp Upshur, blind Candidate Doe awaited us in the Quonset hut. One of the training officers called me into his office and told me that, since we were friends, I was to be his "seeing-eye dog" until they could decide what to do. I protested that I did not wish to miss the training, but the lieutenant quickly shut me up and told me to get on with it. Doe was pathetic, filled with shame that he had failed the course and fearful of his father's reaction. After a day or a little more, he disappeared, probably leaving with his family or heading to the naval hospital, and I returned to the normal training schedule.

At the very end of the training, and after we had passed all the mandatory tests laid out in the training manual, the platoons competed to determine the best performing unit in the battalion. Unfortunately for me, and my fucking clubfoot, I was assigned to the cross-country run, in fatigues and combat boots. It was a misery. The only reason that I managed to finish was my fellow candidates who were running with me. Their competitive juices and desire to win, and the friendships that had built up over the previous weeks, encouraged them to help me along and kept me moving one boot in front of the other, even if it was at a stumble. Still, I held them back and felt that I had let them down. It was the only time during the Platoon Leader Course that I believed that I had failed an exercise. Nonetheless, when my evaluation showed up in the mail at the end of the summer, I had been graded as "satisfactory" and promoted to "Lance Corporal."

That summer of 1966 there was an airline strike when we broke camp. We were in formation when one of the officers read my name among a list of candidates who were to grab their gear and get ready to return home. A two-star general was to fly from Washington, D.C., to Chicago in his government four-engine prop plane. We on the list were to join him because we all lived in the general line of the flight plan. His pilot was to land the plane at major airports between the two cities and drop off the candidates who lived nearby, who from there were to find their way back home. My stop was in a much-maligned city by Lake Erie, Toledo. The plane landed for probably the fourth time since we took off, taxied to the tarmac near the terminal and, while keeping the engines running, opened the hatch and put down the steps while I quickly made my way, followed seconds later by my sea bag with my belongings. As soon as I got clear, the pilot revved the engines, and the general and remaining troops were gone. My parents, having earlier been alerted by me, were waiting in the lounge. My first Marine training had ended.

First Death

The next day I was back working at the factory. (Father saw no reason to extend what he saw as summer fun and relaxation.) I was also immediately faced with a symbol of my mortality. One of my classmates in high school, an attractive young woman and casual friend, whose mother I had taught to swim when I worked as a lifeguard, had just been killed in an automobile accident halfway between Delphos and Lima. Nineteen years of age, and she was dead. She was the first of the inevitable whittling down of our class by accident, war, disease, and age. At the visitation in the Catholic funeral home of Delphos, I met classmates who were participating in the horrible ceremony that is the viewing of the embalmed. Surely this ritual should have died with the Egyptians. Yet here we were, solemnly walking up to the casket with the room-temperature body the texture of a wax block and dressed in its best finery. Where was the smile that had warmed me, the gentle, teasing laugh? They had been wiped out in a microsecond by an event of random horror. Now the family, friends, and priest were talking of a loving god, running beads through fingers and praying to some invisible virgin in the sky while bleating that everything happens for a reason. Bullshit! It was a fucking irrational act of the material universe, a visitation by Our Unholy Lady of Merde in her worst dress. No loving god would have allowed such an abomination. The strong scent of flowers, the murmured clichés of death, talk of better places, how well she looked, the advantage of sudden death, and lack of suffering on the victim's part made me want to vomit. I fled the scene as soon as I could avoid rudeness.

When Julia, Mary and I walked out together, I spurted out a fatuous comment about death, something like "we are born alone, we die alone at an unknown time, and it is not to be thought a great tragedy." After having just trained in killing for six weeks, hearing the nightly death tolls on the television from Vietnam, knowing my destiny had been determined that summer, my attitude about my own safety and death had permanently changed. Or perhaps it was just the death of innocence and religion. For many years to come I was gripped by grim anger, fatalism, and depression that were forged in the forests of Virginia in the summer of 1966. In the next year, a second classmate's death fueled this morbid feeling and propelled me into the most reckless behavior of my life.

But that is a story for another time.

Index

About the Author

R obert Williams was born and raised in Delphos, Ohio, spent four years in The United States Marine Corps, and was educated at The University of Michigan and Cambridge University, England. After training as an NIH Postdoctoral Fellow in Human Genetics at the University of Michigan Medical School, he became the Director of the Histocompatibility Laboratory at Blood Systems, Inc. in Scottsdale where he supervised the genetic testing of families for bone marrow transplants and was instrumental in creating paternity testing protocols that were then accepted by Arizona courts. After a 31-year career and retiring from ASU as a Professor, Williams has become a Special Volunteer for the NIDDK (National Institute of Diabetes and Digestive and Kidney Diseases) for the National Institutes of Health.